THE DIGITAL MARKETER

Ten New Skills You Must Learn to
Stay Relevant and Customer-Centric

LARRY WEBER

LISA LESLIE
HENDERSON

WILEY

To our respective families,
for their unwavering support and enthusiasm.
—LW and LJLH

Contents

Acknowledgments

Writing a book evokes profound appreciation. Like jazz musicians that improvise on established compositions to create new melodies, we are grateful to the many who took the time to share their thoughts and experiences with us, further developing our initial observations into themes, and ultimately chapters. If there is music among these pages, it is due to their generosity.

Multiple business leaders, academics, and specialists contributed to the building of *The Digital Marketer's* melody and supportive harmonies. Mark Fuller (Rosc Global), Len Schlesinger (Harvard Business School), Sally Ourieff (Translational Consulting), Saul Kaplan (Business Innovation Factory), Rick Kash (Nielsen), Scott Epskamp (Leapfrog Online), Diane Hessan (Communispace), Scott Russell (Sparks Grove), Robin Frank (beep beep media), Dan Fukushima (Sparks Grove), Scott Neslin (Tuck School of Business), Peter Henderson (ShapeUp), Elizabeth Zaldastini Napier (Tuck School of Business), Josh McCall (Jack Morton Worldwide), Rodrigo Martinez (IDEO), B J Fogg (Stanford University), Becky Bermont (Creative Leadership), Alan Trefler (Pegasystems), Torrence Boone (Google), Debi Kleiman (MITX), Joi Ito (MIT Media Lab), J P Maheu (Bluefin Labs/Twitter), Wendy Murphy (Babson College), John Maeda (Rhode Island School of Design), Sanjay Dholakia (Marketo), R. Michael Hendrix (IDEO), Scott Ludwig (Skyword), Brian Babineau (Arnold Worldwide), and George Colony (Forrester Research) have all quite generously shared their time and insight.

We are, as always, indebted to Jill Kneerim, Larry's literary agent who heard the melody in this book, and for Richard Narramore, our editor at John Wiley & Sons, who enthusiastically agreed to publish it. Where would we be without Tiffany Colón, our editorial assistant at Wiley, who, like a metronome, kept us on task and on time, and

Lauren Freestone, our production editor, who pulled multiple parts and myriad notes together into one score.

Producing a book takes a tremendous amount of planning and coordination. Heartfelt thanks to Nancy Provost, Larry's trusted executive assistant, and Ginger Ludwig for their orchestration of details, despite their already full agendas, and to Kevin Green at Racepoint Global for his keen insight and creativity that consistently breaks new ground.

Finally, a standing ovation to our respective families. We are always grateful for your accompaniment.

Acknowledgments

Foreword

PR professionals in the technology world are typically gentle, political animals, subtly and quietly steering their clients' offerings into the most flattering light. Then there is Larry Weber. I distinctly remember our first interaction when he brought a client to the old Forrester offices in Harvard Square. No subtlety. No calm nudging. No backroom whispering. It was an all-out, high-volume, lean-in, *Fight Club*, Oxford debate—with Larry passionately advocating for his client and deftly challenging the best arguments of the assembled know-it-all Forrester analysts. It was the first time that I had seen someone from the vendor PR world construct complex and compelling ideas about the future and how markets would transform. This guy was clearly an original thinker.

All of Larry's idea-centric passion and sense of the future shoot out of this volume—*The Digital Marketer*. It's a book with impeccable timing. Why?

Because we are entering what Forrester calls the age of the customer—a 20-year business cycle in which the most successful enterprises will reinvent themselves to systematically understand and serve increasingly powerful customers. Customers will take power from institutions (especially companies) through their access to precise pricing, social voice, and ability to buy anything, from anywhere, from anyone, at any time.

The only way for companies to create a sustainable advantage in the future will be by constructing superior experiences that can win, retain, and serve the newly demanding customer.

And much of that experience will rest on digital. In the future, all companies will be software companies.

To stay relevant in the age of the customer, marketing leaders must be able to adapt to—and exploit—the four market imperatives that are driving the rise of the empowered customer. They must be able to:

- *Transform customer experiences*. Companies must make substantive investments in customer experience to build relationships and amplify fans. In short, companies must transform to become customer-*obsessed* enterprises. Customer obsession focuses strategy, energy, and budget on processes that enhance knowledge of and engagement with customers—and prioritizes them over maintaining traditional (and crumbling) competitive barriers. Marketing leaders must lead the customer-obsessed journey up, down, and across the company.

- *Become digital disruptors*. Digital has unleashed intense and rapid waves of innovation. Disruption requires agility that marketing isn't typically known for, with shorter development cycles and fewer organizational silos. Disruptors spread digital skills and a digital mind-set across strategy and operations, not just marketing or technology. To stand out, you must break your old patterns of doing business to make your customer's life easier. This won't be easy—patterns of work and behavior are difficult to break.

- *Embrace the mobile mind shift*. Mobility has trained people to expect any information or service to be available to them at their moment of need. Context—knowing real-time customer situations, attitudes, preferences, and desires—is key, as is being able to respond to those customer desires at high speed. Few digital strategists have a grasp of just-in-time service, but that's where the mobile battle will be fought.

- *Turn big data into business insights*. Developing true customer insight requires a significant overhaul of your analytics. Marketers need insight across the entire customer life cycle to help grow existing relationships and predict future behavior. Big customer data will be the gasoline that powers all future marketing campaigns.

The age of the customer is demanding a transformation of thought—and herein lays the problem: Only a small minority of marketing executives have any inkling of how they will have to organize and think and perform in the new age. While marketing will take on a new level of importance (one could argue paramount importance), the great majority of marketers are unprepared for the challenge.

Luckily for us and for them, Larry and his coauthor, Lisa Leslie Henderson, have arrived at just the right time with just the right book. *The Digital Marketer* will serve to direct this generation of executives on the task of retooling. From his 10 essential skills to his specific directions for how to build customer experience to his clear explanation of complex technologies like big data, Larry and Lisa present marketers with a manual for survival and success. And *The Digital Marketer's* intriguing examples, references to other experts, and guidance on where to find additional resources extend this book's value beyond its pages.

Forrester has invested much time and energy in researching this tectonic shift in the business environment. We firmly believe in the potential of the age of the customer—or Customer-Centric Era—to reshape how both marketers and technologists define their jobs and the legacies they will leave.

For our clients and the world at large, I am very glad that Larry and Lisa have endeavored to shape and teach the next generation of marketers—a group that will face a series of challenges that did not apply just a few short years ago. No other profession is living through more change, but no other work is more exciting, vibrant, and important than that of the digital marketer.

And now that new generation of marketer has teachers.

—**George F. Colony**
Chairman and CEO
Forrester Research, Inc.
www.forrester.com

Introduction

Almost 35 years ago I began a career in marketing with one blue suit, a typewriter, and some Wite-Out. No mobile phones, computers, social networks, big data, and so on. The landscape has changed radically! We have moved from a media-centric universe to one of customer control.

If this transformation was a new solar system, the customers would be the sun orbited by dozens of planets: Customer Experience, Content, Converged Media, Loyalty, Marketing Automation, Mobility, and so on. *The Digital Marketer* is here to serve as a master guide to this new universe.

Nothing is more important than the customer relationship, so marketing has become the new operating environment of commerce.

I want to thank my family, colleagues, clients, and especially my coauthor, Lisa Leslie Henderson, for their tremendous support.

Enjoy the ride around the stars!

—Larry Weber
Boston, Massachusetts 2014

Chapter 1

The 10 Essential Skills Every Marketer Needs

"In the face of change we have three options: ignore it, grow with it, or drive it."[1]

—**Gerard Puccio, Marie Mance, Laura Barbero Switalski, Paul Reali,** *Creativity Rising*

No one needs to tell us that the world of marketing is changing fast. We are living it. Low-cost and ubiquitous communications technology is irrevocably altering human behavior, causing seismic shifts in marketing philosophy, practices, and careers. At its core, marketing is still about creating and keeping customers, but the how-to questions for accomplishing this have changed considerably.

The Web has empowered people everywhere. Whether in New York or Nairobi, today's customers are connected, informed, and more vocal than they have been in the past. Anyone with a connected device—39 percent of the world as of 2013[2]—now has access to all of the world's knowledge and many of its citizens. With these resources at their fingertips, our prospects and customers can discover and investigate anything and everything, establish decision-making criteria, seek opinions from their peers, evaluate their options, and share their impressions and experience with others, anytime and anywhere. As a result, the relationship between businesses and their customers has been dramatically altered: our customers are now firmly in charge of the buying process.

Digital Has Changed the Game

In the predigital landscape, our prospects undertook a straight-forward purchase journey that we likened to a funnel. The process began with a need or desire that our prospects chose to address. Salespeople were involved early on, helping to establish decision-making criteria. Our job as marketers was to build aware-ness and create materials that made the case for why our solutions should be adopted. Many consumer brands had loyalty programs to encourage retention, but not much attention was devoted to post-purchase engagement.

Digital has dealt us all new cards. Today's customer journey still starts with a need or a desire, but our prospects often undertake an at times lengthy period of silent due diligence during which time *they* discover and evaluate their options via the web. During this period of discovery our prospects' consideration set often grows rather than narrows. According to Google's Zero Moment of Truth study, the average person pulls information from 10.4 sources before making a purchase.[3] Some of the most influential sources are other people's unfiltered post-purchase commentary. Salespeople enter the process at a much later stage for business-to-business purchases; most e-commerce purchases can be made independently.

Marketers have become essential to the purchase process, as more often than not, content is the tool that breaks through this silent due diligence, initiating a conversation between us and our prospects. Recognizing this shift, marketers have become content publishers, experts at creating useful resources that address our prospects' and customers' underlying needs and desires. If these experiences res-onate, we may be invited into the purchase process. Serving as trusted advisors, rather than biased advocates for our company's products and services, we create the conditions for our prospects and cus-tomers to evaluate *for themselves* whether we make the grade.

Social media has multiplied the potential points of connection with our prospects and customers and its interactive nature has turned static text into cross-channel dialogue. As we blog, tweet, host webinars, publish white papers, produce videos, and curate Pinterest boards, we generate living assets that can draw prospects to us. As we come to know these people as individuals through

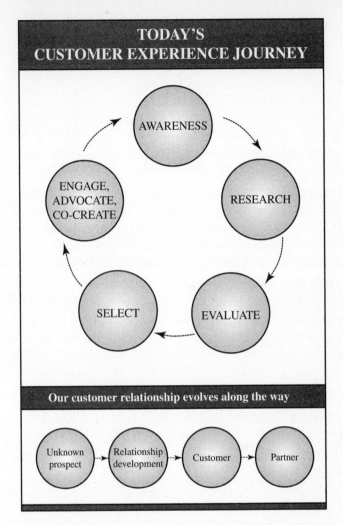

Figure 1.1   Visual of the Customer Experience Journey

careful observation of their digital body language, our encounters become more personalized, incorporating predictive analytics to enhance their usefulness.

Post-purchase engagement with our customers has become essential. Our customers are a primary source of word of mouth—peer-to-peer recommendations—that can make or break future sales. In these later-stage interactions we can learn the details of their

The 10 Essential Skills Every Marketer Needs

experience with us, answer any remaining questions they may have, and mitigate any outstanding negatives. If done right, these can foster positive advocates for our products and services, harness wisdom for our customer service efforts, and generate additional business. Our customers are also a vital source of insight into demand. They may not tell us outright what they want, but they can tell us about their needs and desires. With that knowledge, we can explore latent and emerging demand and co-create new products, services, and experiences that will provide tomorrow's revenue.

Although our prospects may not begin today's customer journey looking to develop an ongoing relationship with us, or with any company for that matter, as we engage in ways that are useful, they often morph from being unknown prospects, to becoming customers, and in many cases, to join with us as partners. As we transform a traditionally passive and transaction-oriented association into a collaborative relationship where we co-create, co-market, and co-serve our brands, our role as marketers expands. We are becoming key drivers of sales, loyalty, and innovation, producers of revenue rather than primarily generators of expenses.

The Disruption of Marketing Continues

Digital's impact on marketing is not yet complete. Innovative technologies and heightened customer expectations are unleashing creativity, spurring imaginative forms of brand expression and interaction. Sensors and near-field communication devices are changing the very nature of products and services, prompting us to reconsider how our companies' value propositions may change when every object—from our customers' homes to their bodies—are connected to the Internet. As the bar is raised, marketers are becoming experience architects, collaborating closely with designers and software engineers.

Widespread adoption of mobile technology has brought new opportunities. The qualities that make mobile a highly engaging, lean-forward medium—touch screens, voice recognition, cameras, and GPS technology—are enabling rich, contextualized experiences. Mobile "always with you" quality has also issued us a new challenge: How to unobtrusively accompany our customers through the course of their days, offering valuable experiences that enhance their lives.

New channels continue to proliferate and are being adopted at record speeds, keeping us on our toes as we evaluate their relevance to our constituents and their effectiveness in obtaining our business goals. Every channel is becoming increasingly visual, forcing us to express our ideas in alternative, visually stimulating ways.

Today's customers live their lives across channels, often incorporating several to complete a single task or transaction. To effectively meet their needs, our companies must be present and available in their preferred channels, offering a seamless, personalized, and often predictive experience. Our ability to offer these contextualized interactions at scale requires that we become adept at big data collection, predictive analytics, and marketing automation, competencies that involve new technology, advanced organizational learning, and high levels of coordination across functions.

New enterprise marketing management systems are emerging to facilitate these personalized interactions, augmenting existing back-office oriented enterprise resource planning (ERP) systems that focus on accounting, manufacturing, supply chain management, and human resources. These new systems are designed to foster information flows and collaboration *across* business functions and our entire demand-related ecosystem in order to more effectively serve our customers.

Native advertising, which when done well mimics organic content, is presenting new targeting opportunities, causing a lot of buzz and a shift in media purchases. Fueled by immense amounts of data on our prospects and customers that is collected, integrated, and analyzed on a moment-to-moment basis, this new form of advertising is prompting marketers to develop converged marketing strategies, blurring the lines between paid, earned, and owned media.

E-commerce has lowered the barriers to entry for competition, establishing a truly global marketplace. Worldwide information flows are turning marketers, possibly inadvertently, into managers of global brands and customer communities. Viable disruptors to established industries can popup anywhere—especially in emerging markets.

Building loyalty in an age when people are inundated with options from near and far and can comparison-shop with ease is a demanding task. As marketers we must continually find ways to stay on top of shifting customer preferences and distinguish our products and services from the growing competition.

Rapid marketplace changes demand that we become more flexible and responsive, challenging rigid corporate cultures and processes. Adopting a more iterative and experimental approach enhances our agility; however, it also requires that we foster a pro-learning environment that values what we glean from our successes and from our failures.

Finally, the pressure on marketers to prove the value of our efforts is tremendous. On one hand, it has never been easier to see the impact of our efforts as digital interactions leave behind a trail of behavioral data. At the same time, it is not easy to piece together this data as it is not captured in a sequential stream from first encounter to sale or advocacy. Closed-loop analytics are making it possible to track the effectiveness of each of our marketing initiatives, but they require software investment and technological know-how.

We Have All Benefitted from the Disruption

As challenging as it is to be a marketer during one of the most rapidly changing business environments in history, both our customers and our businesses have benefitted from the disruption. The numerous changes that digital has ushered in have forced us to move away from our traditional producer-based strategies and tactics, to focus on meeting our customers' needs and desires.

Customer-centricity is an old story. For decades we have known that being as close as possible to our customers and bringing their voice into the center of our organizations has been a winning strategy, but we have not turned that aspiration into reality. The rebalancing of the relationship between companies and their customers has forced the issue, however.

Organizations that have grasped the new reality and are redesigning the way they engage with their prospects and customers are making strides in realizing customer-centricity. They are distinguishing themselves by setting new standards for a customer's experience and often exceeding them. A look at Amazon and Marketo illustrates just how far we have come.

Amazon's customers feel as if the world was made for them. When they arrive on any of the company's sites, they are greeted by name. A robust search engine acts like a personal assistant, quickly locating items from multiple vendors. Tailored recommendations that reflect their prior searches, page views, reviews, and purchases offer suggestions for additional items that may be of interest, presenting relevant options of which they may not otherwise have been aware (see Figure 1.2). To make itself even more useful, Amazon offers its customers the opportunity to proactively rate additional items and express their preferences, enhancing its search engine's predictive ability.

Ancillary features transform a simple purchase into an experience on Amazon. When looking for a book, customers may enjoy videos about the author, the opportunity to "look inside" the book's cover to preview its contents, and the chance to read peer reviews and add their own opinions to the mix. With Amazon's mobile app they can take a photo of an object, and within seconds, a description of the product and a link to where it can be purchased appears on their screen. Items can be bought quickly and easily; 1-Click purchases do

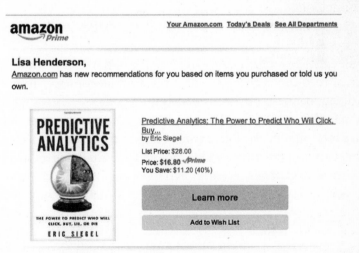

Figure 1.2   Amazon Prompts Purchases with Customized Recommendations

7

not require any additional data input (no names, addresses, or credit card numbers to key in) and Amazon Prime provides free two-day shipping—and complimentary TV, video streaming, and borrowing of e-books. If its customers are not ready to buy, Amazon saves their items for later access on any device.

Amazon's reliability builds trust; their customers know that when they purchase from Amazon their order will arrive intact and on time, if not early. The ability to set e-mail preferences—"We want to stay in touch, but only in ways you find helpful"—and to track orders online go a long way toward making customers feel like they matter. It is no wonder that one blogger wrote, "Amazon is liked so much because it is built to love."[4]

Business-to-Business Companies Are Players, Too

Business-to-business (B2B) companies are also making strides in defining and delivering new levels of customer-centricity. Knowing that almost two-thirds of the research that potential B2B customers undertake takes place before a salesperson is contacted, the marketing automation and revenue management company Marketo creates myriad opportunities for prospects to educate themselves about this emerging field.

White papers, e-books, webinars, and videos are available in a Resource Center located on their website to assist potential customers in their early due diligence. Search engine optimization and contextualized advertising, topics we will explore in the coming pages, ensure that their prospects find their materials.

Once a potential customer has accessed their content, Marketo proactively offers them increasingly targeted content and invitations to events in hopes of being able to build a relationship. E-mail alerts notify prospects of new e-books and webinars on topics in which they have indicated an interest. The company carefully monitors recipient's reactions to determine the next best offer and the appropriate cadence for messages.

Because Marketo's communications are well targeted and well timed, prospects experience them positively, not as spam. Figure 1.3, for example, is a resourceful follow-up e-mail about an event for

Top Presentations from Yesterday's Event

Hi Lisa,

We know it can be hard to carve out time during the work day, so we compiled some of the **most-viewed presentations** from yesterday's Marketing Nation Virtual Event for you to review.

Check out the slides now!

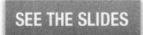

Stay tuned for the rest of the slides and recordings - we will be sending them out in a series beginning in early October.

Please let me know if you'd like to set up some time to learn more about Marketo, or marketing automation in general. If you're ready take a closer look, check out our **4-minute demo** or sign up for a **weekly demo webinar**.

Best,

Figure 1.3   Marketo Nurtures Leads with Personalized E-Mails

which Lisa had signed up for but was unable to attend. Engagement with Marketo also includes access to their social community of over 30,000 Marketo users, as well as on-demand training, and the ability to submit ideas to the company's product management team to shape the future of their products.

Just Ahead: Relief and Reward

We have come a long way during the last two decades. While much complexity remains, we believe that we are entering a time of

9

refinement. After gulping down innovation for two decades, going forward marketers will be able to chew a little more thoroughly. This does not mean that invention will stop, that competition will become less fierce, or that the pace of business will slow. Nor does it mean that those who remain standing have secured a place in the future. It does mean that much of the innovation on the horizon builds and improves upon the seismic transformations that have already altered the landscape. Shakeouts and consolidations will be plentiful as the market integrates. As the dust settles and we gain comfort in our new skills, creativity will flourish.

The ability to create and deliver remarkable customer experience will be the signature of successful companies in this next phase of marketing. It is how we manifest our customer-centricity and what our prospects and customers have come to expect and reward. Organizations that are able to figure out what their prospects and customers want and expect, in terms of products, services, spaces, and the accompanying experiences, and deliver on this insight, will develop a powerful customer experience differential, a key source of differentiation in an environment where commoditization of our best ideas and efforts happens all too rapidly. This differential will drive results—it already is.

Working with five years of data from Forrester Research, Inc.'s Customer Experience Index, a yearly benchmark of businesses' customer experience quality, Watermark Consulting found that the stock performance of companies considered to be customer experience leaders exceeded that of both the S&P 500 and the customer experience laggards.[5] Customer experience leaders had a cumulative total return of +22.5 percent over the half-decade period compared with a −1.3 percent decline for the S&P 500 market index and a −46.3 percent decline for the laggard portfolio over the same period (see Figure 1.4). Here is the bottom line: customer experience matters. Whether we deliver remarkably good or remarkably poor customer experiences, it impacts our results.

With customer experience driving the growth agenda and performance measures for companies going forward, marketers are in the enviable position of holding the keys to the kingdom. To rise to the occasion, we must be able to think and act beyond our traditional

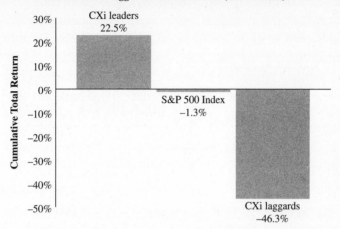

Figure 1.4 Focusing on Customer Experience Pays

Source: **Harley Manning, Forrester Research, Inc. Blog, "When It Comes to Total Returns, Customer Experience Leaders Spank Customer Experience Laggards," Forrester Research, Inc., September 14, 2012.**

turf to proactively build the necessary skills to take our brands and companies to new levels. It is a good time for us to roll up our sleeves, digest what has happened, home the skills that are needed to benefit from these developments, re-energize our creativity, and get on with creating value in this new customer-centric marketing landscape.

What Do We Mean by Customer-Centricity?

Much confusion exists around the definition of customer-centricity. Some false notions of customer-centricity that are expressed with some regularity include:

- Being all things to all people;
- Treating all of our customers the same;
- Attempting to meet every need our constituents have;
- Allowing our customers to haphazardly determine our strategy from minute to minute; or

11

- Blindly copying what Amazon, Marketo, and other market leaders are doing.

We define customer-centricity as helping *our* prospects and customers achieve *their* goals in a way that makes sense for *our* organizations. In this coveted sweet spot, depicted in Figure 1.5, our solutions meet our prospects' and customers' needs and desires. We are operating in a place of shared value, playing on the same team, and pursuing the same goals. That is a powerful combination.

As a result, customer-centricity is uniquely defined for every organization; however, two underlying principles are the same for every organization:

1. Customer-centricity is demand-driven, concentrating on meeting our customers' needs and desires.

2. Customer-centricity is focused, prioritizing our efforts on those customers' needs and desires that we can serve well and profitably.

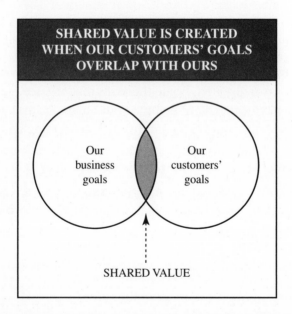

Figure 1.5   Shared Value Is the Coveted Sweet Spot

Walk in Our Customers' Shoes

A deep understanding of our customers, perhaps even better than they know themselves, is a prerequisite to effectively meeting demand. This includes comprehending their needs and desires, motivations, attitudes, and existing knowledge, as well as their ongoing cross-channel behavior, preferences, and the triggers that prompt them to act. Staying current on these variables is a daunting task, as they change often. It is important, however, because this understanding, when coupled with a solid grasp of emerging trends and players in the marketplace, drives today's results and grounds our hypotheses about future demand. Our ability to rapidly test these hypotheses and to translate the resulting insight into innovative business models, products, services, and experiences keeps our companies relevant.

To truly understand our customers, we must shift points of view to see the world through their eyes. Flipping perspectives is hard because we are often entrenched in seeing the world from where we stand. It requires rethinking many tried and true, often producer-centric policies, practices, and frameworks.

To facilitate this flip, creativity and innovation consultant Tim Hurson encourages us to visualize our customers' needs and desires as itches they want to scratch. These itches can be physical, emotional, or psychological and they can be active, emerging, or latent. The most promising business opportunities generally come from addressing emerging and latent itches; who knew we could not live without a mobile phone or tablet until we had one in our hands? To identify the underlying itch, Hurson recommends that we ask, "If your [customer's] itch were a T-shirt slogan, what would it say?"[6] To develop a more complete context for the itch, he challenges us to consider the impact of the itch, what we know about it, who else may be impacted by the itch or influenced it, and our vision for the future in which the itch has gone away.[7]

Applying a different metaphor when he was still teaching, former Harvard Business School professor Theodore Levitt encouraged his marketing students to think of customers as having an underlying job that they are trying to complete. Most of these jobs have a social, functional, and emotional component; Levitt believed that if marketers could understand this context, they would be able to create solutions that would appeal to their customers and prospects. Levitt illustrated this perspective to his students by explaining that, "People don't want to buy a quarter-inch drill. They want a quarter-inch hole!"[8] Applying Levitt's framework, our task as marketers is to understand the job that our prospects and customers are trying to do, and design the experiences that enable them to do so.

Eenie Meenie Miney Mo

Truly customer-centric organizations are able to take this customer understanding to the level of the individual and differentiate their products, services, and experiences accordingly. Differentiating among our customers may at first sound anticustomer-centric, but it truly is not. Our customers are heterogeneous, with different itches and jobs, and varying abilities to scratch and get the job done. As a result, the overlapping area of shared value we have with each of our customers varies. By segmenting and prioritizing our prospects and customers, we can more effectively meet their needs and allocate our resources. This is not earth-shattering news. What is news is our newfound ability to know our customers well enough to pull this off and to have the marketing automation technology to do so at scale.

Consider the case of a luxury boat retailer. While there may be many people who say they want a 50-foot sailboat, a much smaller segment can actually purchase one, and an even smaller set is ready to purchase one now. If we were designing a marketing strategy for the luxury boat retailer, we would recommend prioritizing active engagement with those customers who want to purchase a sailboat, have the ability to do so, and are ready to do so. This would involve a customized flow of content based upon their interest and behavior and engagement with our salespeople when they have been determined to be sales ready.

We would also recommend a nurturing strategy for those prospects who have the interest and ability, but for whom the timing is not right. This would involve a smart stream of content, which becomes increasingly detailed based upon the prospects' actions. A low-involvement, self-servicing strategy would be appropriate for those who are interested, but not yet able to purchase. By knowing its prospects and customers well, the boat seller would be able to design relevant customer experiences that effectively meet the varying needs of the market and most efficiently use its resources.

Realizing the Customer-Experience Differential

Our commitment to customer-centricity manifests itself in our customer experience. When we talk of the customer experience differential, we are talking about consistently meeting or exceeding our customers' expectations for our brands and accomplishing this with more perceived value than our competition. Expectations vary by brand; people naturally have different hopes for shopping excursions to Costco than to Nordstrom; both brands focus on delivering quality, but in very different ways.

Our customers' perceptions of our brands and whether or not they meet the grade are based on their experiences with us. A person's brand experience is defined as the "sensations, feelings, cognitions, and behavioral responses evoked by brand stimuli."[9] These experiences can come in all shapes and sizes. Digital channels have magnified the number of potential brand encounters and have created a digital dimension for every product and service.

Take a Starbucks espresso, for example. There is the robust, slightly bitter drink itself, with its thick, swirled *crema* that floats on the surface and its satisfying aftertaste. People's experience of their espresso extends far beyond the cup of coffee itself, however. It can include searching for a Starbucks location: how easy is it to find digitally and physically? It can include the purchase experience itself, including the design of the venue, the personality and skill of the barista—*Do they remember my drink preference?*—the length of the lines, the comfort of the chairs, the cleanliness of the bathrooms, and the speed of the Wi-Fi connection.

For some customers the quality of the Starbucks espresso experience may also include their mobile phone. The Starbucks mobile app

15

lets them pay by scan, receive personalized text offers, and manage their loyalty points (see Figure 1.6). The espresso experience may also include life between coffees. Starbucks' 35.9 million Facebook fans and 5 million Twitter followers clearly want to engage with the company. For others, purchasing their espresso from Starbucks may be an expression of their values. They may feel connected to the company via its social and sustainability efforts, as represented in the program's tagline, "You & Starbucks: It's bigger than coffee." And that is only a fraction of the possibilities.

Figure 1.6   Starbucks App—Mobile Payments, Automated Loyalty, and Text Communications in One

Source: http://www.starbucks.com/coffeehouse/mobile-apps/mystarbucks

We refer to the sum of these brand impressions over time as the customer experience journey. These experiences can take place while our customers are searching, evaluating, or consuming our products or services, as well as between purchases and even outside the purchase process. Every one of these encounters is considered a touchpoint.

Touchpoints can be static, meaning one-way communications from us, such as when a customer receives a direct mail piece from us, or they can be interactive, like a tweet exchange or a visit to one of our stores. (Recognizing the value of engaging with our customers, most of our static brand experiences now invite our customers to engage with us in more interactive environments.) They may involve direct interaction with our employees in environments like a call center or sales call, or they may stop short of that with a simple download of a white paper. Each of these touchpoints is supported by a complex and interconnected system including Operations, IT, Finance, Human Resources, and Marketing, and by a broader ecosystem, which may include manufacturers, suppliers, media partners, and retailers.

Our prospects' and customers' brand experience include all of the interactions they have directly *with* us, as well as the interactions they have *about* us with their peers. Social media has fostered a recommendation-based global economy, creating unprecedented opportunities for people to seek out information from peers and to influence others. Some of these conversations take place in our branded social environments in the form of a post on our Facebook page or comment on our blog. Many take place in other public and private social environments and plenty still take place around the water fountain or over a cup of coffee.

Each brand experience contributes to people's overall perception of our customer experience (see Figure 1.7). Trust us, customers *always* have a perception of their encounters with us. These responses range from horrible to great or perhaps the dreaded state of indifference. These perceptions are fluid; they can change over time with additional encounters.

These perceptions are significant—they largely define our brands. As our customers write tweets, texts, reviews, upload photos, and

MANY FACTORS IMPACT CUSTOMER EXPERIENCE

Search experience

Community experience

Product or service experience

CUSTOMER

Service and customer care experience

Digital experience (blogs, social, email, website, mobile)

Shopping experience (in-store, ecommerce)

Non-digital marketing experiences

Figure 1.7   Multiple Touches Shape the Customer Experience

make recommendations, they are shaping our brands. This communication amounts to a lot of influence, on par with the big advertising spends of days gone by, because word-of-mouth influence is powerful stuff in a recommendation-driven environment like ours. These perceptions also determine whether our product or services will ultimately be acquired as research shows that brand experience is the single biggest factor in a prospect's decision to purchase a product or service.[10]

Get Customer Experience Savvy—It Pays

Clearly there are many moving parts that contribute to how consumers experience our brands, some of which are in our control and some of which are not. (The manufacturing company John Deere identified over 525 possible touches with its constituents!) These moving parts have to work together, consistently, to deliver remarkable brand experiences that capture our customers' attention and that stand out from the competition in a positive way.

Recognizing the complexity of the task, it is logical to ask ourselves if it is really worth the effort. Rest assured, there is gold in them hills. The customer experience differential represents a large opportunity for multiple reasons:

1. **Customer expectations for brand experience are widespread.** According to a recent study conducted by the marketing agency Jack Morton Worldwide (JMW), over 80 percent of people say that they are more likely to consider brands with differentiated experiences.[11] Although this is true across market segments, people between the ages of 25 and 34 are "most likely to consider, recommend, or pay a premium price based on a better brand experience."[12] Similarly, research undertaken by the strategy consulting firm McKinsey & Company found that customer experience impacts two-thirds of the decisions customers make; price often drives the remaining third.[13]

   Heightened brand experience expectations are not just characteristic of customers in mature markets. In China, for example, 93.8 percent of consumers surveyed said they were more likely to consider brands based on experience, compared with a worldwide average of 80.4 percent.[14]

2. **Few companies have made inroads into realizing the customer experience differential to date.** Although most managers believe that they are already delivering great brand experiences, a 2013 survey undertaken by Forrester Research found that only 8 percent of consumers agreed. In fact, 61 percent rated their experience as ranging from okay to poor or very poor.[15] This is a significant disconnect—and opportunity.

   Forrester also found that some industries are so lacking in customer focus—health insurance plans and Internet service providers are at the bottom of the list, as shown in Figure 1.8—that simply being adequate can create a point

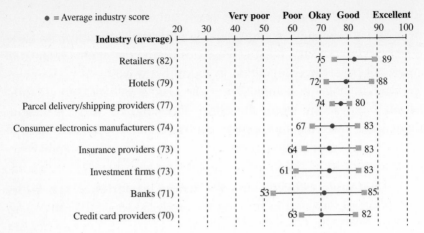

Figure 1.8   Customer Experience Varies across and within Industries

Source: **Megan Burns, Forrester Research, Inc. Report, "The Customer Experience Index, 2013," Forrester Research, Inc., January 15, 2013.**

of differentiation from the competition. In most industries, however, there are one or two exceptional leaders and many others that lag significantly behind.[16]

3. **Remarkable customer experience pays.** Customer experiences with brands impact margins. American Express found that 67 percent of Americans would spend an average of 13 percent more with a company that provides excellent customer service.[17] Not surprisingly, advocacy is also affected. JMW found that 87 percent of those surveyed said they are more likely to recommend a brand based on superior experience.[18] In fact, 79 percent said they would *only* advocate for brands *after* they have a great customer experience.[19]

USAA Understands and Delivers

In the financial services industry, the United States Automobile Association (USAA) leads the pack in terms of customer experience and with good reason: they have made a concerted effort to engage their entire company in the effort. A few years ago the company, which serves military personell and their families, consolidated its customer-experience–related operations under an EVP of member experience. Today, almost half of USAA's employees are on the member-experience team, which is responsible for "setting strategy, monitoring performance, and driving innovation."[20]

To enhance its members' experience, the company recently reorganized its product offerings to better reflect and anticipate the actual steps that USAA members take when purchasing their products. For example, knowing that when their members purchase a car they may be also looking to secure a car loan and insurance coverage, the company now bundles these offerings into an integrated service. Through its mobile app, website, and/or contact centers, or some combination thereof, the company's 9.7 million members and their families can easily find, finance, and insure a car.

Seeing its business through the eyes of its customers paid off. Today, USAA enjoys the highest customer experience rankings across all three industries in which the company is active. These rankings translate into hard cash: the company has enjoyed double-digit increases in auto sales and loans.

What Do Our Customers Want from Us?

People's expectations for brands are increasing; 57 percent of customers say they hold brands to higher standards than they did previously.[21] Our customers become accustomed to the standard of experience offered by companies like Amazon and Marketo, which is always being enhanced. Yesterday's exceptional experiences quickly become today's baseline.

To stay relevant, we have to keep our finger on the pulse of what really matters to *our* customers and build remarkable experiences around that. As a result, the answer to the question—What do our customers want from us?—will differ for every organization; however, there are some basic elements of customer experience that are becoming universal.

Understand and Meet Their Needs

To attract and sustain our prospects' and customers' attention and win their business, we have to offer products, services, and experiences that meet their needs or desires. An understanding of the underlying customers and their needs and desires must accompany this functionality, creating tremendous opportunities for brands that can develop truly empathize with their customers and translate that understanding into products, services, and experiences.[22]

Our marketing must also be purposeful, achieving what marketing consultant Jay Baer describes as, "Youtility," marketing so useful that our customers would pay for it.[23] We can offer entertainment, inspiration, information, or self-actualization, but without being useful, we do not have a shot of being invited in to the customer journey.

Useful does not mean boring. In fact, useful experiences are usually drawn from deep wells of creativity. Take a look at what Nike is doing as an example. Knowing that its customers enjoy the opportunity to express themselves, Nike encourages them to design their own running shoes. By offering them the chance to personalize their shoes on the basis of performance features and appearance, Nike gives its customers the opportunity to say to the world, "This is who I am."

Recognizing the larger aspiration behind their customers' purchase of running shoes, Nike designs experiences that help them reach their fitness goals and enjoy an active life. Runners can map their runs—including elevation details—and track their workout progress through the Nike+ app. When they need a bit of extra motivation to make it up that last hill, Nike's customers can choose a high-energy song from one of the company's playlists. If they have previously alerted their friends of their run on Facebook or Path, they can hear real-time cheers along the way for every like or comment they receive (Figure 1.9).

For their street-soccer fans in Spain, Nike goes beyond the call of duty to provide opportunities for pickup games. Through #MiPista, the company creates temporary playing fields with laser beams projected from a crane onto flat open surfaces below. Using their smartphones, players can request that Nike's traveling team install a

Figure 1.9   Nike Helps Its Customers Reach Their Fitness Goals with its Nike+ App
Source: **iTunes.apple.com/us/app/nike+-running/id387771637**

temporary soccer field and then get to work rounding up players. Within minutes, empty spaces are transformed into illuminated street-soccer fields. Take a moment to enjoy photos on Nike's blog; they are inspiring.[24]

For anyone, anywhere, who is interested in being fit, Nike offers its FuelBand, an electronic bracelet that tracks and measures their movements throughout the day, whether generated from a tennis match, an early morning run, or just walking around the office. Movements are measured in NikeFuel, a proprietary metric that can be evaluated over time, shared with friends, and applied to unlock levels and content on the company's digital game, NikeFuel Missions. It is experiences like these that delight Nike's customers and generate $25 billion a year in revenue.

Offer Relevant Interactions

Today's time-pressed customers want relevance. For many years we have operated under the assumption that our customers want more options; however, research conducted by American psychologist Barry Schwartz found that for most people, having too many options is anxiety producing rather than freeing.[25] Highly targeted experiences that zero in our customer's needs and desires simplify their lives; for many that is considered a gift.

Diane Hessan, CEO of Communispace, which creates private online customer communities for companies, describes this gift in the context of a couple. Tired after a long workweek, they are making plans for Friday night dinner. The man texts his girlfriend asking her to make the reservation at any place she wants, thinking he is doing her a favor by letting her choose the type of food and the venue they will enjoy. Rather than being energized by being given the choice, the woman thinks to herself, "If he really loved me, he would handle this, so all I have to do is show up. I would have even paid!"

What does this mean for marketers? Relevance is nothing short of offering the right experience, in the right format, on the right device(s), when our customers are ready. Relevance increasingly requires contextualized experiences that reflect the individual customer's behavior, preferences, current situation, and are often predictive. This type of personalized marketing experience has long been a dream for marketers, and big data and advanced analytics are now making this dream a reality. From our customers' point of view, relevance means feeling known, not in an invasive or creepy way, but in a way that says, "Can we be of assistance?" It is the difference between being welcome and being annoying.

In the case of Starbucks, relevance could be a personalized e-mail (or SMS text) sent to a customer at the time of day when he or she frequently makes a beverage purchase. The e-mail could feature the signature Starbucks' cup and, as in Figure 1.10, include the customer's name and maybe his or her favorite drink order.

Or relevance could take the form of a personalized video or a Pinterest-like digital bulletin board, sent to a prospect who has recently visited a retailer's website to evaluate and price televisions.

Figure 1.10 Starbucks Customizes Its Customer Interactions

The content could provide additional information about the models that caught their attention, including customer ratings, details about nearby stores where the selected models are presently in stock, and a link enabling an online purchase.

Invite Participation

The interactions that Amazon, Nike, and Marketo enjoy with their customers incorporate another important component of today's customer-centricity: participation. This broadcast era of one-way messaging is gone; effective communication now is about engagement. Customers are often looking for us to provide more than just a product or a service: They are looking for experiences.

Experiences can be digital, physical, or some combination of both. The interactive mobile app, Stylewhile, for example, adds a new dimension to the digital shopping experience.[26] Shoppers can visualize what outfits will look like by dressing an avatar, whose skin tone, hair, and body size can be adjusted to resemble the person for whom the item is being purchased. The app facilitates a fun and novel experience, while removing one of the challenges of purchasing clothes online: visualizing how clothes will actually look.

Similarly, retailers who adapt their in-store experience to leverage the unique capabilities of mobile are finding that it increases sales.[27] The Sprooki shopping app, for example, enhances the in-store experience for shoppers in Singapore.[28] While in or near the mall, shoppers receive deal alerts on their smartphones from participating retailers. If intrigued, would-be buyers can browse and purchase the items directly from their smartphones and pick them up at their convenience.

Creating digital communities around our brands provides our prospects and customers with some of the richest experiences. It might be hard to conceive that people want to connect around diapers, but they do. The Huggies Community, for example, brings together parents to talk about all things child-related. Dell Ideastorm invites customers to cocreate new products and services and to enhance existing offerings. One of the first companies to publicly tap customers for ideas since the site's launch in 2007, the company has garnered more than 15,000 ideas from interested users and implemented close to 500 from them.

Engage Before, During, and After

Our customers want to be educated and engaged on an ongoing basis. According to a study conducted by JMW, this is especially true for customers who say that unique brand experience impacts their brand choice.[29] Many want self-service access to content early in the customer journey, so that they can evaluate potential purchases before they contact a salesperson or walk into a store. Some want ongoing connections after a purchase is made—timely information that keeps them in the know, invitations to special events, and opportunities to share their experience and opinions. By inviting engagement throughout the customer experience journey, we can develop relationship-based loyalty, rather than the more fickle transaction-based version.

To keep its fans engaged, Scrabble set up free Wi-Fi hotspots across Paris in areas lacking coverage. To access the Scrabble network, people were invited to play a digital version of the game, which unlocked the necessary password. The length of time awarded on the network was based on the player's Scrabble score; better spellers were rewarded for their skill with more time. In addition to enabling the brand to connect with its fans, the experience prompted Scrabble players to try the digital version of the game.

Keep It Simple

Ease of use is highly important to today's customers, who have short attention spans and little patience for anything lengthy, delivered slowly, or technically imperfect. The average attention span of adults has decreased from 12 seconds in 2000 to 8 seconds in 2012, giving us the distinction of now having a shorter attention span than a goldfish (9 seconds).[30] The average American in his or her twenties switches media venues 27 times per non-working hour. He or she also multiscreens, browsing multiple screens at once, often absorbing unrelated content simultaneously.[31]

As a result, interacting with us has to be easy, inviting, and hopefully fun, or our customers will go elsewhere. At its best, the technology we employ to engage with our customers should be so simple that it is invisible; the experience that the tools are trying to deliver should be what is remembered. When our customers connect with us in person or over the phone, our employees should be so helpful and the processes so streamlined that people notice—and are perhaps even delighted.

Ease of use also means that our engagement with customers takes place where they are, not where it is most convenient for us to be. We can assume that our customers want to communicate with us in a variety of ways depending on where they are and the nature of the interaction—e-mail, voice, SMS text, apps, call centers, and in person. This means we need to be able to deliver a seamless and interconnected brand experience across channels and devices. While challenging to deliver, this omni-experience can capture the attention of distracted customers by creating a consistent surround sound as they migrate across channels.

Be Real and Be Worthy

Social media offers an interactive marketing experience where we can engage directly with our prospects and customers as individuals. As we draw closer to these constituents, we become more like friends in a neighborhood, rather than buyers and sellers. Many of our communications happen in their Facebook and Twitter streams, right above or below their friends' and family's updates. Mobile devices offer access to our customers throughout their day, whether they are in budget meetings, at the soccer field, or on a first date. This intimacy has changed the social contract between businesses and their customers, requiring a new level of responsiveness, respect, and transparency from companies.

To be worthy of this connection, we must be mindful and respectful of our expanding role in people's lives. Are we truly being useful? Is our cadence right? Are we listening? Are we being too intrusive? Are we being good stewards of the customer data that makes these highly personalized interactions possible? A breach of security or a sense of being too closely observed or intruded upon will turn the dial backwards, perhaps irreparably, in terms of customer-centricity.

Involvement in social environments challenges marketers to be transparent about the ways our companies do business. Everlane, an innovative e-commerce company that creates quality tees, shirts, sweaters, and accessories, has built its brand around this quality. It encourages its customers to "Know your factories. Know your costs. Always ask why."[32] Colorful photos on its website take us behind the scenes to see exactly how their fabrics are created, cut, sewn, dyed, finished, pressed, and packed. Descriptions and snapshots of the factories that manufacture Everlane products tell the story of the

28

company's partners: where they are located, how many people they employ, how Everlane discovered them, and reassurances about the integrity of each partners' workplace. The company also discloses its costs and profit margin, openly making the case for why it can provide quality, value, and ethically manufactured products simultaneously.

Be Meaningful

Everlane is tapping into another key component of remarkable customer experience: a vehicle for people to live out their values. John Maeda, the former president of Rhode Island School of Design (RISD), explains, "What people want today goes well beyond technology and design. What people are looking for now is a way to reconnect with their *values*: to ground how they can, will, and should live in the world."[33] Many of our prospects and customers want us to be meaningful brands, brands with a point of view that is larger than our product lines; brands with a true connection to underlying values, not a superficial greenwashing.

Dove, which manufactures skin and hair care products, is consistently seen as a brand that is making a difference. Inspired by market research that indicated that only 4 percent of women consider themselves beautiful, Dove is committed to "building self-esteem and inspiring all women and girls to reach their full potential."[34] Toward this end, the company launched the Dove Campaign for Real Beauty. Encouraging men and women to "imagine a world where beauty is a source of confidence, not anxiety," the brand has brought discussion of "what comprises beauty?" into the public arena.

Dove continues to push forward the conversation, most recently with its Dove Real Beauty Sketches. In this latest social experiment, Dove uses videos of women describing their appearances to illustrate how they are often their own worst beauty critics. In the video, several women describe their looks to a forensic artist who sketches them unseen, based solely upon their description of themselves. These sketches are compared with drawings created by the same artist with one important distinction: they are based upon strangers' descriptions of the women. The differences are stark; the strangers' images are far more accurate—and attractive.

29

Though these initiatives are at times controversial, Dove is putting a stake in the ground, boldly articulating what it considers to be important. In so doing, the brand attracts and builds bonds with prospects and customers who feel similarly. It has also earned the distinction of being a meaningful brand.

What comprises a meaningful brand? The communications company Havas Media developed the Meaningful Brands Index (MBi) to measure and assess the correlation between financial performance and the benefits brands bring to people's lives in terms of health, happiness, finances, relationships, and community, among others. Their findings are important: Being a meaningful brand is not just a nice idea; it pays. In 2013, Meaningful Brands outperformed the stock market by 120 percent.[35] Dove is among them.

How Remarkable Do We Need to Be?

Throughout *The Digital Marketer* we encourage companies to set their sights on delivering remarkable customer experience. What do we mean by remarkable? We like the definition put forward by marketing guru Seth Godin: "worthy of remark."[36] Remarkable experiences do not have to be accompanied by fireworks or a parade. Some of the most remarkable moments are everyday experiences done well. Think Amazon.

How remarkable do *we* have to be? It depends upon our customers, competition, industries, and businesses. Although customer experience leaders are raising the bar for every organization, *our* criteria for customer experience must reflect our value proposition and the factors that are most important to our customers.

JetBlue is a customer experience leader in the airline industry. The company goes to great lengths to understand the key factors that impact its customers' travel experience, measure those influences regularly, and incorporate this insight into its day-to-day operations. As a result, its everyday experience is worthy of remark. Indeed, as the Twitter exchange in Figure 1.11 captures, one satisfied customer did remark, quite publicly and colorfully, about her positive experience with the airline. Knowing that responsiveness is a key driver of remarkable customer experience, the airline offered a witty reply.

Figure 1.11   JetBlue Delights Its Customers
Source: **https://twitter.com/JetBlue/status/1768096120**

On some occasions, we may choose to take our customer experience efforts up a notch as Morton's Steakhouse did for one its customers, author and entrepreneur Peter Shankman. After a long day of travel and before boarding his last flight, Shankman sent a lighthearted tweet to Morton's Steakhouse, a restaurant chain where he dines frequently, facetiously asking them to meet him at Newark Airport with a porterhouse steak when his plane landed. Two hours later when he landed in Newark, he was surprised and delighted to find that his dinner awaited him. What is more, it was hand delivered to the terminal, free of charge, by a tuxedo-clad server. Shankman summarized the experience in his blog: "I. Was. Floored."[37] That is a remarkable, out of the ordinary, experience.

Whether a unique happening that surprises and delights or the consistent efficient and effective delivery of something more routine, remarkable experiences cause people to take note, perhaps crack a smile, breathe a sigh of relief, or make a remark. That is how good we want to be.

Will We Ignore Change, Grow with It, or Drive It?

Many marketers feel unprepared in this dynamic, confusing, and highly promising environment. The question for each of us is, "Will we ignore change, grow with it, or drive it?" The fact that you are reading *The Digital Marketer* suggests you want to grow and perhaps drive change going forward.

In the pages that follow we explore the 10 essential skills necessary to be relevant in today's marketplace. As marketers we do not have to become experts in all 10 skill areas, but we do need to understand their benefits and limitations, and how they can contribute to delivering remarkable customer experiences. Here is a quick overview.

1. Build a Successful Marketing Career

Success in this marketing landscape requires that we be agile— learning, unlearning, and relearning—in order to be marketers who can adapt to change. It can be a challenge to let go of ideas, practices, and perspectives that have worked well and even made us marketing stars in the past. Research shows, however, that those proven leaders who cannot let go of entrenched patterns, however, do not thrive in turbulent times.[38]

Living in a state of discovery can feel exhausting and unsettling, but consider this: In a world where the terrain is shifting, standing still is an extraordinarily risky proposition. While we instinctually seek safety, a more successful approach is adaptation. As Reid Hoffman, founder of LinkedIn and coauthor of *The Start-Up of You* warns, "Without frequent, contained risk taking, you are setting yourself up for a major dislocation at some point in the future."[39]

Plenty of opportunity exists for those of us who can successfully re-envision our roles and expand our skillsets to match the needs of this new marketing environment. Positions like Content Strategist, Community Builder, Converged Media Specialist, Marketing Technologist, and Manager of Customer Experience reflect some of the new competencies that companies are developing in their quest for customer-centricity. Several new C-level positions that focus on the customer are opening new career paths. (More about this in Chapter 2.)

To take advantage of the opportunities that this new landscape offers we must actively manage our careers to identify the skills and experiences we need, and how we are going to acquire them. Intentionally building our networks creates vital and vetted information flows that keep us up-to-date and augment our resource base. Branding ourselves and being thoughtful about proactively managing our reputation and contributions to the field have become essential. Seeking out developmental relationships including mentors and sponsors can offer necessary support to boost our careers. Finally, consciously putting ourselves in situations where we can feed and flex our creative muscles kindles our imagination, uncovering new possibilities for how we can contribute.

2. Design Valuable Customer Experiences

In an environment in which customer experience is increasingly critical, the thoughtful design of individual customer experiences, and of how multiple touchpoints work together as a whole, is too vital to be left to chance. Knowledge of design thinking, a disciplined process of observation, idea generation, and rapid iteration of products, content, and experiences, jumpstarts our organizations' creativity and transports us beyond our "go-to" options, unlocking new opportunities for creating shared value. An understanding of basic tenants of behavior design and the persuasive impact of technology enhances our ability to create interactions that prompt people to act. Mapping the customer journey of each of our market segments deepens our understanding of when, where, and how our prospects and customers interact with us. By tracking their sentiment across each of these touchpoints, we can evaluate the effectiveness of each of these encounters, prioritize our efforts, and optimize our customer experience.

For example, working with MCorp Consulting, a customer experience and brand consultancy, a large commercial real estate lender that struggled with low rates of customer satisfaction and retention realized significant improvements in its customer experience. By mapping its customer touchpoints, the company was able to evaluate the effectiveness of its interactions and identify those who were most essential for driving customer engagement. Drawing from this insight, the company was able to improve or eliminate underachieving touchpoints, create new processes, redefine roles and responsibilities, and

33

establish relevant metrics, enhancing its customers' satisfaction and loyalty, and increasing overall loan volume.[40]

3. Find Actionable Insight in Big Data and Marketing Analytics

Big data and marketing analytics can be powerful tools for marketers. Indeed, after analyzing more than 250 customer engagements over the span of five years, McKinsey concluded that companies that put data at the center of the marketing and sales decisions have been able to improve their marketing return on investment by 15 to 20 percent—that equates to $150–$200 billion of additional value based on global annual marketing spend of an estimated $1 trillion.[41] Best Buy is among those companies that are realizing gains. As an example, the consumer electronics retailer was able to double membership in its Red Zone loyalty program in three months through a razor-targeted e-mail campaign prompted by insight derived from advanced customer analytics.[42]

Finding the business value in clicks, shares, swipes, and pins is easier said than done, however. It requires an ability to capture relevant data, integrate disparate data sources, maintain and store massive amounts of information, and apply advanced analytics to detect the important signals amid a lot of noise.

How technical do marketers need to become in order to realize this value? Going forward it will be impossible to separate marketing from technology—software, content, creativity, and infrastructure will be completely interwoven. However, this does not mean that marketers must become data scientists. We do need to be capable of broad analytic thinking so that we can ask the probing questions that frame solid data analysis and be able to build and manage technically savvy teams. Given how critical the insights derived from big data and analytics are to the success of our marketing efforts, we must also be informed enough to influence or own the purchase of the necessary technology and ensure that it can be readily adapted for use by front-line marketing managers.

4. Employ Entrepreneurial Thinking for Discernment and Agility

In markets characterized by high levels of uncertainty and rapid change, an entrepreneurial approach to decision-making enables us to act quickly in response to changing market conditions, even in the face of ambiguity. Amazon CEO Jeff Bezos is notorious for his entrepreneurial decision-making style. Favoring intelligent action over intelligent inaction, Bezos has a "ready, fire, steer" style, as opposed to the traditional "ready, aim, fire approach." Bezos encourages his employees to spend less time aiming and more time doing in order to drive creativity and innovation. One of the company's internal awards, "Just Do It," recognizes employees who take the initiative to do positive things for the company without having to involve their boss.

Entrepreneurial decision-making does not mean shooting from the hip. Rather, it means creating evidence for or against our ideas through immediate and frequent testing. This iterative process allows us to continuously act and learn, enhancing our organizations' knowledge, experience, and agility. Entrepreneurial decision-making also includes practices such as determining budgets by defining acceptable losses, pursuing multiple options simultaneously, and building purposeful partner networks. Being able to decipher when to apply entrepreneurial decision-making and when to employ traditional analytic methods is essential for today's marketer.

Consider the experience of the early stage company Carsurfing. Building upon customers' appetite for sharing services, Carsurfing set out to develop a mobile application to facilitate ride sharing to major cultural and sporting events. Before the app was ready to be launched, members of the Carsurfing team noticed a high volume of chatter in social environments about Burning Man, an annual art festival in Nevada. Recognizing the opportunity that the festival presented to test the validity of their product idea, the team moved quickly to temporarily shift their focus from building the app to creating a dedicated landing page for Facebook users that were planning on attending the event. The Company's ability to move quickly paid off.

35

By tapping into the conversations and creating a space for festival attendees to connect, Carsurfing was able to facilitate over 800 rides to Burning Man, attracting its first customers and validating their "barely alpha" product at the same time.[43]

5. Create a Winning Content Experience Strategy

Our customers have changed the way they connect with brands. Traditional broadcast messaging is no longer effective on its own; content now drives our interactions. Our ability to tell great stories and design engaging experiences to catalyze customer connection is critical to our being invited into the customer experience journey. Storytelling is quite different from writing ad copy or press releases. It facilitates our prospects and customers finding themselves in our story and often includes tools that bring them into the experience.

Consider what McCormick is doing to engage its customers around spices, as shown in Figure 1.12. Understanding the truth in

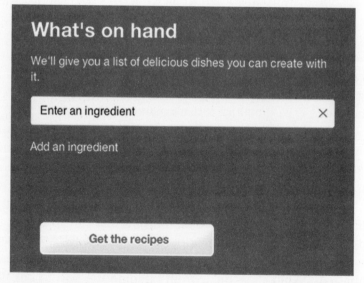

Figure 1.12   McCormick Helps Customers Create Meals with Ingredients on Hand

Source: http://www.mccormick.com

George Bernard Shaw's comment, "There is no love sincerer than the love of food," McCormick makes the world of flavors easily accessible to its customers. Cooks can plan their meals with the help of the company's website—even at the last minute—by simply inputting the food items and spices they have on hand. Acting like top chefs in a quick-fire challenge, McCormick generates recipes for a mouthwatering dinner.

To proactively design multiple menus around its customers' individualized food preferences, McCormick offers Flavorprint™. By filling out a simple digital survey, customers provide the necessary data to generate a footprint of their favorite flavors.[44] Based on this knowledge, McCormick recommends recipes that incorporate those flavors. Who knew that we would like Mojito Lime Grilled Lamb Chops and Smoky Montreal Steak Sauce Burgers? As cooks rate, search, and share recipes and products, Flavorprint™ gets smarter and more accurate with their taste bud preferences. All of McCormick's recipes and seasonings carry a FlavorPrint™ symbol that helps its customers make better selections even when they do not have access to these digital tools.

Understanding the power of peer-to-peer influence, McCormick encourages its customers to socialize their experiences and recipes in McCormick's multiple social environments including Pinterest, Instagram, Facebook, Twitter, and YouTube. Each of these touch-points offers McCormick and its customers an opportunity to get to know each other better and to share their solutions for leftovers, an abundance of zucchini, and a craving for cinnamon with a broader community.

6. Engage Customers via Social Communities

Social media has created virtual neighborhoods where our con-stituents spend an increasing amount of time. Ninety-one percent of online adults access social media at least once a month, and the average online adult spends 37 minutes on social media daily.[45] As a result, these networks and communities have become important touchpoints with our prospects and customers, often vital to cross-channel communication strategies. Conversations flow in these environments and important insights can often be found. In many instances, these networks and communities are influencing the design, manufacture, packaging, delivery, and servicing of our products and services, putting our customers directly in the center of our organizations.

To successfully play in the social sphere, marketers need to be well versed in each community's individual culture and norms of engagement, and be clear about how to best participate. Prioritization is necessary given the sheer number of social spaces where we can have a presence. Engagement involves monitoring the conversation 24/7, actively managing our presence, generating appropriate content, distilling the insight, and sharing what we learn with our broader ecosystem.

In some instances we may choose to develop our own social communities. For example, through the branded social community IBM PartnerWorld, IBM offers a broad range of resources that help its business partners build, sell, and implement IBM-based solutions for their customers. Partners are able to take advantage of IBM programs like *Selling Through Social Insights*, which taps into the power of social listening to increase sales. Social Insights tracks data from over 280 million relevant social sources. The Social Insights dashboard synthesizes "who is talking" and "what is trending" in five strategic subject areas related to IBM products. Personalized recommendations for relevant content, combined with access to relevant IBM experts, provide rich resources for business partners to get up to speed on what is currently on their prospects' minds. Armed with this knowledge, business partners are better able to turn leads into sales.

7. *Maximize Marketing Effectiveness by Integrating Paid, Earned, and Owned Media*

During the past few years, much focus has been placed on the power of owned media—the content that marketers create. Content belongs at the center of any of our experience strategies—it creates the customer experience journey. However, in many cases an integrated or converged strategy in which we combine our content with materials created by our customers (earned media) and amplify it with advertising (paid media) can maximize our impact.

Why is this the case? In a recommendation-based economy, earned media is paramount. It is what people find most credible. When we incorporate our customers' stories into our content, we are harnessing the most compelling advocates for our businesses: satisfied customers. New forms of paid media that draw from reservoirs of social media-derived customer data are creating unprecedented targeting opportunities, offering the promise of being able to reach our prospects and customers with highly relevant messaging in the channels they prefer.

A quick flip through a recent edition of *More* magazine, a magazine for "women of style and substance," illustrates this convergence via traditional media.[46] A two-page advertisement for L'Oréal's Visible Life CC Cream, features celebrity Andie MacDowell, who vouches for the color-correcting cream by saying, "No wonder it's my new best friend." On the adjacent page are before and after pictures of regular women who have experienced "the CC transformation," along with customer reviews from four happy users. Calls to action invite *More* readers to enter a contest to win samples of the product and to learn more about the cream on their website. Earned media (in the form of customer reviews) meets owned media (additional information about the product on their website) meets paid advertising (the ad itself).

8. Drive Sales with Intelligent Customer-Engagement Platforms

Our prospects and customers increasingly expect one-on-one contextualized interactions that reflect their behaviors and current situation–time, location, and device. Creating contextualized experiences is complex. It requires real-time capture of relevant customer data across channels and instantaneous application of predictive analytics to proactively offer appropriate resources. While this is challenging to do for one person, imagine the complexity of delivering contextualized experiences at scale.

To scale one-to-one communication, marketers need integrated customer-engagement platforms that can steward our prospects and customers through the customer experience journey. Smart marketing automation systems can assess where individuals are in the customer experience journey and distribute content specifically selected for them. They also detect potential content redundancies, changes in cadence, and shifts in interest and priorities, based upon behaviors such as clicks, views, shares, time spent with materials and reflect, and adapts content streams accordingly. This means that our customers are only invited into experiences that have a high probability of meeting their needs, avoiding spam.

Marketing automation also allows us to trace the impact of each marketing interaction on our prospects' and customers' behavior, making it possible for us to continually assess and optimize our efforts, and to more accurately demonstrate marketings' contributions to key financial metrics. For many companies, marketing automation has also brought marketing and sales into closer alignment, helping to alleviate age-old conflicts.

9. Build Worthwhile Loyalty and Digital Couponing Programs

Brands can no longer feel certain about their customers' commitment. Loyalty erosion and customer defection are pervasive. Ironically, most loyalty programs do not do much to create loyalty. Although people enroll in the programs, the majority are not inspired to remain active. The best way to create loyalty is to ensure incredible brand satisfaction by creating remarkable customer experiences. For some companies, offering a loyalty program that enhances the customer experience can be a winning strategy.

Starbucks' loyalty program is leading the way. Designed to give its customers more of what they love—coffee—"My Starbucks Rewards" grants free drinks and exclusive offers to customers based upon their usage. The first cross-channel loyalty program in the market, customers are rewarded for purchases made in Starbucks' shops as well as for Starbucks packaged coffee purchased in grocery stores.

The free mobile app automatically tracks and manages rewards, making participation in the program easy. The app also includes a scan-and-go purchase option, locates nearby Starbucks, and provides free downloads of new apps and music. One of our favorite features is the eGift, which makes it possible to send Starbucks' gift certificates to other loyalty members. Students love it when their parents send them a gift certificate for a fortified Red Eye during exams.

For some brands, a couponing strategy works well. A separate strategy from loyalty program offers, couponing may provide just the needed incentive to encourage potential customers to try, share, or act. Digital coupons and apps offer a faster and more convenient way for many customers to clip coupons.

Meijer, which operates groceries and superstores, offers its customers the opportunity to preview and select digital coupons and file them in their digital mPerks account, where they can be instantly redeemed at checkout. Their mobile app includes a find-it feature that makes it easy for customers to locate any item in the store.[47] The program enjoys a redemption rate of up to four times the national average.[48]

10. Ignite Customer-Centricity across the Organization

Customer-centricity requires a higher level of operational maturity than we have needed in the past, because multiple functions impact our customer experience. Acting like symphony conductors, marketers need to be able to collaborate across the entire business ecosystem to facilitate customer-centricity at every important touchpoint. This requires a realignment of efforts, the integrating of many processes and systems, and a shift in many of our organizations' culture. It is a tall order, but as we have seen, companies are rising to the challenge.

What is more, extraordinary value can be created when organizations move beyond their own borders to inspire customer-centricity throughout their larger ecosystems. By sharing end-user data and coordinating their efforts, an entire demand chain composed of manufacturers, retailers, and media companies can develop proprietary insights into demand. This enhanced, customer-oriented view creates unprecedented opportunity and competitive advantage for each partner and the network as a whole.

What's Next?

Overwhelmed? Remember, marketers do not have to be experts in each of these areas. Being knowledgeable in these 10 essential skills will take us a long way toward career success. In the pages that follow, we invite you to explore each of these 10 marketing skills in a way that we hope is useful for new hires as well as for the most experienced marketers. Examples of how large and small companies are putting these skills to work bring them more fully to life. Suggestions for metrics to evaluate success are included, where applicable, and lists of resources accompany each chapter. Hopefully, in the pages that follow, we will convince you that it is, indeed, a great time to be a digital marketer.

Consumers, Prospects, Customers, and Constituents

Throughout *The Digital Marketer*, we refer to consumers as prospects, customers, and constituents. This is intentional. By using the word *constituent*, we are challenging each of us to consider the needs and desires of the multiple stakeholders to which we are accountable—our prospects, customers, investors, regulators, employees, business partners, and more. We also hope to encourage thinking of our customers and prospects as more than transactions. This is not to imply that focusing on sales is not important. A business without revenue is not viable over the long term. A business that focuses exclusively on sales, however, is leaving far too much on the table. In today's connected world, we believe that when you get the relationship right, most everything else—sales, loyalty, and advocacy—will follow.

As a result, throughout *The Digital Marketer* we refer to our lifetime of interactions with our customers as the customer experience journey, rather than the transaction-based consumer purchase journey. This reframing more accurately captures the richness of this more genuine and collaborative relationship.

Throughout *The Digital Marketer*, we often describe the experiences of Larry Weber and Lisa Leslie Henderson, the cowriters of this book. Larry is the CEO of Racepoint Global, an advanced marketing services firm. A globally known expert in public relations and marketing services, Larry has successfully built companies and brands and is passionate about the future of marketing. Lisa is an observer, synthesizer, and writer who draws extensively from her background in marketing and consulting. Lisa and Larry have collaborated on two books to date, *The Digital Marketer*, and *Everywhere: Comprehensive Strategy for the Social Media Era*. To stay current on their thinking, frequent www.racepoint.com/thedigitalmarketer and follow them at @TheLarryWeber and @ljlhendo.

In the following chapter we consider how companies are responding to the customer-centric era.

QUESTIONS FOR CONSIDERATION

- Reflect on a recent experience in which you were the customer. What worked well? What needed to be improved? If you were in charge of improving the customer experience, what would you recommend?

- How important is the customer's experience in your industry? To your company? How well are you delivering? How do you know?

(continued)

(continued)

- How would your customers describe the essential Drivers of your brand experience, the make-it-or-break-it features?
- Which of the 10 essential skills do you want to further develop?
- What is your next step?

RESOURCES

Influencers We Recommend

- *Linda Boff.* As executive director of global digital marketing for General Electric (GE), Boff is the leader of the company's digital-marketing and global-advertising efforts. A self-proclaimed lover of modern art and *Mad Men* enthusiast, you can follow Boff on Twitter @lindaboff.

- *Chip Conley.* Founder and former CEO of Joie de Vivre Hospitality, Conley is a writer and thought leader in creating meaningful customer experiences. His titles include *Marketing That Matters* and *Peak*. Connect with Conley at www.chipconley.com and on Twitter @chipconley.

- *David Edelman.* Coleader of the Digital Marketing Strategy Group at McKinsey & Co., Edelman works across industries to understand the implications of the ever-evolving digital environment on organizations. A Top-5 LinkedIn Influencer, Edelman is a frequent contributor to *Forbes*, *The Economist*, and *Harvard Business Review* blog. Follow him on Twitter at @davidedelman and on McKinsey's *Latest Thinking* blog: www.cmsoforum.mckinsey.com.

- *Seth Godin.* Best-selling author, entrepreneur, and marketer, Godin writes about "the post-industrial revolution, the way ideas spread, marketing, quitting, leadership and most of all, changing everything."[49] Read his latest thoughts, by literally clicking on the image of his head at www.sethgodin.com or follow him on Twitter @thisissethsblog.

- *Harley Manning*. Research director in the Customer Experience practice at Forrester Research, Manning is the coauthor of *Outside In* with Kerry Bodine. Learn the latest on what Forrester is uncovering in customer experience on his blog at www.blogs.forrester.com/harley_manning or on Twitter @hmanning.

- *Scott Monty*. Scott Monty, the global head of social media for Ford Motor Company, writes *The Social Media Marketing Blog*. Monty describes this personal blog as a "series of links about current events and trends in the worlds of technology, social media, mobile, communications, and marketing in order to keep the wider team up to date on the changes, newsworthy items, and content that might be useful in their jobs."[50] Find Monty at www.ScottMonty.com and follow him on Twitter at @Scott Monty.

- *Dharmesh Shah*. Cofounder and chief technology officer of HubSpot, an inbound software company, Shah is a serial entrepreneur, having built and shipped at least 10 commercial products across a variety of start-ups. He is the coauthor of *Inbound Marketing: Getting Found Using Google, Social Media, and Blogs*. Follow Shah on Twitter @dharmesh and read his contributions to www.onstartups.com.

Hashtags to Explore

- #customerexperience
- #cx (customer experience)

(continued)

45

(continued)

- #digital
- #digitalmarketing
- #marketing
- #mktg (marketing)
- #UX (customer experience)

Chapter 2

How Organizations Are Adapting to the Customer-Centric Era

"There is only one boss—the customer. And he can fire everybody in the company from the chairman on down, simply by spending his money somewhere else." [1]

—Sam Walton, founder of Walmart and Sam's Club

There is a shake-up going on in the C-suite. It happens every time there is a game-changing disruption in the marketplace. When Larry first began his career there were only two C-level positions in most companies: the chief executive officer and the chief financial officer. Over time additional people were invited to the table. When information systems were identified as a new source of competitive advantage, the chief technology officer role was born. When software became critical, the chief information officer was introduced. When a renewed emphasis on human assets became a high management priority, the chief people officer position was created. Today companies are introducing several new C-level positions reflecting new priorities on multiple fronts.

Although it goes by several names—chief customer officer, chief client officer, and the chief experience officer—this new position is focused on understanding and enhancing the customer experience, that is, the sum of all the experiences a customer has with a brand over time. Down the hall is the chief design officer (CDO), who is charged with infusing creativity throughout the customer experience, organization, and strategy process. The chief information officer

47

(CIO) is now located next to the chief marketing officer, reflecting the importance of data in driving marketing results. At times this change in location is accompanied by a change in title—but not acronym—as CIO is being redefined as chief integration officer, chief insight officer, or chief innovation officer. Some companies are taking a different approach, installing a chief data officer (CDO) or chief analytics officer (CAO) to transform their businesses into data-driven enterprises, by combining management experience with technical ability.

The thread that runs through all of these positions is a piercing focus on our customers. There is also a recognition that the ability to design and deliver remarkable customer experience requires organizational capabilities beyond most marketing departments. An appreciation for the unique contributions that creativity, data, and analytics make in developing a deep understanding of our customers' needs and desires, in designing the products, services, environments, and experiences through which that demand will be satisfied, and in having the infrastructure and operational ability to deliver them, is also pervasive.

The CCEO: Shifting Our COMPANY'S Point of View

Given the importance and complexity of the customer experience in defining our brands and in our ability to reach key financial goals, it is not surprising that companies are establishing new roles to lead the effort. A common strategy is to begin with an internal advisory group that is charged with developing proof points, building organizational support, and coordinating cross-functional efforts. Over time these consultative models often morph into an operational model, in which related functions are consolidated under one leader who is responsible for managing the customer experience across the organization.

Senior managers with extensive experience that span operations, quality control, marketing, and information systems are filling these roles, which for ease of reference we will refer to as the chief customer experience officer (CCEO). Their rich and varied backgrounds provide them with the credibility and networks to lead the effort across functions, business units, and third-party partners. And they have the ear of their CEOs: Seventy-five percent of CCOs sit on the executive management team of their companies and more than half report directly to the CEO.[2]

Wayne Peacock heads USAA's member experience effort. He is responsible for marketing, sales and service, and enterprise data and analytics across all channels, and he serves on the USAA Executive Council. Initially Peacock was part of an internal advisory group that carried out USAA's customer experience effort, but over time the company's leadership felt that consolidation was necessary to "make it how we operate."[3]

How have members benefitted from the consolidation? By managing this broad portfolio directly, Peacock is better able to focus and integrate each of the underlying function's efforts. Consolidation allows USAA to move away from traditional product-based silos to focus on meeting its members' needs across the customer journey. These needs can vary considerably from the time members are teenagers until the time they retired and are contemplating passing on a financial legacy. As we saw in Chapter 1, being able to combine products from across the organization in ways that makes sense for each member's current life stage needs, allows the company to deliver superior value for its members.[4]

In addition, working with USAA has become even easier. Technology has enabled the company to provide members with an insurance agent or financial advisor anytime and anywhere. Members can buy, finance, and insure their homes and automobiles by phone, mobile device, desktop, or in-person, and take advantage of its low-bandwidth options when they are in remote locations. Through its Virtual Mobile Assistant, a Siri-like function available on its iPhone app, the company is simplifying its overall mobile customer experience making its app more appealing and accessible to a broader base of members, especially the elderly and those with disabilities. Video conferencing technology allows members to talk face-to-face with specialists when needed. Deposits can be made by simply taking a photo of a check or by walking into a branch or local UPS store.

USAA has made financial planning more accessible by creating budgeting and retirement planning tools and an application that consolidates members' financial reporting, including accounts that are held at other financial institutions. A Family Life Advice Center provides useful information on managing key life transitions such as marriage, starting a family, divorce, financing college, and the loss of a loved one. Special digital communities for military spouses and veterans are vital resources where people can "get in touch and help each other out." For these and other ground-breaking efforts, *Fast Company* named Peacock one of the most creative people in business.

So why are companies hiring chief design officers?

The CDO: Expanding Our Organization's Way of Thinking

When we think of design, we often think of making objects more beautiful or functional, but our notion of design is expanding. Today design encompasses the broader strategic process of need finding and problem solving that tees up great products, services, spaces, and experiences, a discipline known as *design thinking*.

Tom Kelley, best-selling author and partner at the design and innovation firm IDEO (and author of multiple books on innovation) explains this shift in perspective about design, "We [designers] used to feel as if we were sitting at the kid's table of the business world. There was serious business going on elsewhere—in the boardroom or a meeting room. The world has changed. Design and creativity are now central to what goes on in business."[5]

Rather than being brought in at the last minute to pretty up an offering, designers are now invited to the strategy table early on to ignite the creative juices of their organizations and enhance their approach to developing strategy. Their customer-focused, bottom-up methodology reaches beyond traditional market research, bringing a new depth of insight to the table.

"In the last decade there has been a realization that our traditional way of developing strategy, which focused on optimizing resources from the company's point of view, is no longer sufficient in and of itself," explains Rodrigo Martinez, life sciences chief strategist and senior portfolio director at IDEO. "To be innovative, we have to work harder, taking a human-centered approach to strategy, asking ourselves, 'What type of experience would it take to really engage our customer? What do we want this specific moment to be like for the people experiencing it?'"

To develop this complementary approach to strategy creation, in addition to collaborating with design-focused organizations like IDEO, companies are hiring chief design officers. PepsiCo recently hired its first CDO to infuse a design mind-set into the culture of the company and into the success of its top 12 brands. Indra Nooyi, CEO of PepsiCo, recently explained why she created this role to *Fast Company*, "Market growth alone doesn't give you enough tailwind. You have to create your own. The way to do that is by designing products for consumers that wow them.... Not just the way they look but that every aspect of what they buy delights them."[6]

Designers are also running companies. Two young designers founded and are managing Airbnb, the digital marketplace for renting spare rooms, homes, and even private islands in over 34,000 cities and 192 countries. Another two sold their start-up, Pulse, the popular newsreader for web and mobile, to LinkedIn for $90 million. No, designers are no longer sitting at the kids' table.

Design Matters in the Big Scheme of Things

Design is a key lever for relevance. It drives macro-level innovation, like new value propositions and product lines, as well as more granular customer interactions. At the highest level, the processes associated with design help us uncover and evaluate new ways to create value—and stay in business.

Saul Kaplan, cofounder and chief catalyst at the Business Innovation Factory, a real-world laboratory for exploring and testing new business models and social systems, observes that "the half-life of a business model is declining."[7] To remain relevant, companies have to move from being "share takers" to "market makers." In his experience, most companies' strategy is designed for winning market share rather than creating the type of disruption that builds or transforms industries. Kaplan warns that twenty-first-century leaders will need to be market makers, able to reconfigure the way their businesses create value multiple times throughout their careers, to stay in business.

In Kaplan's experience, design thinking can help us reach beyond the level of our everyday thinking—survival or problem solving—to be creative and proactive about where undiscovered value lies. It does so by helping us shift our focus from incremental changes to our current business models, to game-changing innovations birthed out of a deep understanding of our customers and their existing, emerging, and latent needs. A more complete exploration of Kaplan's ideas can be found in Chapter 6.

Design Matters on the Day-to-Day Level

While extremely useful at the highest level of value creation, design also reaches down to the deepest level of our experiences with our prospects and customers. "We encounter design, good and bad, with everything we see, touch, and use," explains John Maeda, the former president of Rhode Island School of Design. "It's invisible to most people because it's everywhere—much like the proverbial fish that doesn't know where to find water."[8]

We know when an experience is well designed: it works. It is easy, perhaps even fun. It leaves us confident that we have gotten the best answers to our inquiries and that if for some reason we are not satisfied, we will be able to alter the situation, with the company's assistance. It engages us, perhaps entertains us, and maybe teaches us something about ourselves. And we *really* know when an experience is poorly designed: it does not work. We have to wait on hold only to be disconnected. We click on an offer for a free white paper, but then are required to provide an excessive amount of personal data in return. The app does not load, or the website is not optimized for viewing on a mobile device, or the sales clerk stretches the truth to make a sale.

This is a high-stakes game. Having had a well-designed experience, our customers are more likely to continue to interact with us. This is good news because returning customers enhance our revenues and decrease our costs. (We explain why more fully in Chapter 11.) In addition, satisfied customers typically tell their friends. According to the *2012 American Express Global Customer Service Barometer*, on average Americans tell 15 people about their positive experiences.[9] It works both ways: People also tell their friends about their negative encounters. The same study found that after a negative experience, Americans are likely to tell 24 people. What is more, negative customer experiences often result in the loss of that customer as 90 percent will not come back or buy from us again.[10] The same study found that most companies will not even know that they have lost a customer until it is too late since only 4 percent of dissatisfied customers complain.

Design + Technology = Digital Experiences

Many factors contribute to the design of experiences. Over the last decade, technology has had a profound impact on customer experiences—where would we be without intuitive websites, smartphones, and mobile apps? Design has been central to developing these new products, categories, and markets, and to ensuring that technology is intuitive, working on behalf of the people using it, rather than having them be subjugated by it.

Design combined with technology can create remarkable digital experiences. Take Burberry, for example. In a desire to reach out to Millennials, Burberry, the luxury brand that has been around for more than 150 years, worked with Google to explore how it could deliver a beautiful and romantic experience across screens. "We're constantly thinking about how we translate the emotion of what we create and experience in the real world into the digital space, whether that's capturing the energy and excitement of a live gig, the hum and buzz of anticipation before a runway show, or just the feeling you get when you pull on your trench coat on a rainy morning," explains Burberry chief creative officer Christopher Bailey.[11]

The result: sending a letter sealed with a real kiss to anyone in the world, using a smartphone or webcam. Here is how it works. Using facial recognition technology, a kiss planted on a screen can be transformed into a digital kiss print. Before mailing, the sender has the opportunity to write a message and choose a lipstick shade from Burberry's latest beauty collection. Taking advantage of location data, the sender can watch as their message travels from city to city across a three-dimensional landscape, including local landmarks and street view images. Pretty interesting stuff, no? Send a kiss or at the very least check it out at kisses.burberry.com.

Design + Technology = Hybrid Experiences

Design + technology are being combined to infuse analogue experiences with digital capabilities. Visitors to Disney World, for instance, have come to expect apps that help them minimize wait times, facilitate lunch reservations, and find the quickest ways to maneuver through the often-crowded theme park. Soon they will be able to wear My Magic+ bands that will allow them to accomplish all of the above *and* be able to unlock their hotel room, pay for park admission, concessions, and meals, arrange encounters with princesses and other characters, and secure fast passes for rides. Early testing reveals that visitors to the theme park love the band because it is fun, reduces wait times, and improves their overall experience. Disney loves the band because it allows employees to recognize their guests and personalize their encounters, it generates reams of data about their guests' visit to the park, and its ease of use has families spending more money on their visits.[12]

Strongbow Cider, the leading maker of fermented ciders, is making it possible to set a mood for an entire room by simply opening a bottle. The company has prototyped a bottle cap that allows lights to be dimmed, music to play, and even fireworks to be launched by simply popping the lid on their ciders. The bottle cap is embedded with a radio frequency identification device (RFID) that interacts with sensors in the room, allowing its users to "start the unexpected" once the bottle's seal is broken. The promise of the soon-to-be launched Smartcap is a "fresher start to a more original night."

Similar contactless-connection technology is already being used to facilitate mobile payments. Digital-savvy customers love the ease of being able to pay via a mobile app; it is quick and often facilitates instantaneous coupon redemption and allocation of loyalty points. There are many benefits to retailers as well. At Nordstrom, for example, in addition to accepting credit card payments and sending e-receipts on handheld devices, sales associates can check product availability, place an order for home or in-store delivery, and add customers' purchases to their client-service system without having to touch a register or leave the showroom.

We are only beginning to scratch the surface of the design + NFC technology opportunity. As Padmasree Warrior, chief technology and strategy officer of Cisco, recently said, "We believe that only 1 percent of what can be connected in the world is actually connected."[13] Stay tuned.

Design + GPS Technology = Location-based Experiences

Location-aware devices make it possible for us to send highly targeted messaging to customers when they are in relevant geographic locations or when they have conducted searches with location intent. AisleBuyer found that nearly 75 percent of customers would switch brands if offered real-time discounts and promotions on their phones when they were in the store.[14] That is significant. Capitalizing on this behavior, RetailMeNot, a digital coupon provider, alerts shoppers to in-store deals when they are in the vicinity (see Figure 2.1).

GateGuru takes advantage of location-based technology to make traveling easier. The itinerary for today's trip appears on the home page and is updated in real time to keep us abreast of gate changes, flight delays, and even security-wait times. A map of the airport, complete with a personalized amenity list based on arrival and departure terminals, makes it easy to find food, restrooms, and coffee and to reserve a rental car.

Design + Emerging Technology = Tomorrow's Experiences

Innovative user interfaces like Omnitouch,[15] which turns any surface into a touchscreen, can create a more personal customer experience on phones, tablets, tables, or even windows. Adidas applies touchscreen technology in selected storefront windows, allowing shoppers to explore their products through a life-sized, digitally operated mannequin. Using hotspots located on the glass, shoppers can maneuver the digital model to point out product details and to drag items into a virtual shopping cart. These items instantly appear on their mobile phones, where they can be purchased, saved, and shared with friends.[16]

We are even beginning to imagine interactions *beyond* user interfaces with products like Google Glass. Currently in development, this

Figure 2.1 Mobile Coupons Reach Customers On-the-Go
Source: www.retailmenot.com/mobile

wearable computer in the shape of glasses overlays personal information onto a small screen. Using natural language voice commands, wearers of the glasses can execute requests such as "Take a picture," or "Send a message." It also provides instant access to Google Maps and directions.[17]

Some of the most extraordinary advances in brand experience will come from three-dimensional printing.[18] It is hard to grasp what this process can do because the image of printers transferring ink onto paper is so ingrained in our minds. Three-dimensional printing builds physical objects by molding together layer upon layer of materials—paper, liquid, powder, and others. Lamps, spare parts, and even body parts are being manufactured using this additive process.

Nokia recently made simplified web-based software publicly available that allows anyone with access to a 3-D printer to design and manufacture his or her own cell phone case. Imagine the possibilities for customization, quick prototype building, and onsite manufacturing. To see what is already being created, spend some time exploring the MakerBot and Shapeways communities.[19]

Design Transforms Physical Spaces

While digital technology has enabled and multiplied the number of interactions we have with our customers, physical spaces continue to be a vital component of our overall customer experience. Recognizing the importance of its physical spaces, McDonald's hired former IDEO designer Denis Weil to serve as vice president of concept and design and to oversee the redesign of many of its locations. Weil explains why the company is redesigning many of its restaurants around the world to *Fast Company*, "If Martians came down to Earth and visited a McDonald's, a post office, and a bank, they wouldn't be able to tell the difference. They would just see that everything starts with a line, has a counter that acts as a divider where the money exchanges, and has something hidden going on way in the back."[20]

A visit to one of the updated restaurants in Boston reveals many key changes. Spacious dining-in spaces complete with Wi-Fi and electric outlets reflect the company's effort to rebrand McDonald's as a place to eat and work, rather than just get drive-through food. To reduce customers' waiting times, the company has redesigned the way purchases are made. Rather than waiting in line while their food is being prepared, customers receive a number and are encouraged to get their drinks and settle in at their table until their number is called.

Retail store spaces remain important even in the age of e-commerce. Today's sophisticated customers toggle back and forth between in-store and digital environments throughout the customer experience journey. Creating a truly integrated shopping experience across channels that is continually informed by customer behavior data is increasingly important.

57

H&M's new flagship store in Times Square shows what designers can create when they combine fashion, technology, and physical space. A Social Media Lounge creates an inviting environment where shoppers can sit for a spell while enjoying free Wi-Fi access, the chance to listen to music, and even a photo studio. Cash registers and sales advisors are located inside the dressing room area to simplify checkout. One of our favorite features is a virtual runway upon which customers are encouraged to strut their stuff. People on the street can enjoy the show as runway performances are projected onto gigantic outdoor LED screens that face Broadway and 42nd Street.

Design Includes Event Making

Sometimes design is about creating physical events, short-term encounters when we invite customers into our world for a first-hand experience with our brands. Red Bull, which makes energy drinks, has made a name for itself by creating adrenaline-pumping extreme-sports events.

As part of its Red Bull Cliff Diving Worldwide Series, every year, some of the world's best high divers come to Boston to jump off of the Institute of Contemporary Art building into the Charles River below. These divers are flipping, twisting, and folding from heights that are equivalent to an eight-story building at speeds of between 53 and 62 miles per hour before impacting the water. The event is a major touchpoint for Red Bull fans in Boston, for fans located near the tour's event locations across four continents, and for anyone tuning in digitally. If you missed it, no worries. Find the link to some incredible photos in our endnotes.[21]

Armed with a better understanding of how critical design is to our ability to offer excellent customer experiences, the rationale for appointing a chief design officer is clear. But why is the chief information officer title being renamed chief integration officer, chief insight officer, or chief innovation officer?

The New CIO: Developing New Sources of Insight

Information technology is a vital part of the foundation upon which customer-centricity is built. Talk of big data is everywhere and with good reason. McKinsey recently described this nascent field as "the next frontier for innovation, competition, and productivity" and a "vital factor of production" on par with labor and capital.[22] As an indication of the potential, McKinsey estimates that by fully employing big data, a retailer could increase its operating margin by 60 percent and that the U.S. health-care industry could realize more than $300 billion in value annually.[23]

The opportunities being unlocked by truly data-driven companies are so fruitful that, even at this early stage, it is clear that companies across every sector and leaders of every function are going to have to get in the game—including us marketers. As we explore more fully in Chapter 5, data and advanced-marketing analytics are helping us better understand and prioritize consumers, follow their journeys, predict what they may want or need next, and design and deliver individualized-customer experiences. They can also help us to find patterns and trends in the market, our categories, and adjacent spaces, and to evaluate our marketing efforts with much greater certainty.

Realizing these gains is easier said than done, however, because big datasets, by themselves, do not have much value. Value is created when the data is analyzed and insights are derived that allow us to make better business decisions. This insight then has to be disseminated across our ecosystems, ingested, and put into action to have an impact on our day-to-day operations.

How well are we doing? Like any new undertaking there is often considerable learning to be done before the results live up to the expectations generated by the initial hype. A recent study by the Economist Intelligence Unit, which provides forecasting and advisory services, found a "notable gap between the value markets put on big data and businesses' ability to glean insights."[24] Many executives (45 percent) perceived marketers' "limited competency in data analysis as a major obstacle to implementing more effective strategies."[25]

Optimism continues to run high, however. Eighty-five percent of respondents to a survey conducted by IDG Research Services and Kapow Software believe that big data has the ability to help businesses make more informed decisions.[26] A majority (75 percent) view projects as successful or somewhat successful to date.[27] We believe that as an analytical mind-set and capabilities are more

How Organizations Are Adapting to the Customer-Centric Era

widely and deeply developed across our organizations, big data will indeed become a key driver of business value.

Solid executive leadership is required to realize this opportunity. In addition to keeping all the existing enterprise systems running and preventing any security breaches, the new CIO needs to be able to build a broader analytics foundation than is currently available in most companies. This includes putting new technology infrastructure and tools in place to gather disparate data, coordinating data analytic efforts, building consensus around the focus of business analytics throughout the organization, and being a champion and enabler of a more data-driven mind-set across departments. This person also has to be obsessed with customers and committed to driving business results with data in real time.

The jury is still out on who is the best person to fill this role. Some companies are expanding the job description of their existing CIOs. Others are asking their CMOs to take on the job. Shiv Singh, PepsiCo's director of digital, North America, forecasts a consolidation of the CMO and CIO roles. As Singh said during a recent Social Media Insider Summit, "Forget the CMO—the next big industry title will be the CMTO [chief marketing and technology officer]. Each time I catch up with my CMO, I ask her how much she is learning about marketing technology."[28] Other organizations are testing new positions such as the chief digital officer and the chief analytics officer, staffing them with people who have both technical know-how and marketing and management expertise.

What's a Marketer to Do?

With all of these new C-level positions, is there still a place for marketing at the table? Absolutely. The emergence of CCEOs, CIOs, CAOs, and CDOs illustrates the new opportunities available for marketers. We believe that the traditional CMO position can ultimately morph into any of these roles; however, marketers will need to proactively build the requisite skills. We need to get in the game now and take ownership of what is to be.

This may or may not be music to the ears of marketers who are already under a lot of pressure. It can be overwhelming to learn new mind-sets, skills, and processes, even as we are being asked to do our current jobs and measure the value of our contributions. Given the plethora of imperatives for action, it is challenging to place bets on what to emphasize first. But we can do it. Remember the big picture: to know our customers thoroughly, to build profitable relationships with them through great customer experiences, to have our finger on the pulse of demand, and to inspire our broader ecosystems in the endeavor. That combination will make us invaluable to our organizations.

Understand Our Customers Thoroughly

To lead the customer effort, we need to know our customers inside and out. Charles Eames, the world-renowned designer, once said, "Never outsource understanding," and we could not agree more. Drawing from new and traditional sources and ongoing engagement, we can continuously build a living and breathing context for our customers: what are their needs, desires, motivations, and existing beliefs? What are their preferences for communication and purchasing? What makes them act? What gives them meaning? As our organizations' reach extends into new markets and cultures, this ability to create relevant contexts for our customers is even more important.

Keeping our finger on the pulse of cultural zeitgeists, those movements that are defining the spirit of the time, combined with ongoing conversations with our customers, can help us anticipate where demand may be heading next. What music and philosophies are gaining steam? What consumer-electronic trends and devices might our customers take a cotton to next? What new products or solutions are being developed around the world, and especially in emerging markets, that may change the rules of the game for everyone?

Know How Our Customers Experience Our Brands

We also need to know how our customers experience our brands throughout the customer journey. What attracts people to us and how do they find us? What inspires them to engage? This includes the big notions like our sense of purpose and smaller, concrete things like search terms. Drilling down further: What are our customers' typical journeys? Who and what are the key influences along the way? Which are our most vital interactions? What touchpoints are redundant or missing or need to be improved? What do our customers value in an experience with us? How do we know? What back-end support is needed to deliver excellence in each of these interactions? How does our marketing spend match up to where our customers are spending the most time? While we can answer these questions at a given point in time, really knowing our customers is a dynamic proposition; these questions need to be asked and answered regularly.

Build Customer Relationships

Ultimate job security and satisfaction comes from our ability to transform key-market segments into relationships with real people who feel a connection with us—and to be able to do so at scale. This requires us to reenvision our role as marketers to be one of trusted advisors rather than pushers of sales. As Gary Vaynerchuk, a wine connoisseur and social media expert you will get to know in Chapter 3, says, "The one who cares the most, wins. It's about relationships, not platforms. It's about having real friends."[29]

Being able to develop and implement thoughtful customer experiences that coordinate our interactions with each of our market segments across channels fuels these relationships. To pull this off, we need to be creative and data analytic savvy, so that we know the types of experiences that we can deliver. We also need to work with IT to develop an integrated and intelligent customer engagement platform to be able to offer these contextualized experiences at scale.

Coordinate Moving Parts and Integrate Opposites

Designing and delivering remarkable customer experiences is complicated; it involves managing and integrating multiple moving parts: customer service, sales, web design, fulfillment, IT, e-commerce, and more. Each of these parts has to work together consistently to create and deliver the customer experience differential. Just as data scientists consider a variety of inputs to find the signal in the noise, we work across functions to uncover patterns, synthesize points of view, and keep our organizations focused on our constituents.

In addition to coordinating efforts across our organizations, we often have to juggle seemingly opposite influences. We say seemingly opposite, because we know that connecting ideas, objects, and processes that do not normally go together can be quite fruitful—like peanut butter and chocolate before Reese's Peanut Butter Cups.

For example, analytics and creativity are two seemingly opposing efforts. Pitting analytics and creativity against each other makes no sense; they need each other. Analytics uncovers the deep insights that fertilize our imaginations and can evaluate the effectiveness of our creative endeavors. Similarly, in an experience-based environment, creativity fuels our connection with our customers. It also spawns innovation, which directly impacts our competitiveness.

Speed and accuracy are two other seemingly opposite forces. By employing entrepreneurial decision-making techniques, however, we can learn by doing. As we translate our thinking into immediate action, we create evidence, improving our accuracy and speed. This too positively impacts our competitiveness.

Be a Curious Expert

Scott Bedbury, a former marketing executive at Nike and Starbucks, made a comment that has stuck with us: "Show up stupid. Be forever curious."[30] This is great advice. Even as we become the customer experts in our organizations, we must give ourselves permission to always look with fresh ideas, to never get stale in our view, or too sure in our ways. While it is helpful to be aware of how things have always been done, we cannot let our organizations be limited by it. To be successful in this marketing landscape we must ask questions, then reframe the questions, and ask again; it is a proven way to uncover unforeseen answers and opportunities.

Tina Seelig, who teaches about creativity and innovation at the d.school at Stanford University, has found that reframing questions is a great way to unlock the imagination and create fresh solutions. In her book *inGenius* she illustrates how different the range of possible solutions can be simply by changing the way a question is

How Organizations Are Adapting to the Customer-Centric Era

answered. For example, she asks, Which of the questions below is more thought-provoking?

- What is the sum of 5 plus 5?
- What two numbers add up to 10?[31]

Similarly, in his book *Think Better*, Tim Hurson, whom we met in Chapter 1, encourages people to use the word: *else*. "How *else* might we solve this problem? Who *else* might be involved? What *else* haven't we thought of yet?"[32] In his experience, the best ideas generally come when people hit the "we-are-dry" stage. Up to that point most ideas are generally regurgitations of existing patterns. Following a similar path, at IDEO, they continually ask themselves, "How might we?"

Keep the Faith

Yes, it is a buyer's market. And yes, our companies are actively contemplating who can best lead their efforts in this new landscape. That means it is a great time filled with opportunity for retooled marketers as well.

In the pages that follow, we explore the 10 skills we believe are necessary for marketers to be relevant and customer-centric, offering a vantage point from which each of us can individualize our game plans. Chapter 3 focuses on building a successful marketing career.

QUESTIONS FOR CONSIDERATION

- How is your company's leadership changing?
- Who is responsible for leading the customer effort? Your data analytics and insight effort? Innovation?
- How is strategy developed in your organization? Is it grounded in a deep understanding of customer demand?
- What intrigues you most about the opportunities facing marketers? What makes you uncomfortable?
- What is your next step?

RESOURCES

Influencers We Recommend

- *Kerry Bodine*. VP and principal analyst in Forrester Research's Customer Experience practice, Bodine is also the coauthor of *Outside In*, the customer experience book from Forrester. Stay current with Kerry's thinking at www.blogs.forrester.com/kerry_bodine and on Twitter @Kerrybodine.

- *Joi Ito*. As director of the MIT Media Lab, Ito is a leading thinker and writer on innovation and how the Internet is transforming society. Some of his publications include *Ryu Murakami X Joichi Ito* and *Freesouls: Captured and Released*. Enjoy his thinking at www.joi.ito.com and on Twitter @joi.

- *Tom Kelley*. Kelley is the author of *The Art of Innovation* and *The Ten Faces of Innovation* and the coauthor of *Creative Confidence*. A partner at IDEO, Kelley is also the author of *The Art of Innovation*, *The Ten Faces of Innovation*, and the coauthor of *Creative Confidence*. Learn more from Kelley at www.ideo.com and by following him @TomKelley74 and @kelleybros.

- *John Maeda*. The former president of the Rhode Island School of Design, Maeda is a design partner at the venture firm Kleiner Perkins Caufield & Byers. A thought leader in design, technology, and leadership and their convergence, his recent publications include *The Laws of Simplicity*, *Maeda@Media*, and *Redesigning Leadership*, the latter of which he coauthored with Becky Bermont. Catch his thoughts at www.creativeleadership.com and www.maedastudio.com. Follow his tweets @johnmaeda.

- *Wayne Peacock*. As chief member officer of USAA, Peacock is trailblazing new ways to deliver exceptional customer experience. *Fast Company* named him one of the most creative people in the United States. Follow Peacock on Twitter @wayne_peacock.

(continued)

How Organizations Are Adapting to the Customer-Centric Era

(continued)

- *Mauro Porcini*. The chief design officer at PepsiCo, Porcini's former employer described him as "an infectious agent for design." Follow Porcini on Twitter @MauroPorcini.

- *Tina Seelig*. An expert in creative thinking and entrepreneurial mind-sets, Seelig serves as executive director of the Stanford Technology Ventures Program, and is the author of numerous books, including *inGenius*, *What I Wish I Knew When I Was 20*, and two manuals on the chemistry of cooking. In her spare time, Seelig also enjoys painting and staying stay current in neuroscience. Enjoy her insight on Twitter @tseelig.

Hashtags to Explore

- #creativity
- #design
- #designthinking
- #innovation
- #3DPrinting

Build a Successful Marketing Career (Hint: Standing Still Is Extraordinarily Risky)

"There are costs and risks to a program of action, but they are far less than the long range risks and costs of comfortable inaction."

—President John F. Kennedy

In 1995 Andy Grove, the cofounder of Intel, caused quite a stir when he shared his vision of how globalization and the Internet were going to impact the workplace, "As a general rule, you have to accept that no matter where you work, you are not an employee; you are in a business with one employee—yourself. You are in competition with millions of similar businesses, millions of others all over the world, picking up the pace, capable of doing the same work that you can do and perhaps more eager. The point is, the clichés of globalization and the information revolution have real meaning—potentially deadly meaning—for your career."[1]

The past few years have proven that Grove knew as much about where careers were heading as he did about transforming the chip industry.

Successful career management in today's marketing environment asks five things of us.

1. That we take charge of our own careers and develop them as if they were small businesses.

67

2. That we are self-aware and know our talents and interests, as well as areas in need of growth (we all have them).

3. That we articulate our personal brand and market ourselves as we market our brands.

4. That we are connected and actively build and nurture our knowledge networks.

5. That we be resourceful.

Me.com

When we speak of taking charge of our careers and developing them as if they were small businesses, we are not suggesting that each of us should start our own company, although in some circumstances that may be the right course of action. Rather, we mean that as a human resource manager for our business with one employee, we think through and proactively seek out the skills, experiences, and exposure that we need to grow with or drive change. Wearing our marketing hats, we consider our abilities and interests and brand ourselves accordingly, creating a public presence for ourselves in selected social environments. As business development people, we cultivate a network of people who can help us grow with and even drive change. As chief customer officers we contemplate how we are constantly adding value to our clients—our employers—anticipating and meeting their next need. And as customer service reps, we routinely seek feedback from those around us on how we can improve.

For some of us this imperative feels freeing and perhaps obvious. For others it feels like a breach of a contract. Many of us grew up with the understanding that companies offered job security, steady income, and stability. We expected 40 to 50 hour workweeks, training and professional development guidance and resources, and a mutual long-term commitment to each other. Then the Internet came along and the story changed.

Expect a Unique Career Trajectory

Going forward few marketing career paths will resemble straight lines from start to finish. Great marketing careers will include jumps, backward steps, and several shorter lines. Today the average American professional changes jobs seven times throughout his/her career and that number is expected to increase. Our careers may include stints with big companies, small start-ups, and even time working as freelancers in the gig economy. We may work in traditional marketing roles but also spend time in data analytics and customer experience. In order to thrive in this environment, we have to proactively manage our careers, not by attempting to plan out every step—it is simply not possible, nor advisable, in a rapidly changing climate—but by fully exploring, experimenting, and contributing to the environments where we are today.

Consider the career path of Scott Russell, director of customer experience services at Sparks Grove, a strategic marketing consultancy and division of the North Highland Company. An undergraduate marketing major, after attending business school, Russell joined the consulting firm Accenture where he worked in systems development to improve financial companies' performance and operational efficiency. After a few years he moved to Ernst & Young, where he focused on process improvement and design consulting, before starting his own consulting business, where he enjoyed engagements with Cingular, Equifax, and EarthLink, among others. Later he joined forces with the consulting firm North Highland with whom he had worked on several projects.

Five years ago when the market began to see the value in improving the customer experience, Russell saw the opportunity to combine his background in process improvement with marketing. What does a background in process improvement have to do with marketing? Everything. For starters, he was comfortable with data, its power and limitations, and how to collect it and make sense of it. Second, he had an end-to-end view of systems, an essential ability for marketers who are concerned about the customer experience, as well the ability to drill down at any given point in a process to see how people, technology, processes, and content work together—or not.

Today Russell directs North Highland's customer experience efforts. "It's a cross-functional discipline that plays to my background, the needs of the market, and to the way I am wired," he explains. Russell could not have anticipated this move early in his career, as the field did not exist, but by continually building skills in areas that created business value, and by staying aware of developments in the broader marketplace, he was able to create a state-of-the art marketing opportunity for himself and for North Highland.

Know Thyself

The aphorism "know thyself" is not new—it was originally inscribed in stone on the Temple of Apollo in the fourth century BC—but its message is still highly relevant, essential even, for marketers. Indeed, some 2,400 years later, Dr. Ella Edmondson Bell, a career development expert at the Tuck School of Business at Dartmouth, instructs her students that "success starts internally" and encourages them to invest time throughout the course of their professional lives developing self-awareness.[2]

As we better understand our strengths and weaknesses and are able to compare our perceptions of ourselves with how others see us, we have the chance to become more authentic, capable, and confident. Knowing who we are and what we want grounds us in an environment that is continually shifting. This clarity is priceless. It provides focus that helps us flourish in a world of far too many variables and makes us the kind of people others trust and with whom they want to work. It is the basis for goal setting and for productively managing our careers and our responsibilities. What is more, self-awareness provides us with the insight that is necessary to proactively manage and brand our own image and identity, an important ability in today's marketing landscape.

There is no magic pill that we can take to become aware; it is an ongoing process that is informed by work- and nonwork-related experiences. Cultivating self-awareness takes intentionality. It requires us to seek out honest feedback, reflect on our experiences, and routinely ask ourselves questions such as, "What is my story? What captures and retains my attention? What bores me to tears? What are my strengths? What areas do I need to develop? What do people think of when they think of me? What makes me unique?"

Suffering from self-awareness block? Asking a couple of people who know us well to share their impressions of our strengths, weaknesses, and general characteristics can spur some thoughts. Take what they have to say under consideration. Does what they are saying make sense? Is the feedback consistent across friends and acquaintances and with how we perceive ourselves?

Keeping an About Me board on Pinterest, the online pin board, is a great way to easily assemble a visual picture of ourselves. It is fun and easy; no content creation is required, just scrolling through photos and graphics, choosing those that catch our eyes and describe us, and pinning. Over time a clear image emerges. Adding to our boards keeps them current, generating a useful resource for shaping the future. Lisa maintains a Pinterest board that visually identifies topics about which she is interested in writing. When she contemplates taking on projects, she refers to the board, to ensure that her potential commitments are aligned with her professional goals.

Magic happens when self-awareness intersects with knowledge of the surrounding marketing landscape. Like Scott Russell, who was able to see how his interest and experience in process improvement translated into the emerging field of customer experience, self-awareness makes it more probable that we will be able to identify emerging marketing opportunities at which we will excel. Being in the right place at the right time is a function of knowing ourselves well enough to say "Yes!"

Brand or Be Branded

In addition to us knowing who we are, to be successful marketers, other people have to know who we are as well. Like the brands that we market in our day jobs, it is useful to think of ourselves as personal brands. Consider the following questions: What is my story? If I were a brand, how would I describe myself? Describing our brand and our brand attributes flows naturally from the self-awareness work we have undertaken.

But it is not enough to answer those questions for ourselves. We also have to consider how others might describe us. After all, our personal brands are the sum of the experiences that people have of us, not what we think of ourselves or hope that others will think of us. These experiences that comprise our brands take place when people interact with us, hear about us, view our online profiles, and review the content that we have created and shared. Hopefully these experiences, or touchpoints, are an accurate representation of us. To ensure that this is the case, each of us need to be proactive about developing our personal brand.

Developing Our Personal Brand

Robin Frank, a personal branding and social media strategist, offers a four-part framework to assist people in articulating their brands and developing a personal branding statement. Part one asks us to describe who we are and what we most want people to remember about us. This is a short, hopefully catchy, statement, what some may call an elevator pitch that prompts people to say, "I get this person." Frank would describe her who-am-I statement as: I am a navigator. I help people find their way.

The second part of the models gets at what we do: how we add value, what are our distinctive benefits, and how what we do is different from what others like us do. This is tantamount to the unique value propositions that we define for our brands. Frank's what-I-do statement would be, "I help people imagine and create their brand online quickly and efficiently."

Part three of the framework, which is perhaps the most important, reflects our passion, why we do what we do. In Frank's experience most people tend to skip over articulation of their why, seeing it as less significant. However, Frank will tell you it is essential: What generally grabs people's attention and makes us memorable is not what we do, but why we do it. This is where our personal values, our vision, and our enthusiasm comes though. If you ask Frank why she started her company, beep beep media, she will tell you: I love to help people achieve their goals.

Finally, the fourth part of the schema is being able to articulate what our goals are, what we are trying to accomplish. This determines how and where to focus our personal-branding efforts, including what type of a digital presence makes sense for us individually.

Interested in taking a quick quiz to assess the strength of your brand and digital presence? William Arruda and Deb Dib are personal-branding experts and the authors of *Ditch Dare Do*; they offer a 32-question, digital-brand quiz that gets at the essentials at ditchdaredo.com/quiz. Answer the questions, press submit, and within a few hours you will hear back with a personalized evaluation and suggestions for any improvement. It is a good way to assess where we are, and for some of us, to initiate a motivational conversation with ourselves.

Remember, however we define our personal brand, it must be authentic; it should ring true to who we are and how we live. It needs to be consistent both online and offline, manifesting itself in how we answer our phone, what we retweet, and even the community organizations with which we engage.

Our Networks Are Verbs

Self-awareness and personal branding are foundational, but they are not enough. Our careers are social endeavors; with few exceptions, none of us is an island. We are greatly enriched and impacted by the ecosystem of resources and support that surrounds us. People in our networks serve a variety of purposes. Some stimulate our thinking, providing us with vetted information flows that help us expand our understanding, narrow our options, and make better decisions. Others support us personally or provide insight into our careers. Regardless of the stage of our marketing careers, each of us can benefit tremendously from having a solid network of people around us for whom we can be mutual resources.

A word of caution: Building our networks is not about quantity; it is about deepening our connection with people that we may have just met or that we may have known for our whole lives. Our networks are verbs, not nouns; we interact with them; we do not own them. A successful strategy for managing these living and breathing entities is to be mutually beneficial, not transactional, and to actively cultivate this network regularly, not just when we need to ask something of those with whom we are connected. A good rule of thumb is to try and give something of value in every interaction—not gifts, but information, inspiration, or a useful introduction.

73

Identifying Our Networks

A good place to begin to build our networks is by taking a simple inventory. Start with our closest relationships, the people we know, our friends and family. Add in school friends, parents of our children's friends if applicable and relevant, and people with whom we worked or volunteered in the past. Think of people we may have met while traveling, or in a cycling group, or with whom we may attend church or temple. Do not forget former bosses, friends with whom we may have gone to camp, or fraternity brothers or sorority sisters. Add colleagues from work and clients—even competitors.

Wendy Murphy, an assistant professor of Management at Babson College and an expert in developmental networks, recommends mapping these contacts visually. By placing ourselves in a circle in the center of the page and drawing lines extending from that circle outward to form pie-shaped pieces, we create spaces in which we can classify our relationships: friends from childhood in one triangle and colleagues from work in another. From there we begin to add names to each section. We have found it fruitful to return to this exercise multiple times to create a more complete picture.

Continue to add new contacts as appropriate, such as the people throughout our organizations with whom we interact on projects and those who we connect with at meetings or conferences. Seek out diversity. While our close-knit group of friends and colleagues may always be there for us, they may not be the most effective in helping us stay on the cutting edge of what is happening in the marketing world because we probably see the world too similarly. Friends and acquaintances who live in different parts of the world, work in different industries, explore different interests, and even vote for different candidates, offer us the opportunity to broaden our horizons, and we can do the same for them. Research shows that these weaker ties are more likely to provide information about jobs that lead to employment than closer friends, because they have access to a different pool of resources. On a broader scale, societies in which people have multiple weak ties that complement their strong ties have been found to be more innovative.

Murphy teaches her students to proactively expand their networks by working though their existing weak and strong ties. In

74

one exercise she asks students to identify a goal they would like to tackle. Once the opportunity is identified, Murphy asks students to pinpoint which individuals in their network will be able to help them achieve their goal and how. If the assistance they need to accomplish their goal is not readily available in their networks, she challenges them to consider how they could leverage their existing network to fill the gap. Who might they know that would be willing and able to connect them with someone who could help? How would they go about reaching out to them and making the request? Finally, Murphy challenges them to act.[3]

We can all benefit from undertaking this exercise. As we set out to write this book, we combed our networks to see what individuals would help us be able to move the conversation about new digital marketing skills forward. In addition to giving us plenty of food for thought, many of those colleagues introduced us to people they knew, people to whom we would otherwise not have access and who challenged us to think differently and more completely. The result is *The Digital Marketer*.

Taking Our Brands and Networks on the Road

Digital channels play such an influential role in today's business world that marketers have to be active in social media. Two types of social environments comprise social media: social networks and communities. What is the difference?

When we move our personal networks into digital spaces like LinkedIn, Facebook, or Twitter, we are joining robust, public, social-networking venues. Although these networks may be huge, they are manageable because we only engage with a fraction of the entire network—our friends, colleagues, and acquaintances. (There are many more social networks besides these big three, which we discuss more fully in Chapter 8.) Our digital networks are places of connection centered on us. That is why they are so interesting!

Social communities, on the other hand, are places of connection around an interest, need, event, or shared purpose. It may be a hobby, an illness, a lifestyle, a business issue, or political cause. Unlike social networks, people who join social communities may or may not know each other when they join. They may be involved in multiple communities depending upon their interests, time, and qualifications.

Why is it important for us to be active in social media? These social networks and communities offer a vehicle for us to nurture our relationships, tap the wisdom of our networks, monitor the latest developments in our fields, share our experience, and contribute to the conversation. It is also where the action is. According to a recent study conducted by Forrester Research, fully 100 percent of business decision-makers surveyed use social media for work purposes.[4] Almost all (98 percent) read blogs, watch videos, and listen to podcasts; 75 percent comment on blogs and post ratings and reviews, and 79 percent of those maintain a profile on social networking sites "all in the context of their business activities."[5]

Not surprisingly, patterns of use in these social spaces is highly individualized. For the most part, people take a cafeteria-style approach: They pick and choose which social networks and communities they want to be a part of based upon specific personal and business goals. Often people's personal and business goals differ; as a result, the communities they join for business purposes may not be the ones they use for personal reasons.

What social media should marketers target? It depends upon our goals and the industries in which we operate. A high-tech marketing vendor, for example, would want to be a part of Spiceworks, a social community where over 2.5 million information technology folks gather to talk all things tech. A broader swath might enjoy being a part of the Marketing Profs community, a professional development resource for marketers.[6] At the end of every chapter in *The Digital Marketer* we offer suggestions for social media and other resources that have been useful to us. Check them out and see what resonates.

In terms of social networks, given LinkedIn's high level of adoption among business people, we recommend that every marketer join. There are many other social networks beyond LinkedIn—Google+, Twitter, Pinterest, Instagram, TenCent, Mxit—that can be richly rewarding, but a description of them is beyond the scope of this book. Membership and the cultures of each of these networks and communities vary significantly, so it is wise to invest some time up front to see which ones meet your needs.

Getting the Most Out of LinkedIn

A few statistics to set the stage: LinkedIn presently has over 225 million members in 200 countries.[7] This network is growing with more than two professionals joining every second. The fastest growing demographic is students and recent college graduates, of which there are over 30 million members. Sixty-four percent of LinkedIn members are located outside of the United States.

LinkedIn is a great tool for marketers. It can help us stay connected with, learn from, and bring value to our friends, colleagues, and acquaintances. Easy to join, with permission, the site will tap the contacts in our digital address books and invite them to connect. (Chances are many are already active on the network.) Perusing our contacts' connections can jog our memory as to other relationships we may have and with whom we want to invite to connect. As we meet people with whom we want to stay in touch, we simply send an invitation.

Staying Current

One of the beauties of LinkedIn is the news feed that allows us to stay current with our connections. Regular homepage updates alert us to what our contacts are sharing, recent job changes, LinkedIn groups they may have joined, and any queries they may have made of their networks. LinkedIn Pulse's news stream offers a broader perspective, personalizing content from influencers in our industries to our homepage, placing rich resources literally at our fingertips. Brands and companies also have pages. If we choose to follow them, their updates will be posted directly to our homepages.

Communication works both ways; what we share also reaches, and hopefully enriches, our network. It is helpful to build our presence and nurture our network regularly. Listening and adding value where we can by uploading useful presentations we have made, webinars in which we have participated, or blog posts we have crafted, and answering others' questions or commenting on their posts when we have something relevant to contribute, are great ways to add value. Always be mindful that this is a professional network—what we publish should reflect that intention—and that cadence matters. Spam helps no one.

Job search and recruitment are another way that companies and job seekers put LinkedIn to use. In addition to being a vehicle by which we can engage and share knowledge within our networks, our LinkedIn profile is a digital résumé that can help generate career and business opportunities. A living document, this résumé is updated daily, capturing our interests and abilities in what we choose to share and publish and by the groups that we join.

Joining Relevant LinkedIn Groups

There are LinkedIn groups for everything and they can be useful places to identify trending topics, pose questions, offer answers, post job listings, and network in general. The quality of LinkedIn Groups can vary greatly—most are user generated and managed—so be judicious. A handful of corporate-sponsored groups exist that are usually quite well run. Examples include Staples (Small Business Network), Citi (Professional Women's Network), and American Express OPEN (business owners). Alumni groups for schools and former places of employment are often useful. Myriad marketing-related groups exist. A few that we have joined include Social Media Marketing, Marketing 2.0, Market Profs, Inbound Marketing, Social Media, and Future Social Media.

To find relevant groups, search LinkedIn Groups with the keywords that describe your interests. To add a geographic location to the search, simply add an *and* to the search: social media *and* Boston. LinkedIn will also make personalized suggestions if you click on the Groups You May Like feature. To find out more about a group, click on the group name in the Group Directory. You will see a listing of the members, how long the group has been around, and who is the manager. Joining a group for a trial period gives us an opportunity to determine if it is worth our time or not.

But I Want to Have a Life

There is only so much time in every day and we can waste a lot of it in social environments, so being smart about where we spend our time and efforts is important. One way to reduce time commitment is to observe rather than contribute across our social media profiles. However, the beauty of social environments is the multidirectional flow of conversation. If we choose to add to that conversation, we can become a part of the fabric of these communities. Our thought leadership and industry expertise can add value and move the dialogue forward. Participating also allows us to engage in dialogue with people in the industry to which we may not otherwise have access.

To facilitate a more active engagement, Robin Frank suggests that we create simple content calendars to organize our contributions in a proactive way and with a cadence that our followers, friends, and connections will appreciate. An easy way to do this is to schedule our social media listings ahead of time with a dashboard tool like Hootsuite. The tool lets us manage up to five social media for free and provides analytics to better understand our activity.

How much is enough content? We are fans of the notion of the *minimum effective dose* (MED). A pharmacology term that has been made popular by author Tim Ferriss, MED refers to the smallest dose that will produce a desired outcome. In the case of building our brands, it is the minimum amount of work necessary to achieve whatever goal we have set. If we are starting a new business, or looking for more clients, more effort may be required. In addition to participating in the ongoing conversation, we recommend taking time to monitor what is being said about you and your company on a regular basis. (Suggestions for how to do this using Google Alerts follow.)

Are a Personal Blog and Website Necessary?

To blog or not to blog, that is the question. It is quite easy to set up a personal blog these days on WordPress or Tumblr and therein lies the challenge. At last count, WordPress has over 63 million blogs and Tumblr reports 101.7 million, and they are not the only games in town. It is very hard to get noticed in such a crowded space. However, if there is a compelling business reason to start one, it may be worth it.

For many years, Gary Vaynerchuk worked to transform his family business from a local wine shop, the Wine Library, to a national industry name. Things really began to take off when he began publishing

79

a daily video blog about wine, Wine Library TV. The goal of the vlog, which also came to be known as The Thunder Show because of his noticeably heated passion about wine, was to develop a story around Gary and the wine shop.

To accomplish this goal, Gary reviewed wines and gave advice on wine appreciation and related topics. He built quite a following over the years, which substantially increased the revenues of his family-owned wine shop and launched him as both an influential wine critic and social media guru. Today he runs a social media consulting agency and has published a book, *Crush It!*, in which he explains how to make a living from following a passion, just as he has done. As for the concern about launching a new blog into a crowded space, Gary writes, "Quality is a tremendous filter. Cream always rises, my friends, no matter how many cups of coffee you pour."[8]

How important is a personal website? Less and less important. Some people are consolidating their personal digital presences via an online calling card like Aboutme.com and flavors.me; however, as the go-to destination for finding other professionals, LinkedIn has largely done away with the need for a personal website.

Be Resourceful

Being resourceful means being do-it-yourself learners who are on top of what is happening in our companies and our industries. Andy Grove is a master of self-learning, a true autodidact.

When Intel was founded in 1968, Grove was one of three employees and the only one who had much interest in managing the company, according to his biographer, Harvard Business School professor Richard Tedlow. Having only graduated from City College of New York with a degree in engineering a few years before, Grove had limited management experience. In Grove's words, "I was scared to death. It was terrifying. I literally had nightmares. I was supposed to be director of engineering, but there were so few us of us that they made me director of operations."[9] But he taught himself by experimenting and pulling in resources where necessary to help him learn what he needed to know, a process he continued throughout his career. Today, Grove is considered one of the greatest managers in American business history.

Like Grove, our job includes tapping multiple resources to stay in front of the curve as to what is happening in our organizations and categories both domestically and internationally. Needless to say, our investment in our own education does not stop when we formally leave school. Many of us continue to take classes. We personally have tapped the resources of HubSpot's Inbound Marketing University, HootSuite University, Quick Sprout University, and Marketing Profs University. Through online resources like LearnStreet.com, Coursera.org, edx.org, and udacity.com, marketers are learning the basics of programming and web construction.[10]

Our informal schooling continues daily in the form of blogs, tweets, white papers, shares, conferences, conversations, and simply exploring in digital spaces. As we regularly expose ourselves to a variety of relevant sources of information, we become knowledgeable and expand our capacity to think afresh, increasing our value to our companies. This customized lens continually helps us to focus and see clearly. Tapping international sources is equally important as many disruptive innovations in our own industries are being launched across the globe, a topic we will address further in Chapter 6.

Few of us have unlimited time to search the web to stay up to date, however. Fortunately there are great tools to streamline that process. We have already discussed how LinkedIn can be useful, but here are a few other helpful tools:

- **RSS feeds**, or rich site summaries, bring content updates to us rather than having us go in search across the web. By simply subscribing to a company's or an individual's RSS feed, an update arrives in our e-mail every time content on a site is changed. These feeds can be consolidated into an RSS reader such as Digg Reader, Feedly, NewsBlur, or Flipboard, among others. Some of these readers incorporate Facebook and Twitter streams into the mix as well. (Note: These feeds may be censored depending upon the country we operate in.)

- **Google Alerts** monitor the web for new content based upon a given query, as Figure 3.1 shows. It is a good idea to set up an ongoing monitoring of us, our competitors, key influencers

81

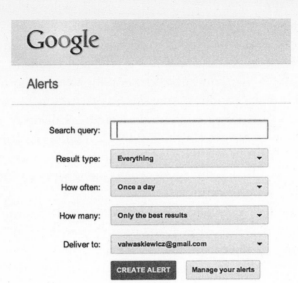

Figure 3.1   Alerts Keep Us Aware of Content Changes

we have identified, and perhaps our favorite band or sports teams. Similar tools include Social Mention and Talkwalker.

- **Twitter Lists.** We are fans of the microblogging site Twitter because it often breaks news faster than most traditional media sources and it makes it possible to learn directly and in real time from people and organizations both inside and outside of personal networks. Many key opinion leaders are active on Twitter, including government officials, business leaders, and journalists, as well as celebrities and sports figures. Forming a Twitter list of favorites in a dashboard like Hootsuite makes it possible to quickly scan recent content from our favorite people and organizations.

- **Twitter Chats.** Unlike our content feeds that flow organically, Twitter chats are an organized conversation around a specific topic. Each chat has a specific hashtag (#) and meeting time during which a conversation takes place. Some of these chats take place regularly—the #socialmedia chat, for example, meets every Tuesday at noon EST—some just facilitate conversation during a discrete webinar or conference. For an always-expanding list of Twitter chats refer to tweetreports .com/twitter-chat-schedule/. Be sure to use the hashtag to follow and contribute to the conversation. Several tools exist to separate these conversations from our primary news stream to make them easier to follow including TweetChat, Twitterfall, and Hootsuite.

Learning in Atypical Classrooms

It is not enough to just think about new marketing developments; it is critical that we gain experience with the technologies and techniques about which we read, to have a firsthand understanding of why they are newsworthy. We typically spend a couple of hours every day playing in digital spaces, exploring new apps and experimenting with platforms, seeing firsthand how organizations are creating content and experiences and how social networks in different parts of the world meet their constituents' needs.

Transcending corporate silos by regularly connecting with people across our organizations is well worth our time. Noontime walks, lunches, or catching a drink after work are terrific forums to learn about the challenges and opportunities facing customer-service persons, developers, or human-resource personnel. How are they driving customer-centricity in their respective areas? What bridges may we help build between marketing and the other functions to improve our constituents' experiences? Expanding beyond our own organizations helps us gain a broader prospective. There is more than one way to approach a challenge, and it is helpful to see how other organizations tackle similar problems and opportunities.

Making a special effort to cross age groups pays off in spades as well, especially if we approach each person humbly and with a willingness to learn. We try to connect regularly with young adults to see what is captivating their attention and what no longer does. Remember that people under the age of 30 founded Google, Facebook, and Twitter. If you are under 30, remember, wisdom often accompanies age.

Spending Time with Creative Folks

Our calendars are filled with meetings with entrepreneurs and their early stage companies. Whether or not the companies are ultimately

83

successful does not matter; they are already bringing a different way of viewing the market to the table, which is invaluable. Joining innovative industry groups and staying close to innovation centers in universities can bring us in contact with these connections.

Several years ago Larry helped to found MITX, the Massachusetts Innovation and Technology Exchange. Dedicated to building a thriving innovation community at the intersection of marketing and technology, today MITX is the largest nonprofit of its kind. MITX offers ongoing classes and events, including the annual Future M festival, which brings together people who are pushing the boundaries, shaping the future of marketing. Through its MITX Up program, the nonprofit works with local accelerator programs to identify the most cutting-edge and innovative start-ups, some of which we will hear more about in the pages that follow. Seasoned marketers can roll up their sleeves and help these start-ups solve their marketing challenges through MITX-sponsored Marketing Hackathons. It is great fun, cutting edge, and brimming with fresh ideas.

For many years Larry has also been involved with the Media Lab at the Massachusetts Institute of Technology (MIT). One movement in particular with which he has enjoyed collaboration is One Laptop Per Child (OLPC), a nonprofit that develops and distributes inexpensive laptops to children throughout the developing world.[11] He should not have been surprised when several years ago his daughters, after returning home from a school trip to South Africa, approached him about finding a way to bring these laptops to the Kliptown Youth Program,[12] an after-school program where they had volunteered while in Soweto. Working as a family, and with the support of many others, they were able to help establish a computer center with over 200 laptops in this financially impoverished community. Through this involvement, Larry was introduced to Paul Harris, the founder and former CEO of FirstRand, a financial services group in South Africa, whose foundation helped to fund the center. Harris later invited him to join the board of Mxit, the largest social network in South Africa, an opportunity that has broadened his understanding of the global social media landscape.

The bottom line is simple: We need to be active in likely *and* unlikely places. Some of the most fecund moments take place when we connect ideas and objects that normally do not go together.

Doing Something Creative Every Day

Creativity is key to staying relevant. Tina Seelig, who we met in Chapter 2, teaches about creativity and innovation at Stanford University. Seelig believes that "creativity allows you to thrive in an ever changing world and unlocks a universe of possibilities."[13] We all are naturally creative—really! It is not just the domain of a lucky few.

Doing something creative every day can develop our creative muscle and mind-set so that we can think better, take more risks, and become more flexible. This can be as simple as cooking something new, using colored markers at work, taking an improvisation class, adding an interesting photo to Instagram daily, flipping through Pinterest, or attending a storytelling festival. It could be redesigning everyday experiences in our minds, such as a better floor plan for the grocery store or a more effective backpack for carrying heavy textbooks. Whatever crosses our paths and inspires us will work.

Taking the time to look around while on business trips and vacations can also stir our creative juices and spark insights that we can bring into our work. For example, on a recent trip to the Philippines, Lisa spent some time in local sari-sari stores—small convenience stores that are often located in people's homes in low income or rural areas. Observing the shoppers make purchases in extremely small quantities—this is what they could afford and store—it became clear to her that consumer product companies hoping to sell into this market would need to repackage their goods into very small units.

As our companies enter new venues, marketers need to reach beyond our experience, and rethink what is essential: What bells and whistles actually create value for our customers? Careful observation can provide a context for our marketing efforts and spark the creativity that finds untapped ways to create value.

Taking Time Off

It may seem oxymoronic to recommend taking time off while talking about being resourceful, but it really is not. Many of us are operating in a state of overload these days, and it is not useful for us personally or for the organizations for which we work.

Leslie Perlow, a Harvard professor and author of *Sleeping With Your Smartphone: How to Break the 24/7 Habit and Change The Way*

85

You Work, says that when we are trapped, "we don't think about better, faster, and more effective ways of working. Rather, we just keep working more and more, perpetuating and amplifying the bad intensity of our work."[14] As an antidote, Perlow recommends that we each take one pre-planned night off a week. E-mail, voice mail, and work activities are prohibited. In her experience, those people who commit to this change are more excited to go to work, more satisfied with their jobs, and feel better able to achieve work/life balance.

A recent study undertaken by KRC Research of 404 creatives across the United States and the United Kingdom affirms the connection between time, space, and creative mojo. A frightening 50 percent of people surveyed believe the industry has grown less creative in the past decade. Many affirm that they still have great ideas, but 60 percent say they do not have enough time to bring them to fruition. Three out of every four who have time constraints believe they are stuck in a rut with too many competing priorities to make time for reflection.[15]

Cultivating Developmental Relationships

Jim Atchison, SeaWorld's chief executive, believes in mentors. A company man, Atchison has spent his entire career at SeaWorld, starting as a parking attendant at the age of 18. In addition to spending time every day in the parks talking with visitors, which was critical to his understanding of what is important to SeaWorld's customers, Atkinson sought out good mentors who coached and encouraged him along the way. "My best advice for others is to look for people who can be sounding boards and use them judiciously," Atchison said. "Don't be afraid to ask for opinions and advice. You can accelerate the progression through your career if you listen to others who have been there before."[16]

We, too, have had good luck with mentors. One in particular, Harry Figgie, Jr., helped Larry to claim his talent in uncovering and articulating companies' stories, back when Larry was still teaching English literature and writing to high school students. Although Figgie had a reputation for being a ruthless manager, from day one he gave Larry the opportunity to contribute to his portfolio of companies, which included Rawlings Sporting Goods, American LaFrance fire trucks, and Fred Perry Sportswear, a priceless gift for any 23-year-old. At a time when most heads of companies were focused on manufacturing, Figgie was relentless about understanding demand. No doubt that Larry's customer-centric orientation was greatly shaped by this early mentor and boss.

Mentoring is mutually beneficial to mentee and mentor. According to Wendy Murphy, mentees benefit from greater clarity about professional identity, increased satisfaction, higher salaries, faster promotions, and additional career opportunities. Mentors report higher career satisfaction and salaries, and more recognition, visibility, and meaning in their work.[17]

Having multiple mentors is common and recommended; on average most people early in their career say they have four or five mentors, but in Murphy's experience, as they advance and if they dig down a little deeper, they tend to have 12 to 15 developmental relationships. They may not be in day-to-day contact, but they are there as important go-to resources. Diversity among mentors is helpful; it broadens perspectives and provides access to a broader network of resources. Murphy recommends having mentors at different stages of their careers and from inside and outside of the organization for which you work. Peer mentors are often the most useful.

Most people find mentors on their own, rather than through official mentor programs. Even if our companies assign us a mentor, it is important to scout out other developmental relationships as they serve different roles. Official mentorship programs are usually designed to help new hires become acclimated to the organization's culture and internal workings. Self-sourced mentors often help us address personal challenges and advance our careers.

As you might expect, a key criterion to look for in a mentor is someone we admire, a role model for some aspect of our lives. Having someone that we trust and with whom we can communicate candidly is essential. Murphy encourages us to be patient; cultivating developmental relationships can take time. A good place to start is by asking people to lunch and connecting at events and company meetings. Reciprocity is vital; offering our talents, when relevant, is appropriate. Above all, Murphy cautions us to perform. People want to help those who are motivated, positive, and going places.

Sponsorship Takes It Up a Notch

Sponsors are a slightly different form of developmental relationship. A recent *Harvard Business Review* article describes *sponsorship* as "active support by someone appropriately placed in the organization who has significant influence on decision-making processes or structures and who is advocating for, protecting, and fighting for the career advancement of an individual."[18]

A formal and professional relationship, sponsorship's purpose is to strategically develop talent, usually in large organizations. Sponsors publicly endorse our authority, skills, readiness, and contributions. They provide concrete problem-solving and strategy planning for our advancement.

Studies conducted by the research firm Catalyst reveal that sponsorship can be especially important for women.[19] When women have mentors that are highly placed in organizations, they are as likely as men to get promoted. Without sponsors, even with the benefit of mentors, women often lag behind.

Generally sponsors and their protégés find each other by working together. Protégées are selected for their outstanding performance and loyalty. Sponsors are matched based on position of power and specific experience in areas where a high-potential candidate has gaps. Murphy describes a healthy sponsorship relationship as providing both people with valuable feedback and personal and professional satisfaction; a connection characterized by mutual trust, honesty, communication, and commitment to the relationship.

Sponsorship is not without controversy. Some view it as anointing people for promotion; a formalization of the old-boy network. Sponsorship is also a risky game. By aligning themselves with us, sponsors risk their reputational capital. They put us in the center of vital organizational networks and advocate for us: our success is their success. By aligning ourselves with them, we are jumping on their ship, choosing to sink or sail with them. Choose wisely.

Empowered and Vulnerable

Retooling can be challenging. If we have not had to do it yet, it is quite likely that we will sometime in our careers. Understanding what it is like for those who are in the midst of remaking themselves is a valuable resource from which we can draw when it is our turn. Empathizing with those who are doing the work right now can be rewarding and an authentic way to nurture others within our networks.

Acknowledging our emotions surrounding the task of retooling is helpful. For some of us there is a feeling of elation, a sense of what is possible. For others, it feels mostly uncomfortable. If we are really honest with ourselves, chances are we feel both feelings to some degree.

Being in learning mode can be exhilarating, but it can also be quite uncomfortable, especially if we have been experts in the past. Expect to feel afraid and vulnerable. Andy Grove was. But that is not where his story ends—or ours.

Being active in digital spaces opens a world of possibilities; however, we can also feel nervous and unskilled. Some of us grew up in a more private and less connected environment; life on LinkedIn and Twitter can seem very public. Expect to feel exposed. But also know that communicating in these environments does not have to be self-aggrandizing or involve revealing our dirty laundry. It is about articulating who we are, what is important to us, and the value that we bring. For those of us who grew up texting, tweeting, and documenting our lives continually on Facebook and Instagram, we may need to professionalize our image.

Freely sharing ideas and connections may be fruitful, but it may also feel like we are giving away our best resources. Scarcity and protectiveness have been pervasive philosophies in the business world in the past; however, today's business environment rewards connection and generosity. The best ideas are often developed in community, building off of the ideas of one another.

In an interview in the *New York Times*, Susan Credle, chief creative officer at the advertising agency Leo Burnett USA, spoke of how she tries to build a culture of generosity throughout the company. She tells her employees, "You are not competing with each other in here. If you think you win when your idea wins out over your neighbor's, that's a pretty small gain…I would suggest that if you look at something and you have a better idea, that you generously give that idea to someone and make them better. Because if we all do that, we all win. The minute you're the only good thing at this company, we're done. So can you do it? Can you be that generous?"[20]

While we may feel afraid, vulnerable, unskilled, and exposed, rest assured that we can make the transition. Our skills and even our deep-seated feelings are not fixed in stone. Stanford psychology Professor Carol Dweck studies the impact of our mind-sets on our ability to learn and grow.[21] As it turns out, our mind-sets matter. If we have a growth mind-set, believing that we can develop new qualities and skills through dedication and effort, we realize that belief. We can enjoy learning and acquire the resilience that is essential for great accomplishment. If on the other hand we have a fixed mind-set, where we believe that our intelligence or talent is a fixed trait, we will be stuck in the past, ill equipped for this new marketing world. Want to learn more? Dweck offers a simple test of our mindsets and tips for how to shift toward a growth orientation at mindsetonline.com.

There is an old saying that says, "Smooth seas do not make for skillful sailors." Now is a great time to rig our sails and enjoy the ride in these chaotic, yet exciting new waters. In the next chapter, we turn our attention to new skills that facilitate designing remarkable customer experiences.

QUESTIONS FOR CONSIDERATION

- How should I keep investing in myself? What do I need to learn or do?
- Who can help me understand or affirm what I need help me develop?
- Have I mapped my personal networks? Who might I want to add?
- How would I define myself as a brand? Is this consistent with how others see me?
- How robust is my digital presence? Does it accurately represent me?

- What resources comprise my daily briefing dashboard? What resources do I want to further investigate or incorporate? How can I simplify this process so that it is not a time drain?

- Am I part of an ongoing, albeit not constant, conversation with members of my network? What might I commit to doing to enhance these relationships?

- Is this a good time for me to seek out a mentor?

- Do I have a fixed or growth-oriented mind-set?

- What is my next step?

RESOURCES

Influencers We Recommend

- *Marci Alboher*. A former corporate lawyer who now writes and speaks on workplace issues and careers, Alboher is the author of *One Person/Multiple Careers: A New Model for Work/Life Success* and *The Encore Career Handbook: How to Make a Living and a Difference in the Second Half of Life*. Explore her work at www.heymarci.com and follow her on Twitter @heymarci.

- *William Arruda*. An expert in personal branding, online identity, and career management, Arruda is the author of *Career Distinction* and the coauthor of *Ditch Dare Do*. Learn with him at www.williamarruda.com, @williamarruda, or on his blog at www.thepersonalbrandingblog.com/tag/william-arruda/.

- *Ella L. J. Edmonson Bell*. A specialist in career development, Edmondson Bell teaches at the Tuck School of Business and is the author of *Career GPS: Strategies for Women Navigating the New Corporate Landscape* and *Our Separate Ways: Black*

(continued)

(continued)

and White Women Struggle for Professional Identity. She puts a special emphasis on articulating the experience and challenges of women of color. Follower her on Twitter @CareerGPSBook.

- *Brené Brown.* Brown is a professor, author, and storyteller whose groundbreaking research on vulnerability, courage, worthiness, and shame have made her a favorite of many. Her 2010 TEDxHouston talk, *The Power of Vulnerability*, is one of the top 10 most-viewed talks on TED.com. Enjoy her blog on www.brenebrown.com and follow her on Twitter @brenebrown.

- *Marcus Buckingham.* The author of several books, including *First Break All the Rules* and *Now Discover Your Strengths*, Buckingham is a pioneer of the idea that people are more effective, successful, and fulfilled when they play to their strengths rather than trying to shore up their weaknesses. To learn more about his work, go to www.tmbc.com or follow him on Twitter @mwbuckingham.

- *Deb Dib.* A personal branding expert and coauthor of *Ditch Dare Do*, Dib offers plenty of insights on her blog, which can be found at www.executivepowerbrand.com, or gathered by following her on Twitter @DebDib and @CEOCoach.

- *Carol Dweck.* Stanford professor of psychology, Dweck is the author of *Mindset: The New Psychology of Success*. Helpful tools for assessing and changing our own mindsets are available at www.mindsetonline.com.

- *Reid Hoffman.* The founder of LinkedIn and a partner of Greylock Ventures, Hoffman recently coauthored the book *The Start-Up of You*. Learn more about the book at www.Startupofyou.com, @startupofyou, and #startYOU or follow Reid directly on Twitter @reidhoffman.

- *Herminia Ibarra.* A professor of Leadership and Learning at INSEAD, Ibarra has a special interest in professional development and women's careers. Her latest book, *Working Identity: Unconventional Strategies for Reinventing Your Career*, focuses on how people are reinventing themselves at work. Named one of the top 50 management gurus, Ibarra dreamed of being an organizational professor at the age of 13.

- *Wendy Marcinkus Murphy*. As an assistant professor of Management at Babson College, Murphy thinks a lot about organizational behavior. Specifically, her research focuses on mentoring and developmental relationships, gender in the workplace, identity issues, and the work–life interface. Her work appears in a variety of publications including *Career Development International*, *Journal of Management*, *Human Resource Management*, and *Journal of Family Issues*. Learn more about Murphy at www.babson.edu.

- *Daniel Pink*. Best-selling author of five books, Pink's titles include *Free Agent Nation: The Future of Working for Yourself*, *Drive*, and *A Whole New Mind*. A great thought leader, Pink was the former chief speechwriter for Vice President Al Gore. Follow him at @Danielpink or at www.danpink.com.

- *Dan Schawbel*. A Gen Y career and workplace expert, Schawbel has written several books on personal branding including *Promote Yourself* and *Me 2.0*. One of the *Forbes 30 under 30*, you can follow him on Twitter @DanSchawbel or at www.danschawbel.com/promote-yourself.

- *Simon Sinek*. The author of *Start with Why: How Great Leaders Inspire Everyone to Take Action*, Sinek's TED talk on inspiration is the seventh-most-viewed video on TED.com. To learn more about his work, see www.startwithwhy.com and follow him on Twitter @simonsinek.

- *Gary Vaynerchuk*. The cofounder and CEO of a social media branding agency, Vaynerchuk is also a video blogger, and co-owner and director of a wine store. His book,

(continued)

(continued)

Crush It!, describes how he used social media to create a personal brand for himself and for his family's wine business, www.winelibrary.com. His latest book is *Jab, Jab, Jab, Right Hook: How to Tell Your Story in a Noisy World*. To learn more about Vaynerchuk, see www.garyvaynerchuk.com or follow him on Twitter @garyvee.

Hashtags to Explore

- #personalbranding
- #career
- #careeradvice
- #startYOU

Chapter 4

Design Valuable Customer Experiences

"Design in its simplest form is the activity of creating solutions. Design is something that everyone does every day."

—Frank Nuovo, former chief of design, Nokia

You know that you are doing something right when companies across several industries try to emulate you, going as far as citing your company in their brand profiles. Such is the case with eyewear purveyor Warby Parker.

A collaboration among four classmates from the Wharton School, Warby Parker was founded with a simple, game-changing idea: "to create boutique-quality, classically crafted eyewear at a revolutionary price point."[1] An analysis of the cost structure of the industry, a summary of which is openly available on their website (see Figure 4.1), revealed that this was in fact the case. By designing their own eyewear, carefully selecting manufacturers, utilizing the highest-quality materials, and engaging customers directly through their website, Warby Parker could substantially reduce the cost of a pair of prescription glasses.

Warby Parker's success is only partially due to economics. The company is also superb at understanding its customers and building a brand that truly inspires them. Their glasses, website, newly added retail spaces, blog, and other social media presences embody their "vintage-inspired with a contemporary twist" brand aesthetic.

In addition to quality glasses at an affordable price and a compelling brand with which to identify, the young company also offers its customers a sense of purpose. Committed to making the world

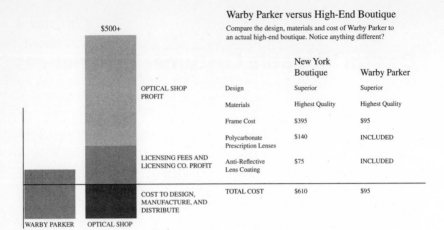

Figure 4.1 Warby Parker Openly Compares Industry Cost Structures

Source: **www.warbyparker.com/how-we-do-it**

a better place, the company offers a Buy a Pair, Give a Pair program that provides glasses to people in need. In an effort to be a carbon-neutral company, Warby Parker actively works to reduce greenhouse-gas emissions across its manufacturing, shopping, and retail operations; it also purchases carbon offsets.

Customers enjoy the company's fun and easy shopping experience and the way it reduces the risk of online glasses purchases as captured in the Post-it note message below (see Figure 4.2). Their e-commerce site allows shoppers to filter their options by shape, color, and material; acting like a salesperson in a high-end boutique, the site makes recommendations for similar frames based on their choices.

Customers can also upload a photo of themselves for a virtual try on (see Figure 4.3). To get their friends' opinions, they can share the image on Facebook or Twitter. For people who want to physically try on their frames, Warby Parker makes it a cinch. They can come in to one of their retail stores or try five frames for five days (with free shipping) through the company's Home Try-On program. If they choose the latter, customers are encouraged to post photos of them

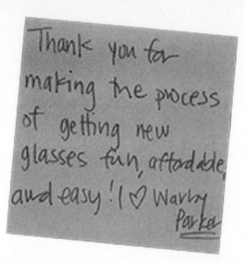

Figure 4.2   Why Customers Love Warby Parker

Source: www.warbyparker.com

Figure 4.3   Virtual Try-On Simplifies Online Purchases

Source: Warby Parker

Design Valuable Customer Experiences

wearing the frames on social media to get feedback about potential purchases from their friends and from Warby Parker employees. After making a selection, if their customers are not completely satisfied, the company accepts 30-day returns, no questions asked.

Recognizing that its customers shop across channels, Warby Parker has recently opened several boutiques located in fashionable locations across a smattering of cities and multiple showrooms within partner stores. The spaces reflect both the essence of their brand and the neighborhoods in which they are located. Inspired by classic libraries, its flagship store in Soho features shelves lined with books from small presses and rolling library ladders. The company has its own version of the pop-up store: the Warby Parker Class Trip. Traveling across the country, this completely reimagined yellow school bus—it looks like a Classics' professor's library inside—takes the company and its products to customers' hometowns, creating a media buzz everywhere it goes.[2]

Frameworks for Thinking about Customer Experience

Fabulous customer experiences like the ones Warby Parker creates do not happen by chance. A combination of creativity, deep customer understanding, knowledge of behavior design, intuitive websites and supporting infrastructure, data analytics, integrated online and offline presences, useful and engaging content, helpful customer-facing employees, and more give shape to the interactions that delight our customers. When they come together, it seems almost effortless, as if there is nothing to it—although we know better.

In an environment where businesses compete on the basis of customer experience, tools that provide proprietary insight into our prospects, customers, and their experiences with our brands are highly valued. They can make the difference between experiences that appears to be effortless and those that take entirely too much effort. Three tools that we have found to be especially helpful in designing and evaluating our customers' experiences include design thinking, the Fogg Behavior Model, and customer-journey analysis. The success of companies like Facebook, Apple, Instagram, USAA, and Google can often be linked to some combination of these tools.

Generating Remarkable Experiences
with Design Thinking

Big data, which we explore more deeply in the chapter that follows, provides us with unprecedented information about our prospects and customers and their attitudes and behavior. New insights are being uncovered as we combine data streams and test relationships among variables with advanced analytics. However, even when marketers have the benefit of insights derived from big data, we often still need tools that help us reach deeper than the numbers to truly understand the spoken and unspoken needs and desires that our customers and prospects are trying to satisfy. This depth of understanding, which some call empathy, is often the source of current and future innovation and the basis for our most successful marketing efforts. Design thinking can get us there and provide a disciplined process through which we turn that insight into game-changing customer experiences.

Design thinking facilitates our organizations' ability to think creatively and to put our customers at the center of our efforts. Based on the methodology that designers have typically undertaken in approaching product innovation challenges, the design-thinking process has been successfully used to create new products, to improve the interactions between people and products, and to analyze and enhance people's relationships with each other.[3] It is especially powerful in environments that are in constant change, when the way things have always been done is no longer especially useful. Although many organizations have adopted the process, it is often associated with the d.school at Stanford and the design and innovation firm IDEO. (The link between the d.school and IDEO is strong; Stanford professor David Kelley cofounded them both.)

Design thinking is inherently a social process. It brings together a diverse group of people from a variety of backgrounds to contribute their unique perspectives to the challenge at hand. Engineers, marketers, artists, doctors, designers, writers, CFOs, creative technologists, and ethnographers are some of the types of people who may all have a seat at the same table. Why is this necessary? There is a saying at IDEO that succinctly summarizes the reason: "All of us is smarter than any of us." When managed well, this diversity of thought generates new combinations of ideas.

99

But having a diverse group is not enough. Creativity only happens when we can be vulnerable, and this can only happen within a nonhierarchical environment. As Rodrigo Martinez, IDEO's life sciences chief strategist, who we met in Chapter 2, warns, "hierarchy kills innovation."

Design thinking pushes participants to think holistically by incorporating both divergent and convergent thinking. Divergent thinking is curiosity in action. An expansive process, the goal of divergent thinking is to generate many ideas in a short period of time. The reason: It takes a lot of ideas to come up with the one that sticks. Convergent thinking is its partner. An analytical framework for deciding among options, we employ convergent thinking when we synthesize the output of divergent processes, reassembling insights and observations in new ways. Convergent thinking reduces options, nudging us forward toward solutions. Both types of thinking are necessary to successful innovation.

Most of our companies are adept at convergent thinking. For the past several decades, our management tools and processes have emphasized efficiency, streamlining processes, and continuous incremental improvement. We are less skilled at divergent thinking. Rather than considering how to improve what is already in place, divergent thinking often threatens the status quo, with the goal of finding new ways to bring value. The combination is what creates thoughtful and disruptive innovation, which is precisely why many companies are eager to understand design thinking and incorporate it into their corporate DNA.

How does the design-thinking process work?

An Exploratory Process That Transforms Needs into Demand

Design thinking begins with inspiration, flows into synthesis, develops into ideation, and concludes with implementation of a solution. Inspiration involves exploring the challenge, the problem to be solved or the opportunity to be tapped. Synthesis creates a point of view that frames the parameters for the solution. Ideation involves generating, enhancing, and testing potential solutions. Implementation

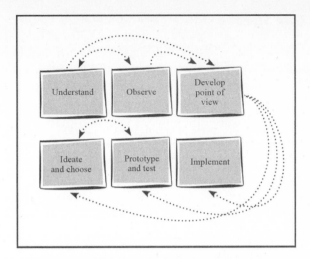

Figure 4.4   Design Thinking Is a Fluid Process

brings it all together in real life.[4] Do not be fooled into thinking this is a linear process; organizations cycle through these spaces multiple times as their thinking progresses and their ideas are improved (see Figure 4.4).

Develop an Understanding

One of the hallmarks of design thinking is a rigorous focus on clearly articulating the challenge that is to be solved or the opportunity to be created. Experience shows that, more often than not, impactful innovation comes from reframing a problem rather than solving the existing problem in a different way. Toward this end, the process kicks off with an invitation to explore, to uncover and closely examine the underlying customer need or desire to be addressed, rather than tackle a predefined problem. This openness to discovery is important: It creates space to think anew.

The brief is a vehicle through which the design process begins. It outlines the constraints surrounding the process that are to be balanced and a framework for evaluation. Midcourse adjustments are often made to briefs to reflect a growing understanding of the situation.

Design Valuable Customer Experiences

Roll Up Our Sleeves

Ethnographic research, or direct observation of our customers and the context in which they are trying to meet their needs and desires, is central to the inspiration phase. Tim Brown, who runs IDEO on a day-to-day basis, explains, "They only way we can get to know them is to seek them out where they live, work, and play."[5]

We prime the divergent-thinking pump when we spend time with the people for whom we are creating solutions—our prospects and customers—to better understand their needs, desires, motivations, and beliefs. Ideas begin to flow when we are able to break down a process, product, situation, or topic into smaller pieces to truly understand what is going on. Time and time again, standing back and taking a fresh look brings a different perspective to the table than our traditional market research.

Standing back suggests that ethnographic research is passive observation. It is not. Sometimes it involves intentionally putting ourselves in our customers' shoes, electing to be a patient in the emergency room of the hospital for which we run marketing, or shopping on our own e-commerce site in addition to our competitors. It may involve observation of other industries to see how similar challenges are identified and addressed. It always engages our customers to help define problems and generate potential solutions. Observing extreme users of products—the obsessives and the deviants—is a common practice; there is much to be learned from those who consume differently.

Develop a Point of View

"An idea is our imagination's way of responding to a gap," explains Gerald Puccio, chair of the International Center for Studies in Creativity at Buffalo State.[6] Looking to reconcile the gap in our understanding that stems from the information uncovered during our observations, our imaginations begin to form new associations and connections. In the synthesis phase, we try to discern the signals from the noise, imagine how the pieces fit together, and begin to frame the underlying story. We move from specific observations to broader generalizations: what have we learned that is relevant to

The Digital Marketer

our broader customer base? Buoyed with these insights, we define the problem and develop the design principles for solutions.

Generate Possibilities

Brainstorming begets solutions. At this stage the process brings together people from diverse backgrounds to generate and build on each other's ideas. Great care is taken to ensure that this time of divergent thinking is convergent-thinking free. While complementary, these two ways of thinking cannot exist simultaneously. Like the game Rock, Paper, Scissors, when paper always trumps rock and scissors always beat paper, critical thinking will always sabotage divergent thinking. Here is why: Young ideas are partially formed. As such they are easy to judge. If we judge them early on, they will never be able to be developed to a place where they may be credible.

To protect this time of divergent thinking, we work hard to create a nonjudgmental space with the necessary psychological safety to encourage prolific idea generation. Formal rules govern the seemingly freewheeling process. At IDEO they are written on the wall: Defer judgment. Encourage wild ideas. Stay focused on the topic. Build on the ideas of others.

This is a fun and optimistic time. It has to be. As author Helen Keller once wrote, "No pessimist ever discovered the secret of the stars, or sailed to an uncharted land, or opened a new heaven to the human spirit." It also gets very visual as Post-it notes capturing ideas and images cover entire walls.

A variety of materials are on-hand, to create prototypes. The goal of this learning by doing is to find out what works and what does not while the consequences are low. Sometimes prototypes take the form of physical objects; other times they may be drawings such as wireframe mock-ups of new mobile apps; still other times they come to life through storytelling and role-playing. Brown explains why prototyping is so important: "This shift from physical to abstract and back again is one of the most fundamental processes by which we explore the universe, unlock our imaginations, and open our minds to new possibilities."[7] Through this experimentation we create new knowledge and move ideas forward.

Evoke the Power of Convergent Thinking

As the process continues, we switch gears, adopting convergent thinking, as we shift from generating options to making choices.[8] One of the classic tools of the IDEO brand of design thinking is the butterfly test. Having ingested the group's range of ideas, which have been captured in Post-it notes or prototypes, participants are asked to identify those ideas which they believe hold the most promise. Each participant receives a small number of Post-it notes, which serve as ballots. The wisdom of the group surfaces as members attach Post-it notes to the ideas they believe should move forward.

Prototyping becomes important again as the group begins to refine solutions; however, the purpose and level of detail of these models change. Early on prototypes are quite simple and are designed for learning. At this stage, prototypes become more elaborate and are designed to explore marketplace viability.

Move from Insight to Impact

Finally, the design is refined and a road map for implementation is created. This is not to say that implementation starts at the end of the design-thinking process. Rodrigo Martinez explains that implementation actually begins at the very beginning, with careful selection of the people on the project team, and remains on the group's radar screen through the entire process. By ensuring that key decision makers from our companies are on the team, buy-in is being built while the vision unfolds. Top-down and bottom-up insights are combined in the process, which, in Martinez's experience, "infects the rest of the organization with the right behaviors, like a virus."

Applying Design Thinking to Marketing

ShapeUp is the leading provider of social networking and incentive-based employee wellness solutions. Founded by two medical doctors, the company has pioneered an innovative approach to behavior change that leverages the power of social networking, gaming, and financial rewards to improve the health of large populations and reduce health-care costs across the globe. Through fun challenges created via the ShapeUp platform, companies can encourage their employees to exercise more, eat healthier, and improve their overall well-being while building camaraderie among coworkers. More than 270 employers and health plans use ShapeUp's social-wellness platform and health plans; nearly 10 percent of the Fortune 500 are ShapeUp customers.

High employee engagement is critical to the success of ShapeUp's programs. Convinced that design thinking would facilitate their ability to think more expansively about engaging employee populations, ShapeUp worked collaboratively with IDEO. To kick off the engagement, members of the IDEO team reviewed ShapeUp's existing marketing materials. They also interviewed employees who use the product and human resource managers who are the primary purchasers of the product to develop a deeper understanding of the underlying needs and desires of both parties. As the process got underway, a cross-functional group of ShapeUp employees of varying seniority combined forces with the IDEO team, creating an eclectic group from which ideas flowed.

Together the group concluded that ShapeUp could benefit from creating marketing experiences that would appeal directly to the end-user. Prior to the engagement, ShapeUp had developed a library of marketing materials that was consistent with the branding of the ShapeUp platform; however, the content was largely product-focused. IDEO proposed a set of core design principles that would flip perspectives, showing employees how they would benefit from participation in ShapeUp's platform.

Incorporating this learning, today ShapeUp's marketing materials emphasize ease of participation and communicate a fun, lighthearted tone, which is consistent with how its customers experience the product. To encourage ongoing employee engagement, ShapeUp also helps its clients establish Pinterest-like communities, where employees can post stories of how they are improving their health. Reflections submitted on the "How Do You Shape Up?" sites personalize the ShapeUp experience and illustrate its effectiveness, acting as a powerful recruitment tool. It also promotes sharing and expands the experience to include spouses and dependents. Is the new approach

Design Valuable Customer Experiences

working? As one employee posted, "When your children say, 'Mom, when can we get up before the sun comes up and go to a race again?' you know you have created a healthy lifestyle."

Going Viral

The underlying principles of design thinking—customer-centeredness, diverse groups working together, experimentation, ideation, proto-typing, and divergent and convergent thinking—can also be put to use in other contexts to great effect. Imagine the potential of this type of thinking could spread to all corners of our organizations—if it was part of our corporate culture and DNA? That is precisely why companies like McDonald's and Pepsi are bringing designers into the highest level of management and why the president of Stanford University wants every Stanford student to have firsthand experience with the design-thinking process before they graduate.

Although David Kelley originally saw his work in developing design thinking as bringing together diverse groups of people to identify and solve challenges—which it does well—he now envi-sions the process more broadly, as building the creative confidence of individuals and organizations.[9] In *Creative Confidence*, the book that he recently coauthored with his brother, Tom Kelley, a partner at IDEO and author of *The Art of Innovation*, they provide numerous examples of design thinking at work. Specific strategies to unleash creativity in our organizations and us are sprinkled throughout the text. They also offer suggestions for how to successfully navigate corporate cultures to introduce design thinking.

The Science of Behavior

Marketers have traditionally been experts at convincing our prospects and customers to buy our products and services. In recent years, these persuasion techniques have become less effective as empow-ered customers, who have grown tired of producer-centricity and hard sells, turned a deaf ear to conventional marketing messages. Our prospects and customers still have needs and desires that they want to address, however. If they believe that we can help them meet their goals, we may be invited into their purchase journey, where we have the opportunity to authentically and simultaneously meet their goals. However, our customers and prospects may still need nonintrusive prompts that encourage them to act quickly.

An understanding of the emerging discipline of behavior design, which is being pioneered by innovator and social scientist Dr. B. J. Fogg, can help us create customer interactions that more effectively help our prospects and customers scratch their itch or finish the job they set out to do, while also prompting them to take action sooner rather than later. Fogg's work in this promising field incorporates insights from the Persuasive Technology Lab that he directs at Stanford University, where he explores the relationship between computing technologies—everything from websites to mobile devices—and persuasion. In Fogg's experience, these inherently neutral tools can be powerful instruments.

Under Fogg's leadership the lab develops insights into how technology can positively change what people believe and do. Projects are designed to help people take action to bring about essential changes in health, business, education, and safety. Changes that they want to make, as opposed to manipulating them to do things they do not want to do.

The Secret to Eliciting a Target Behavior

The first step in designing effective customer experiences is being clear about the target behavior we are trying to elicit. For instance, looking to improve the health of their patients, a health-care provider asked Fogg to design an experience to help reduce their patients' stress. The goal of reducing people's stress was too broad and difficult to measure to be successful; however, focusing on a smaller, near-term objective, proved more useful.

What would qualify as a smaller, near-term objective? Early testing found that the health-care provider's patients could be prompted to do 20 seconds of stretching a day. While the goal of stretching for 20 seconds a day may not sound like a very impactful way to reduce stress—wouldn't a more aggressive goal such as running two miles a day seem more appropriate?—it was the foundation upon which more advanced behaviors would eventually be built. In Fogg's experience, if we ask people to do something that they will not be able to successfully complete, we will adversely impact their future motivation to act.

Next, we have to create the conditions under which the target behavior is likely to be elicited. Fogg has found that for a target behavior to occur, three factors must be present simultaneously and in sufficient quantity: (1) motivation, or the desire to act; (2) the ability to act; and (3) a trigger to act now. These three factors are summarized in the Fogg Behavior Model, represented by the formula: $B = mat$, where B is a desired target behavior, m is motivation, a represents ability, and t stands for a trigger or prompt (see Figure 4.5). A dynamic relationship exists between motivation and ability, which allows one factor to be traded off for the other.

Motivation

Truly useful customer experiences help our customers meet their goals, whether those goals are purchasing a new pair of eyeglasses, becoming more fit, discovering new authors, or nurturing leads. When our prospects and customers have confidence that we can help them meet their goals, we have tapped into something powerful: Motivation. They have a reason to act.

Fogg has identified three core motivators: sensation, anticipation, and social cohesion. Each of these motivators has two opposing dimensions: Sensation is marked by pain and pleasure, anticipation

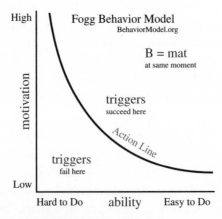

Figure 4.5   The Fogg Behavior Model

Source: http://www.behaviormodel.org

The Digital Marketer

by hope and fear, and social cohesion by acceptance and rejection. By creating conditions that impact these motivators, marketers can influence people's motivation.

Marketers have traditionally spent the lion's share of our efforts trying to influence our prospects' and customers' motivation. Ironically, Fogg has found that motivation is the hardest of the three "mat" factors to influence. It requires careful design and caution as experiences that impact motivation often result in people feeling manipulated. Indeed, research shows that efforts to impact people's motivation can lead to the exact opposite behavior, a response knows as reactance.[10] Here is the good news: In many cases, attempting to augment our prospects' and customers' motivation may not be necessary. If they are already using search engines and social networks to seek out solutions when they discover us, the requisite motivation may already be present. In those cases, focusing on increasing their ability to act, or creating a well-timed trigger to encourage them to act now, may be a more effective use of our time and resources.

This was the case with Fogg's stress-reducing intervention. Because people were already motivated to reduce tension by daily stretching, the experience did not have to try and increase the group's motivation by showing graphic images of stress-induced heart attacks or even compelling personal accounts of improved health. Instead, Fogg turned his attention to examining the group's ability to stretch for 20 minutes a day.

Ability

Many times people may really want to do something, but are unable to because their do not have the necessary ability. They may want to buy a new car, but do not have the cash. They may want to read a whitepaper, but they do not have the time to fill out the contact form. In Fogg's experience, in addition to time and money, ability also includes having resources like the necessary skills, the physical or mental capability to act, or the strength to go against a social norm or engage in an activity that is outside of one's normal routine. Often experienced designers overlook the ability factor, assuming their audiences are more capable than they really are.

How can we increase our prospects' and customers' ability to act? One of the most successful techniques is to make acting easier for

Design Valuable Customer Experiences

them. For example, if people have high motivation to do something that they find hard to do, by simplifying it in a meaningful way, we increase the chance of evoking the target behavior. By bundling their automobile services into an integrated service, USAA made it easier for their members to purchase a car, secure a car loan, and obtain insurance coverage. Similarly, Starbucks' app allows their customers to purchase coffee with their phones (no cash or card required) and automatically manage their loyalty points and offers. Amazon's 1-Click Shopping option and Amazon Prime make purchases almost effortless. According to a recent article in *Time*, on average people spend as much as 150 percent more at Amazon after becoming Prime members.[11] They also "stop shopping anywhere else," preferring to take advantage of Amazon's free and speedy shipping.[12] As Fogg says, "Simplicity impacts behavior." Indeed, the success of most mobile apps can be linked to their ability to make things easier for people.

Simplifying can be complex. Fogg has found that everyone has a different simplicity profile. What may be simple for a 15-year-old girl may be different than for a 15-year-old boy, or for a 50-year-old and vice versa. To enhance our target customers' ability to purchase or use our products or services, we have to understand their perception of simplicity. In Fogg's experience, this perception is a function of their scarcest resource at the moment—time, money, physical or mental effort, or their ability to go against the grain or try something new.

Trigger

Perhaps the easiest way to elicit a target behavior is by providing a well-timed trigger that gives people a prompt to act now. A handshake is an effective trigger in many cultures; it encourages people to respond. A ringing phone can be an effective trigger, if people can hear it and are able to pick up. Effective triggers can also be an event, a call to action, a request, or an offer delivered via phone, email, text, post, pin, and more. To be effective, people must be familiar with the technology that delivers the trigger. As Fogg cautions, "The combination of a new behavior and a new channel never wins."

As Figure 4.5 illustrates, triggers must fall above the motivation/ability threshold to be effective. If we ask people to do things that are too hard and for which they have little motivation, even the most exceptional triggers will fail. Similarly, if we continually offer triggers to people who may have the ability to act, perhaps make a donation to a cause, but have very little interest in the cause, our triggers will amount to nothing more than annoyances. In these cases, the triggers are cold; they do not produce positive results.

In the case of the stress-reducing intervention, Fogg chose text messaging on mobile phones as a daily trigger to remind people to do their stretching. Because the target population was already in the habit of texting, this channel was an effective choice. Had the group not been adept at texting, a different trigger would have to be employed. Did the intervention work? Yes. The majority of people successfully completed the two-week challenge and were willing to continue. In Fogg's experience, simplicity is how long-lasting habit change is born. He also encourages us to start small and experiment quickly, building on each success, rather than being too ambitious upfront.

Facebook and LinkedIn are quite adept at designing triggers. To encourage users to log in, Facebook sends e-mails notifying them of updates to their page, such as friend requests and messages (see Figure 4.6). Similarly, LinkedIn delivers updates to their members when one of their connections changes jobs or has a birthday, or when they receive a new connection request or endorsement. Through LinkedIn Pulse, which was created by one of Fogg's students, the network dispatches personalized news content based upon members' professional interests, prompting further engagement.

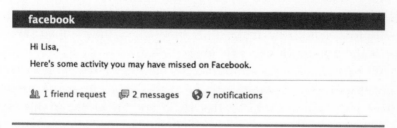

Figure 4.6   Facebook Designs Triggers to Prompt Engagement

Design Valuable Customer Experiences

Using $B = mat$ *to Understand What Works*

In recent years, the use of software to create persuasive experiences has spread well beyond the confines of Fogg's laboratory. Consider how the fuel gauge in the Toyota Prius inspires eco-conscious car owners to drive more efficiently, reinforcing its brand promise. Or how simple widgets that are well-placed on a blog post encourage people to share compelling brand content with their friends on the social networks of their choice. Similarly, by improving its customers' success in meeting their fitness goals via its runners' app and Fuel-Band, Nike simultaneously prompts their customers to purchase more athletic shoes and gear, while also creating a brand preference for Nike. These are "win-win" scenarios for brands and their customers made possible by creating the necessary conditions for eliciting mutually-desired behaviors.

Using the Fogg Behavior Model as a guide, we can create experiences that are likely to elicit target behaviors. We can also evaluate why our customers or prospects may not be responding to our marketing efforts. For example, if our customers are not sharing our content, it could be they do not have the ability (add share buttons), they do not have the motivation (create content that they are inspired to share), or they do not have an effective trigger (ask them to share or interact with them in a more preferred channel). If we want to stop or reduce a behavior, we can use the Fogg Behavior Model, only in this case, our focus will be on removing one of the three factors (mat).

$B = mat$ *Explains the Success of Instagram*

Another one of Fogg's former students, Mike Kreiger, is the cofounder of the popular photo-sharing application Instagram and a self-proclaimed behavior geek. A snapshot of the company shows the thoughtful use of behavior science.

When Instagram was introduced to the marketplace, it was not a novel idea. People were already in the habit of sharing photos online through other vehicles like Flickr and Shutterfly. In this case, the presence of competitors was a benefit; they had already built the market. In terms of the Fogg model, Instagram's prospects already had the necessary motivation and ability to use the new app.

To encourage prospects to switch, Instagram addressed all three variables of the Fogg Behavior Model. Its multiple filters made photos taken on mobile devices appear to be professional quality—so much so that during a recent Fashion Week, *Vogue* conducted photo shoots exclusively via Instagram[13]—increasing the value and fun of the app relative to those that people were already using. The ease and speed that photos could be uploaded and shared across multiple networks made taking pictures simpler than its competitors, enhancing people's ability and motivation to use the app. Finally, seeing friends post their filter-adjusted pictures on Facebook created triggers that prompted people to download the app and get snapping and sharing right away. Did it work? Eighteen months later the app was sold to Facebook for a quick $1 billion. Today the company has over 150 million active members and over 16 billion photos have been shared.

To continually improve its customer service, Instagram creates new uses and activities while being careful to maintain its simplicity. As Fogg cautions, "Each time you add something to your customer experience, you increase the likelihood of failure." Users can now post videos and choose to share photos and videos privately with selected friends through Instagram Direct. On Thursdays people participate in one of the most popular hashtag-based games: Throw Back Thursday. Instagramers are encouraged to post nostalgia-inducing photos of days gone by and tag them with the hashtag #TBT. People love the game: over 63 million pictures have been tagged with #tbt or #throwbackthursday on Instagram.[14]

To learn more about Fogg's work, see bjfogg.com and read his books: *Persuasive Technology: Using Computers to Change What We Think and Do* and *Mobile Persuasion: 20 Perspectives on the Future of Behavior*. To learn to create habits quickly and easily, check out Fogg's breakthrough method at tinyhabits.com.

Getting Our Arms around Our Customers' Experience

To improve our customer experience, we must also have a clear and fact-based understanding of how our customers experience our brands. Poor customer experiences are costly. Forrester Research found that 79 percent of online shoppers who have unsatisfying web experiences are unlikely to make a purchase from that same site in the future.[15] Similarly, ineffective or redundant interactions waste resources and can be annoying to our prospects and customers. Missing touchpoints may leave an important customer need unmet or thwart their ability to progress along the experience journey. Well-designed interactions, on the other hand, can improve our prospects' and customers' perception of our brands and draw them closer to us.

How do we know how customers *really* feel about our brands? Quantitative data, such as our churn rate, which measures attrition, captures our customers' overall satisfaction with our brands. The only drawback: it gives us this knowledge after the fact. Our former customers have already voted with their feet. Having tools that can help us assess customer satisfaction long before that point is reached is fundamental to being able to realize the customer experience differential.

Perception-based surveys that proactively generate customer satisfaction scores (CSAT) assess our customers' overall satisfaction with our brands and uncover any gaps between their expectations and their actual experience. Net promoter scores (NPS) that are derived from asking our customers, "How likely are you to recommend us to a friend?" allow us to consider customer satisfaction from a slightly different vantage point: what they are likely to do next as a result of their interaction with us.

In addition to understanding our customers' overall satisfaction with our brands, there is much to be learned from analyzing their experiences with us on a more granular level. One way to do this is through customer journey analysis. This systematic process connects our customers' perceptions of us with the interactions that formed those impressions. An important vantage point, this is where people are delighted, nonplused, or disappointed. A place of emotional connection, these are the moments when our prospects and customers decide to further engage with us—or not.

Analyzing our touchpoints can be a complex exercise—there are often more potential touchpoints than we think. The global delivery company, FedEx, for example, identified 200 possible touches it could have with its customers. Clearly, we cannot analyze or optimize everything at once; some prioritization is necessary. How do we know where to focus our efforts? By determining which interactions are most important to our customers. Identifying the typical journeys that our customers take with us can point us in the right direction.

Mapping Our Customers' Journeys

A *customer journey map* is a visual representation of the interactions our customers have with us over time from *their* point of view. In addition to capturing the interactions themselves, the mapping process records the device or setting in which they took place, the specific channels utilized, and the stages in the customer journey that a customer enters and exits, sometimes multiple times along the way. It also includes our customers' underlying motivations, the questions they were hoping to answer at each stage, and their feelings about the encounter. Armed with this insight, we can do more of what is working, and fix what is not.

The mapping process begins with identifying the steps a representative customer would take in engaging with us. These steps should include actions taken even before our customers approach us—how they became aware of their need or desire—and continue through the customer experience journey to the point of sale and later stages of engagement.

Altimeter Group, which provides research and advisory services on social business strategy to companies, estimates that some customer journeys can have as many as 75 digital variances when you consider all of the content sources, channels, and screens that are now available for every touchpoint.[16] The more precise we can get at identifying the steps that all of our prospects and customers are undertaking, the more accurately we can design customer experiences to accompany them along the journey. Path analysis facilitates our ability to map these journeys with more certainty and clarity.

Comparing and contrasting what our customers may be trying to achieve with our goals for the same touchpoints shows us where important gaps may be. Is our content answering our customers' questions? Are our steps actually encouraging prospects to continue forward? How effective are our triggers? Are our steps actually encouraging prospects to continue forward?

Design Valuable Customer Experiences

We answer these questions using both quantitative and qualitative information. Descriptive metrics derived from operational data—call center reports, web and mobile analytics, customer billing systems, customer relationship management systems—explain who, what, and where. To understand our customers' motivations and feelings about what happened when they acted, and what they are likely to do next, we use qualitative research such as CSAT surveys, NPS, customer interviews, and focus groups. We also mine social media chatter, call center transcripts, and discussions in our customer communities that can help us ascertain customer sentiments, which they may not share with us directly.

Creating multiple maps to represent the journeys of our target market segments paints a more complete picture of our customer base and teases out differences among segments. This is especially important for companies that offer different experiences to customers based upon their lifetime value and for companies operating in global or multicultural markets where contexts may vary significantly. An investigation of the competitive landscape to see how important customer experience is in the industry and who is doing it well provides further context for our efforts.

Like design thinking, the customer journey mapping process works best when it is undertaken with stakeholders across the organization. Inclusiveness ensures that the right data is captured—much of the necessary data resides across business functions—and that there is validity to the results. It is also important that the spirit of this process be positive, not a time to point fingers, but an opportunity to harness support and insight for improving our customers' experience. Finally, these customer journey maps are meant to be working documents for everyone involved, a catalyst for optimization and further inquiry, not documents to be filed away.

Maps, Cell Phones, and Upgrades

To understand how customer experience mapping works, we asked Sparks Grove, the marketing division of the consulting firm North Highland, to create a simplified map (see Figure 4.7). This particular map captures the story of a cell phone purchase undertaken by a fictional character, John. The journey begins while John is watching

PUTTING IT ALL TOGETHER

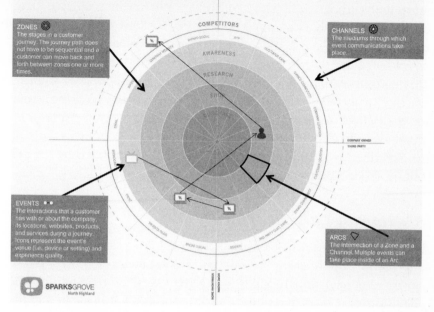

Figure 4.7 The Customer Journey Tells an Important Story
Source: Sparks Grove

Monday Night Football. Too tired to find the remote or to move, John remains on the couch during the commercial break, half watching the ads. However, one commercial piques his interest—an advertisement for a new model of his cell phone. The commercial makes the latest version seem useful, sleek, and fun. John is inspired to get up, go to his computer, and do some research. At this point John's experience with the cell phone brand is neutral. He is intrigued; but by no means convinced.

John picks up his laptop, conducts a search about the new phone, and finds several glowing reviews on an independent technology website. The reviews address his concerns about usability and confirm the features that he found most appealing. John's experience is positive; however, he wants to see the phone in person before he makes a purchase.

Energized, John heads over to his service provider's local retail store the next day to check out the phone. After playing with it for a

Design Valuable Customer Experiences

few minutes, he is convinced; he wants the phone. John's enthusiasm turns to disappointment when he learns that while he is eligible for an upgrade, he will have to pay an additional $200 to get that particular model. He walks out disgusted. His experience is decidedly negative.

When John returns home, he has an inspired thought. He picks up his computer and searches for the phone on a superstore website. He can hardly believe his luck when he finds that they have the phone in stock and that he can have it for $99 with two-day delivery. John purchases the phone on the website and looks forward to its arrival. He is thrilled with the superstore but remains disgruntled by the cell phone service provider.

Reading the Customer Journey Map

How does the customer journey map tell John's story? John's initial interaction in purchasing a new cell phone takes place via a television commercial, which builds his awareness of the new model. The television icon marks this initial step on the map. It is located in the arc that represents the intersection between the awareness zone and the broadcast channel, where he was first engaged.

If we follow the arrow, we are led to John's next stop: visiting an unaffiliated tech website to learn of others' experience with the phone. A computer icon captures this interaction. Having begun the research process, the computer is located in the arc at the intersection of the research zone and an unaffiliated website channel.

John's next step takes place in-store. He has moved from research to shopping mode; as a result, the self-icon is placed in the arc representing an in-store channel and shopping zone. Following the arrow, we see that this step leads to a purchase. Unfortunately for the cell phone retailer, the purchase takes place on a competitor's website, as indicated by the rather long arrow extending away from the in-store channel.

Drilling Down: Touchpoint Analysis

Many companies choose to take the mapping process one level deeper, identifying the internal processes involved with each interaction and how information travels. *Touchpoint analysis* essentially explores a single interaction or sequence of interactions that take place during the customer journey from the company's point of view. It provides a comprehensive picture that generates insight into what organizations do that may cause a customer to act in a particular way.

Figure 4.8 captures the actions taken by a company after they received a call from a customer who discovered fraudulent charges on their audio conferencing account, through to the fraud being verified, and a credit issued. A quick glance illustrates how much of a cross-functional organizational effort it takes to create and deliver a unified brand experience.

Optimizing Our Customer Experiences

Once our representative journeys are mapped, we have to determine which interactions to optimize. Scott Russell, director of customer experience at Sparks Grove, explains that the key to successful optimization is to prioritize improvement initiatives with customers' needs, goals, and preferences in mind. If an experience is negative, but it is not that important to our customers, it may only need to be improved to a neutral state (see Figure 4.9). On the other hand, if the interaction is highly important to customers, then it needs to be improved right away.

Russell recommends using the Kano model to frame our optimization efforts.[17] Originally designed for prioritizing features for product updates, the Kano model can prevent us from succumbing to the got-to-have-it-all mentality. According to the model, a product, service, or experience can be evaluated in terms of three attributes.

1. *Basic attributes* are must-have features. These are the components of an experience that must be present. It could be a steering wheel on a car, a website that has zero downtime, or an app that loads in three seconds or less. Providing these features does not make our customers love us, or even like us, but without them we can be assured that they will not give us the time of day.

2. *Performance attributes* are features in which there is a direct correlation between our customers' satisfaction and how well we are able to deliver. In terms of improving our customer experience, it could mean reducing the wait time at a store,

Design Valuable Customer Experiences

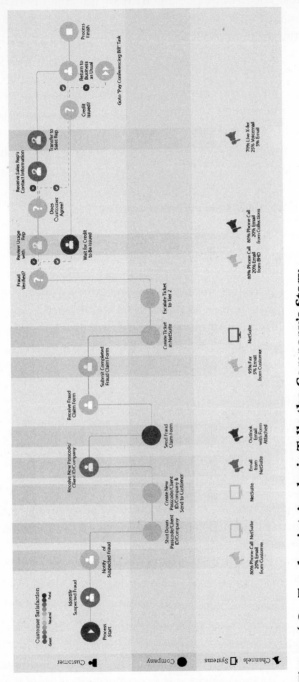

Figure 4.8 Touchpoint Analysis Tells the Company's Story

Source: Sparks Grove

CONSIDER CUSTOMERS' PRIORITIES WHEN OPTIMIZING

	Action to be taken	
Level of customer importance	Unimportant	Important
Negative current experience	Improve to neutral	Improve to excellent
Neutral current experience	Do not bother	Improve to excellent

Figure 4.9   Optimization Matrix

Source: **Adapted from Sparks Grove**

increasing the fuel economy of a car, or improving the battery life on a mobile phone. Often on the top of our customers' minds, these are incremental improvements to our experience, rather than new game-changing advancements. However, if we do not perform well on them, our customers will be disappointed.

3. *Delight attributes* create experiences that surprise and often captivate our customers. They are often unexpected, the result of innovation that reaches beyond the incremental. This could be introducing the iPhone, offering mobile-payment options on an app, or offering virtual-try options on an e-commerce site. This is where real differentiation lies.

Being early to the game matters here. In markets characterized by intense competition, today's delight attribute becomes tomorrow's performance attribute, and next week's basic attribute. For example, offering Wi-Fi in coffee shops has gone from being a key point of differentiation to part of a baseline experience. This is why getting there first has become so important.

Drawing upon customer insight, we can use the Kano model to classify aspects of our customer experience as basic, performance,

Design Valuable Customer Experiences

and delight. In terms of prioritizing our efforts, preference is given to basic attributes; if they are not present and glitch-free, we are already out of the game. Our choice for performance offerings is governed by our customers' needs and not what our competitors are doing. With these essentials in place, we can turn our attention to designing delight attributes.

With the Fogg Behavior Model as a guide, we can develop a plan of action for those touchpoints that are high value and need improvement. Can we make the interaction easier? More appealing? Might we be able to reach people at a more opportune time or through a preferred channel? Sometimes the solution may include technology; other times it may involve people, communication programs, or process reengineering, or a combination of all of the above.

Customer journey analysis is an ongoing process as our customers' behavior and channel preferences change frequently. It pays to continually engage, measure, learn, and adapt.

How can big data and analytics contribute to our design of valuable customer experiences? We tackle that question in the chapter that follows.

QUESTIONS FOR CONSIDERATION

- How do you currently observe your customers' world and the needs and desires they are trying to address? What methods have been most effective?

- What aspects of design thinking might be useful to your organization?

- How do you currently evaluate your customers' experience with your brand?

- How might *the Fogg Behavior Model* improve your interactions with your customers?

- What is your next step?

RESOURCES

Influencers We Recommend

- *Warren Berger*. An author and speaker, Berger has spent his career profiling creative people and companies. His most recent book is *A More Beautiful Question*, which explores the power of inquiry and its ability to spark fresh ideas. *Glimmer* focuses on design thinking. For more information see www.warrenberger.com, www.amorebeautifulquestion.com, or follow him on Twitter @warrenberger.

- *Tim Brown*. Brown serves as the CEO and president of IDEO and is the coauthor of *Change by Design*. Follow his thoughts at www.designthinking.ideo.com/IDEO and on Twitter @tceb62.

- *BJ Fogg*. Director of the Persuasive Technology Lab at Stanford, Fogg works to use technology to create lasting behavior change. His Tiny Habits™ methodology outlines a simple way to bring new behaviors into people's lives. Get to know his work at www.behaviormodel.org, www.tinyhabits.com, and www.bjfogg.com and follow him on Twitter @bjfogg.

- *Tim Hurson*. Creativity and innovation consultant, Hurson is the author of *Think Different: An Innovator's Guide to Productive Thinking*. There is much to be learned from the man who challenged us to think of a customer's needs as an itch. For a taste see www.timhurson.com or follow him @tim_hurson.

- *David Kelley*. As cofounder of IDEO and the d.school at Stanford University, Kelley has made many contributions to design thinking, including bringing human-centered methodology and a culture of innovation to the field of design. He recently coauthored *Creative Confidence* with his brother, Tom. Follow Kelley on Twitter @kelleybros.

(continued)

Design Valuable Customer Experiences

(continued)

- *Steven Johnson.* The author of eight books and a regular contributor to the *New York Times*, *The Wall Street Journal*, *The Financial Times*, and *Wired*, Johnson explores the intersection of science, technology, and innovation. *Where Good Ideas Come From* explores creativity suggesting that innovation is a gradual process of proving a slow hunch, rather than a singular moment of inspiration. For more information see www.stephenberlinjohnson.com and follow him on Twitter @stevenbjohnson.

- *Harley Manning.* Manning is research director in the customer experience practice at Forrester Research and coauthor of *Outside In*. Learn the latest on his blog at www.blogs.forrester.com/harley_manning or on Twitter @hmanning.

- *Rodrigo Martinez.* Martinez is responsible for design+biology @IDEO and tackles interesting challenges in health care, life sciences, wellness, and financial services. If you can't attend his frequent lectures at MIT and Harvard, nurture your creative juices by following him @RodrigoATCG.

- *Gerald Puccio.* Puccio is the chair of the International Center for Studies in Creativity at Buffalo State and the coauthor of *Creative Leadership Skills* and *Creativity Rising*, among other books. Catch his TED talk on "Creativity as a Life Skill" and begin to think differently by following him on Twitter @pucciogj.

- *Bruce Temkin.* Temkin is the customer experience transformist and cofounder of Temkin Group, a customer research and consulting firm. Keep up with Temkin's insights on the blog at www.temkingroup.com and @btemkin.

Hashtags to Explore

- #creativity
- #customerloyalty

- #custexp (customer experience)
- #CX (customer experience)
- #CXO (customer experience optimization)
- #design
- #designthinking
- #innovation
- #UX (user experience)
- #UI (user interface)

Design Valuable Customer Experiences

Chapter 5

Find Actionable Insight in Big Data and Marketing Analytics

"Judge a man by his questions rather than his answers."

—Voltaire

"We will share the risk and the reward." These are not words that marketers typically hear from their partner agencies, but this is exactly the business compensation model that Leapfrog Online offers its clients. The marketing company, which develops and optimizes digital sales channels for Fortune 500 brands, is compensated not just for its ideas, but also for how those ideas deliver against its clients' goals, be they an increase in revenue, number of customers, or loyalty.

How does Leapfrog Online do it? By truly owning the customer experience journey, which for a direct marketing company like Leapfrog Online, starts at the moment a prospect engages with its client's brand and continues until a purchase is made. This sounds relatively straightforward; however, to pull it off requires the highly coordinated management of myriad interconnected details across multiple media and response channels in real time. Leapfrog Online's success is a testament that it can be done.

The process begins and ends with data. Data informs the company's customer understanding, segmentation, targeting, media planning and buying, and how it assesses, refines, and optimizes every interaction along the customer journey. What is more, data is fundamental to understanding the chemistry among customer touchpoints. Without this broader perspective, interactions are optimized for one channel—search results, web traffic, conversions from e-mail viewed on mobile devices—but not for the customer. "Driving scale through digital channels means owning the full lifecycle, and making decisions based on the full chain-of-events—not one link at a time," explains Joel Grossman, senior vice president, who leads the team responsible for the development, delivery, and optimization of Leapfrog Online's digital platform.

Closing the loop between marketing and sales is also critical to being able to manage the end-to-end process. A state-of-the-art customer engagement platform that integrates with its clients' backend systems and tracks each and every customer interaction, online and offline, creates a leak-proof flow of information. Measuring results across every stage and channel reveals how customers are responding to messages and the format in which they are being delivered, making real-time adaptations possible. "Once you're tracking your customers it's easier to make decisions about where to focus marketing effort and investment," explains Scott Epskamp, president and cofounder of Leapfrog Online.

How might Leapfrog Online help build a clients' business? Time Warner Cable (TWC), which provides digital voice, video, and data services to individuals and businesses, worked with Leapfrog Online and Google to develop a mobile channel to better engage and respond to its customers. Recognizing that the channel could be used for both educational and sales purposes, Leapfrog Online and TWC designed an integrated, end-to-end mobile strategy that aligned the mobile customer experience with the customer's underlying need.

Customers were routed to different mobile experiences depending upon whether they were looking to make a purchase or obtain customer care. Each path incorporated click-to-call features that allowed customers to reach TWC quickly and easily by phone if they desired. Incoming calls were filtered to either sale or customer service representatives and were picked up in less than 30 seconds. Leapfrog Online continually monitored the effort, integrating mobile and call-center data, and adjusting budgets, keywords (for search ads), and call-center staffing to match customer demand. The result: a streamlined customer experience that now accounts for over 10 percent of TWC's online sales and continues to grow.

Find Actionable Insight in Big Data and Marketing Analytics

The combination of knowing how to collect and leverage relevant data, a proprietary engagement platform, and proven optimization techniques, allows Leapfrog Online to go all in with their customers, linking its performance to their success. Together with its clients—brands such as Culligan, Comcast, Fifth Third Bank, Terminix, and DeVry University—Leapfrog Online is fully accountable to clearly defined and measurable outcomes.

Will more agencies follow Leapfrog Online's lead, tying their compensation to performance? "The market is moving in our direction and the drive for accountability in marketing spend continues to increase," explains Epskamp. Furthermore, as advertising becomes increasingly digital, and data and analytics more integrated and accessible, it is hard to image how agencies will be able to ignore the trend.

The New Face of Market Insight

The design of remarkable customer experiences begins with customer and marketplace insights. It always has and always will. Viral videos, memorable taglines, and actively used apps all start with a solid understanding of the person and the environment for which they are designed. It is logical: The more insight we have into our prospects and customers, the better we can meet their needs; the better we understand what is going on in the marketplace, the faster and more appropriately we can act. What is changing is the underlying data with upon which our decisions are based, the analytics we use to find meaning in the data, and the type of customer experience we are able to deliver as a result.

For many years our market research was derived from customer surveys, panel data, third-party transaction data, and our own often siloed customer databases, which we supplemented with qualitative data. We made key business decisions based upon what we would now consider limited information, years of experience, and a good amount of intuition. Today we are gathering data from seemingly everywhere: e-mails, texts, searches, product reviews, recommendations, customer service records, and more. This explosion of new types of information is known as *big data*.

Big data has captured the attention of organizations and institutions across multiple industries. Being able to investigate large datasets is intriguing because it holds the promise of predicting behavior with much more accuracy than is possible using smaller volumes. We can also integrate datasets to create synthetic data, data that cannot be obtained by direct measurement, from which we can often obtain deeper insight.

Until recently, big data analysis was theoretical at best because datasets were too complex, large, and cumbersome to capture, manipulate, analyze, and access using conventional databases. Developments in cloud-storage capacity and the ability to process information efficiently using tools like Hadoop, which allows companies to distribute computing tasks across servers to simplify data, are critical innovations that are making it possible for us to gain business value from the reams of data we are capturing.

Although we are still in the early stages, it is clear that organizations that are able to master the big-data and analytics opportunity will reduce their time to insight and increase the relevance of their interactions significantly. Excited by the potential, companies are investing substantial time and funds into capturing, managing, analyzing, and interpreting these new forms and combinations of data. Marketing initiatives are driving much of this activity. Gartner, the information technology research and advisory firm, projects that by 2017, CMOs will spend more on information technology than the traditional CIO.[1] The goal, of course, is not to just purchase technology, but to be able to find the big insight within the data, and to apply that insight in concrete ways to deliver remarkable customer experiences.

What Exactly Is Big Data?

A clear definition of big data has yet to emerge; most definitions are descriptive. One of the properties of big data is its size, hence, its name. To get a sense of the magnitude of big data, consider the context provided by Eric Schmidt, Google's chief executive officer: "Between the birth of the world and 2003 there were five exabytes of information created. We [now] create five every two days."[2] (See Figure 5.1.)

Without even knowing what or how big an exabyte is, it is clear that the amount of data that is out there has grown significantly.

```
An exabyte is
1,000,000,000,000,000,000 bytes

A zetabyte is larger
1,000,000,000,000,000,000,000 bytes

(One byte is equivalent to a single letter or number.)
```

Figure 5.1   How Big Is an Exabyte?

By 2015, it is estimated that nearly eight zetabytes of digital information will be created and shared.

What is fueling this growth in data? We are. As we go about our days, each of us leaves a digital footprint. Our individual and collective footprints are growing, as more devices and sources are added. If we pay by credit card for our gas or groceries, we generate transaction data that is collected by companies. If we are part of a loyalty program, every time we purchase anything, even if it is by cash, our purchases are recorded and captured by companies' data systems. If we visit a given website, our activity—what we viewed, and for how long, and what search terms we may have used to arrive there—is captured. If we like a photo on Instagram, update our status on Facebook, tweet, or share our location though our mobile phones, it is recorded. If we sign on to any of these sites or apps via Facebook or Twitter, even more data is shared.

A plethora of data is also being generated from the Internet of things—smart devices imbedded in objects—and from traditional secondary sources such as census data, macroeconomic data, psychographic data, weather patterns, and Dun and Bradstreet and Experian reports. It is not surprising that as marketers we often feel as if we are drowning in data.

Another characteristic of big data is its complexity. For years now, companies have been analyzing what is known as structured data. Transaction records like those we generate when we use a credit card or a loyalty card are considered structured because the data fits into traditional numerical-based database-management programs. Today over 80 percent of data is considered unstructured; our clicks, texts, searches, book reviews on Amazon, and blog postings are more complicated in form and cannot be stored and managed in traditional ways. To take full advantage of big data requires us to be able to combine structured and unstructured data and analyze these enhanced data streams. To do so we must be able to transform unstructured data into structured numerical data.

Speed is also a property of big data. Continual updates to data—think how often our phone-location data changes—and the frequent introduction of entirely new data sources, such as the latest mobile applications, add an additional layer of complexity to the puzzle. Our ability to extract insight from this data and act on it, in some cases in real time, can be what makes it possible for us to see an opportunity before our competition, make use of data before its shelf-life has expired, and provide remarkable experiences for our customers.

Where Is the Insight?

Big datasets in and of themselves do not have much value. The ability to analyze data, find the signals amidst the noise, and apply those insights to business decisions quickly is what makes them useful. Without reliable analytics, big data is a big nada. Fortunately business analytics are evolving to keep up with big data's multiple new forms and sources.

Dr. Michael Wu, principal scientist at Lithium Technologies, which develops customer experience software, provides a helpful overview of the three types of business analytics—descriptive, predictive, and prescriptive—in his blog, The Science of Social.[3] According to Wu, the majority of business analytics used by companies today are descriptive; derived from operational data, they report what has taken place. Descriptive analytics answers questions like, "How many page views, shares, checks-ins, and replies to blog posts have we received?" This highly useful data that helps us evaluate the effectiveness of our marketing efforts. Filters can be applied to consider data from different perspectives and discover important influences. For example, a geo-filter allows us to consider how many people in a specific location shared our content. A weather filter allows us to explore the impact of weather conditions: How did a week of heavy downpours impact sales. While descriptive statistics are informative, Wu cautions

131

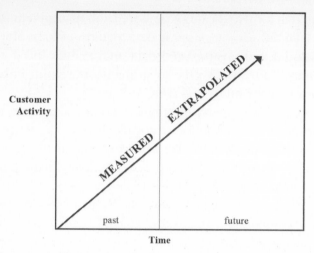

Figure 5.2   Predictive Analytics Are Based on Measured Data

Source: Adapted from Michael Wu, "Big Data Reduction 2: Understanding the Science of Social" (blog), March 25, 2013. http://lithosphere.lithium.com/t5/science-of-social-blog/Big-Data-Reduction -2Understanding-Predictive-Analytics/ba-p/79616

they do not explain why events occur or predict what might happen in the future.

About 20 percent of business analytics are predictive; they try and forecast what may happen in the future (see Figure 5.2). How is this possible? Data scientists are not clairvoyant; they are just highly adept at building models from historical data to generate data about the future. As Wu explains, "It's using data you have to predict data that you don't have."[4]

Marketers have been using a form of predictive analytics for years when we create time-series analysis to discern patterns in data and build trend lines based upon those findings. Today's predictive models take more underlying data sources into account and are updated rapidly, improving their validity and impact.[5] For example, using predictive analytics we can discern what products a consumer may purchase next or where a prospect is in the purchase process, when might they convert, and why. Predictive analytics can help us identify customers who are likely to defect and, of those, whom we might be able to persuade otherwise.

Prescriptive analytics takes future planning one step further, to identify an optimized course of action. It does so by generating multiple futures based upon different choices of action and evaluates the outcome. As Wu describes, "A prescriptive model can be viewed as a combination of multiple predictive models running in parallel, one for each possible input action. As such prescriptive models use existing models as well as action and feedback to guide the decision maker."[6] To learn more, see Wu's most recent book, *The Science of Social 2: Social Strategies for Long-term Business Advantage and the Science Behind How They Work.*

Where Does Big Data End and Small Data Begin?

A clear delineation between big data and small data does not exist. The difference is primarily a function of the amount of data under analysis, its form, and at times, its speed. As a rule of thumb, Thomas Davenport, professor of Management and Information Technology at Babson College and author of numerous books on the subject, describes small data as a terabyte (10^{12} bytes) of structured data or less. In contrast, big data is larger and more complex. As Davenport explained in *Harvard Business Review,* "If your organization stores multiple petabytes [10^{15} bytes] of data, if the information most critical to your business resides in forms other than rows and columns of numbers, or if answering your biggest question would involve a 'mashup' of several analytical reports, you've got a big data opportunity."[7]

Say Good-bye to Traditional Marketing Research?

Will big data render traditional market research obsolete? After all, some of the data that has traditionally been collected through traditional marketing techniques can now be readily captured through big data. Rather than making survey research irrelevant, Bill Pink, senior partner, creative analytics at the global research agency Millward Brown, believes that big data will have the opposite impact.

"What matters is our ability to answer questions," Pink explains. In his experience, big-data assets generate more questions than answers, and those questions need to be answered via traditional

Find Actionable Insight in Big Data and Marketing Analytics

research forms. "Big data is the passive monitor and surveys become the focused, ongoing probes into changes and events that require exploration."[8]

Consider customer-journey and touchpoint analysis, for example. Although big data illuminates the paths customers take and the devices they utilize, more traditional forms of research are still necessary to uncover the whys. Similarly, a considerable amount of noise exists in customer sentiment that is captured via social media. In Pink's experience, "when market researchers apply their experience around understanding consumers and proven constructs of brand success such as levels of differentiation, dynamism, and salience to big-data assets, the results have clear meaning and often align with offline measures of equity and behaviors."[9]

Rather than killing traditional marketing research, Pink believes that big data has liberated it. Because big data captures consumption data, follow-up surveys can be shorter and focus on key issues, enhancing their accuracy and appeal to customers. Insights derived from big data can be incorporated into survey design to drill down further and improve findings. This creates a blend of research curation and creation that better serves the brand and its customers. That is, of course, if the research is designed well and properly addresses the business issue at hand.

What is more, mobile is bringing new creativity to traditional survey design, creating opportunities to gather responses during experiences, rather than in hindsight, and to incorporate sound, photographs, and videos into feedback. Care must be taken to customize survey features to mobile—if surveys do not render properly people will not take them—and understand any new bias that mobile may add in terms of representation and fullness of attention.

Diane Hessan, CEO of Communispace, which creates and manages private online customer communities for leading brands, whom we met in Chapter 1, agrees that big data alone does not capture the whole picture. "With big data, companies can know everything their prospects and companies do, but that does not mean that they *know* them or know why they behave the way they do. Being able to talk with your customers on a daily basis is the difference between research and game-changing insights," Hessan explains.

What Are Marketers Doing with Data and Analytics?

The full impact of big data is yet to come; however, a sampling of what some marketers are working toward by applying analytics to their big and small datasets follows.

Developing a 360-Degree View of Our Customers

One size fits all does not fit anymore. People are more likely to respond to brand experiences that are tailored to their individual needs and desires and to interactions in which they are remembered and rewarded for their previous actions. What is more, for maximum effect, these experiences have to be integrated and adapted across channels. Not being aware of a recent customer service challenge, for example, can leave a salesperson blind to a customer's reason for not renewing a contact. Customers generally perceive our companies as single entities; a salesperson's lack of knowledge of what has transpired with customer service can increase the customer's dissatisfaction, making them feel even more insignificant to the company. In a different scenario, if we know what a customer has viewed on our website, we can tailor our messaging to reflect those interests. If we are aware of their past purchases, we can make more intelligent recommendations.

Scott Epskamp encourages us to invest adequate time discovering the true nature of our customers and their preferences across channels and throughout the sales cycle. In his experience at Leapfrog Online, without this knowledge it is impossible to optimize our marketing and sales efforts for the customer. Instead we optimize for the channel. He cautions against having a digital bias: "While digital might make the most sense for information building, interacting live with a sales rep at the right stage of the sales cycle could make the difference between a research project and a sale."

Piecing together a comprehensive view of our customers that makes this level of customization possible requires us to be able to combine traditional demographic data (for example, age, income, occupation, home ownership, nationality, and residence) with behavior captured from across relevant online and offline touchpoints—call center data, web analytics, social engagement—in real time. To build

135

contextualized experiences requires that we also have access to situational data such as our customers' location, the time of day, and the device they are using, and even what the weather is like where they are located. Building a comprehensive view does not mean that we capture all the available data that is about our prospects and customers, only relevant information. We do not need to know everything that our customers discuss on social media, only that which is applicable to our business.

Most companies are not yet at the point where they can match every customer interaction to an individual person. For example, if we visit a company's website three times, once on a mobile phone, once on a tablet, and once on a desktop, most companies' systems will think these were visits from three different people. *Customer stitching* is the process of being able to link all of these devices to a single user. In the absence of this capability, we do not have an institutional memory of our interactions with our customers; it is very easy for us to inadvertently make them feel insignificant.

Many firms may need to upgrade their technology to realize the benefits of big data. According to SCRIBE's *2013 State of Data Integration* report, only 16 percent of companies surveyed have fully integrated systems.[10] Web-derived data often resides in a different system than data derived from call centers or social media, which limits our ability to form a comprehensive view. Further, data streams may not be organized using the same definitions; systems may define a lead or a customer differently. Solving these infrastructure challenges upfront is critical to our ability to create reliable analytics, to integrate data at the level of the individual, and to deliver a more remarkable customer experience.

Fill in the Blanks

How do we build an enhanced view of our customers in the absence of complete data? In some cases we can obtain third-party data to augment our customer profiles. An e-mail address, for example, can help us incorporate new data into a customer record.

Analytics can be used to create synthetic data, a proxy for authentic data that simply does not exist. For example, data fusion is a process that integrates multiple datasets of different, yet similar survey respondents, to develop a deeper understanding of a targeted group of customers. Data fusion works when there are strong underlying common characteristics between the two groups of survey respondents and those common characteristics explain the consumer behavior being evaluated. Validation techniques are used to prove the model and evaluate the reliability of results.

Data fusion is often used in marketing to make inferences about media exposure and buying behavior for a given segment. By merging data about a given segment's media behavior (TV viewing, for example) with a data stream about a similar segment's buying behavior (purchase of an over-the-counter pain reducer), we can extrapolate what the TV viewing behavior of people who purchase a given over-the-counter pain reducer may be. If we are marketing over-the-counter pain products, this information would allow us to make more informed choices about where and when we might advertise on TV in the absence of data obtained by direct measurement.

Smarten Segmentation

Segmentation is a process of breaking down an overall market into smaller groups based on common needs and motivations. When broken down in meaningful ways, segmentation allows us to prioritize our efforts and design more effective products, services, and marketing experiences for each targeted group or individual.

In the past we segmented our prospects and customers by demographics, reflecting how data was collected and how media was purchased at the time. Our segmentation became increasingly sophisticated when we augmented this data with transaction records from loyalty programs and credit-card purchases. Today we are able to segment our customers and potential customers in even more useful ways. In addition to being able to describe who our customers are and what they buy, we are able to get at the where, how, and why underlying their behavior.

Rick Kash, the vice chair of Nielsen and coauthor of *How Companies Win*, illustrates how segmentation has changed using the dog food industry as an example.[11] Working with demographic data, we have traditionally segmented the dog food industry into categories like "owners of medium-sized dogs," "owners of large

137

dogs," or "owners of small dogs." Today, we can view the industry in terms of what actually influences customer behavior: the types of relationships owners seek with their dogs (the why). This leads us to market segments with personas, or representative archetypes, such as "Pampering Parents," "Performance Fuelists," and "Minimalists." This additional dimension is critical; it allows us to more clearly identify each segment's needs and desires, the triggers that prompt them to act, and the owners' criteria for making purchase decisions. This proprietary insight is a very real source of competitive advantage in a time when customer-centricity matters.

A closer look at Pampering Parents, for example, reveals a market segment that treats their dogs like children. Often empty nesters, these people generally own small purebreds. They purchase dog food on the basis of their pet's taste preferences, rather than on price or nutritional value. Viewing their dog as a love object, these pet owners have low price sensitivity. In contrast, Minimalists view their dogs as functional objects, low-cost employees, or living, breathing alarm systems. This market segment skews toward large, rural households with utilitarian hounds. Highly price sensitive, these owners look to buy the least expensive dog food brands in the largest sizes. A third segment, Performance Fuelers, are people who live active, healthy lifestyles and view their dogs as partners in their outdoor activities. This group wants the best for their dogs, and they define the best dog food on the basis of nutrition and taste. Performance Fuelers tend to be single or young families with large purebreds.

By segmenting the dog food market in this way, differentiated product and marketing strategies for each segment become clear. One brand will not satisfy the Pampering Parents and the Minimalist segments; however, one company can, by offering several distinct products, each with its own packaging and marketing strategies. Kash refers to each of these groups as demand profit pool, reflecting the basis upon which they are derived—by their demand rather than their demographics—and the potential profitability they represent. In his experience, at least six different demand-profit pools comprise most markets or demand landscapes. Predictive analytics allow us to determine how likely a customer or prospect is to be a part of a given demand pool, linking our customer base to our strategy.

Improve Targeting

More precise knowledge of prospects and customers, including their preferred communication channels, allows us to customize key elements of our content experience efforts. When situational data is layered on top, we can further refine customer experiences to reflect where people are, what they are doing, the devices they are using, the time of day, and even the weather.

For example, to drum up business during the off-season, an indoor waterpark resort applies a geofilter to its data to target parents of students residing in zip codes where school is cancelled due to inclement weather. Targeted web display ads served to parents when they are online, encouraging families to grab their bathing suits and head over for some indoor fun, have increased attendance by 30–50 percent.

Combining customer data with advanced analytics creates even more powerful targeting opportunities. *Next-best offer* (NBO) *analytics* help us estimate the probably that a customer will be interested in a targeted offer. When the rules and algorithms of NBO are combined with search engines, we can create cross-selling experiences such as, "You may also like…," which often result in higher average order sizes and happy customers. For instance, the fashion retailer Forever 21 posts personalized recommendations for items on the bottom of their "reset your password" page, knowing that they have your attention and some degree of purchase-intent.

At-risk models can help us identify changes in customer-usage patterns, making it possible for us to predict when a customer may be losing interest and target interventions to retain their business. Using IBM's Centralized Customer Decisioning Platform, which consolidates customer data and provides marketers with what-if analysis tools, a financial institution was able to increase its retention offer acceptance by 33 percent.[12]

Prioritize Customers

Customer-centricity involves accurately identifying the value of our customers and generating appropriate opportunities and experiences for those whom it makes sense for us to serve. Segmentation focuses our efforts and enables us to better prioritize at the segment level. We can go one level deeper by using predictive analytics to score each of our customers in terms of their own customer lifetime value (CLTV).

The CLTV represents our best estimate of a customer's financial value to us over the lifetime of our relationship. (It does not quantify their contributions to product innovation or advocacy.) A predictive measure of future profitability, CLTV has its roots in past purchase behavior, but is adjusted to reflect future expectation of value. If we have faith in our estimates, CLTV can help us allocate our resources more effectively, offering our most valuable customers differentiated, premium experiences. It also allows us to quantify our companies' overall customer equity. The sum of all of our CLTVs, customer equity is an alternative and customer-focused method of measuring corporate value.[13]

Given the importance of referrals to our ability to generate revenue for many of our businesses, we may also choose to estimate a customer's referral value or CRV as this often differs from their CLTV. V. Kumar, J. Andrew Peterson, and Robert Leone presented a methodology for calculating CRV in an article in *Harvard Business Review*.[14] According to their model, a customer's CRV is calculated by estimating the number of successful referrals that he or she may make. Value is calculated differently for referrals for business that would have come in anyway (in which case we only count the acquisition costs we saved) and those that would not have joined without the referral. Our most effective prioritization efforts would capture both our customers with the highest CLTV and those with the highest CRV and encourage them to refer and spend more, respectively.

Working with customer data from a telecom company, Kumar et al. found that they were able to successfully influence customers in each of these groups through targeted marketing efforts. By offering financial incentives for referrals, they were able to encourage customers with high CLTV, but low referrals, to make successful referrals. Similarly, by offering cross-selling and up-selling opportunities to high CRV customers, the team was able to increase their average CLTV. Interestingly, when combined, these marketing techniques also improved the CLTV and CRV of the company's least valuable segments.

Identify Influencers

Today's customers trust recommendations from third parties, making influencer marketing one of the most effective ways to attract prospects and customers. Knowing where influence lies allows us to identify, engage, and support people who have credibility, sizeable networks, and an ability to motivate those networks to act on our behalf. Influencers can be journalists, experts, analysts, regulators, members of our broader customer ecosystem, and even family and friends. Their influence varies depending upon the type of purchase and where a prospect or customer is in the experience journey. Nurturing shared-value-based relationships with influencers can help us build brand awareness, create and activate content, spread the word about product launches, and be a partner in crisis management, product development, competitive analysis, and event promotion.

Social listening and social network analysis, which helps us predict someone's potential to influence based upon their connection and interactions with others, can help us do both. Popular blogger outreach identification tools include Klout, Inkybee, BuzzStream, and GroupHigh. Using GroupHigh's influencer software, the family entertainment company, Chuck E. Cheese's, was able to enhance the effectiveness of its social media strategy, of which 40–50 percent is focused on influencer relations. By identifying and analyzing family-focused bloggers with adequate social influence and engagement, the company was able to build relationships with more than 650 influencers and generate more than 75 million monthly unique visitors to their website.[15]

Capture the Voice of Our Customers

To be successful, our companies must offer our customers products, services, environments, and experiences that we know they what, not what we hope they want or think they want. By interjecting our customers' voice into our business decision-making we can improve our relevance to our customers.

Well-managed *Voice of the Customer programs* (VoC) that define customer insights clearly and have processes in place for taking action can help make this possible.[16] Most VoC programs utilize

Find Actionable Insight in Big Data and Marketing Analytics

surveys, e-mails, and customer comment cards to better understand their customers' experience. Increasingly, companies are establishing customer communities to provide ongoing connection with customers and prospects. This running dialogue allows us to get to know them in a way that is not otherwise possible, yielding macro- and micro-level insights. We can explore ideas for new products and services innovation as well as test incremental improvements in our content or advertising. (We explore customer communities more fully in Chapter 8.)

Tracking and analyzing customer sentiment as expressed in reviews, ratings, recommendations, and comments in social media is another essential component of our customer listening effort. Social media monitoring allows us to identify what is being said about our products and services, brands, companies, competitors, and industries; anything really. Social media tools, such as Sysomos, Radian 6, Social Mention, Lithium Technologies, ViralHeat, and Meltwater Buzz, mine this unstructured data to determine underlying attitudes. As we saw with IBM Social Insights, social monitoring allows us to proactively address prospects' and customers' needs and desires and to incorporate their sentiments into our messaging and other engagement efforts. To truly reflect the market's feelings, sentiment analysis needs to incorporate offline sources of information as most word of mouth takes place face to face.

Measure and Optimize Our Marketing Efforts

According to Gartner's *U.S. Digital Marketing Spending Survey*, on average marketers spend 25 percent of their budgets on digital activities[17]—which should make it easier to evaluate our efforts as we can quantify clicks, views, shares, and track how people are discovering us. However, today's marketing mix is complex and interconnected, making it challenging to evaluate the effectiveness of our marketing efforts with certainty.

Closed-loop analytics measure the value of each digital marketing interaction toward a desired outcome, allowing us to identify what is working and what is not and make mid-stream adjustments. This end-to-end picture also allows us to accurately demonstrate marketing's impact on key business performance measures like revenue, profit, loyalty, and advocacy metrics we analyze in more depth in Chapter 10. Using webtools like Google Analytics, we can optimize our marketing efforts by running comparative champion-challenger analyses of our content in real time. (More details follow in Chapter 6.) Similarly, dynamic optimization of ad content allows us to break ad content into layers, so that we can overlay customized features and test the effectiveness of variations.

How Analytics Savvy Do Marketers Need to Be?

Marketers are not expected to build complex models; however, we are expected to be data and analytics savvy. This includes understanding what analytics can and cannot achieve, knowing the necessary questions to ask when designing and evaluating a project, having a basic comprehension of the math and statistics underlying models and are used to evaluate their validity, and being confident about making decisions based upon the output.

Our longer-term goal is to move essential, everyday analyses into the hands of marketers and line-of-business managers so that we can act quickly on marketplace developments. To do so requires that complex models be transformed into highly interactive tools, with graphics-based user interfaces that make it easy for laypeople to visualize, understand, and further explore data. As this becomes a reality, and data visualization tools are making it possible even today, marketers will need to get increasingly comfortable with conducting basis analytics.

Toward this end, a great resource for marketers is *Keeping Up with the Quants, Your Guide to Understanding + Using Analytics*, a book coauthored by Tom Davenport and Jinho Kim.[18] Their accompanying website, keepingupwiththequants.weebly.com includes detailed analyses of cases and the opportunity to query the authors directly specify data-analytic challenges.

Tackling an Analytics Project

A considerable amount of upfront work is required to ensure the success of any data-analytics project. Experience shows that organizations that spend enough time upfront developing a clear sense

143

of what they want to achieve have considerably more success in the end.

One of our first considerations is identifying and garnering buy-in from the key decision makers related to the challenge being addressed. By involving key stakeholders in the process, we can improve our chances of understanding the underlying challenge and having access to the necessary data and resources to effectively address it. Understanding and managing stakeholders' expectations for the project and agreeing early on ways to provide regular feedback help ensure that our findings are implemented.

Essential questions for the stakeholder group to ask at the onset of the project include, "What is the problem we are trying to address?" and "How will this undertaking create business value?" In the absence of clarity about these questions, even the most sophisticated analytics will amount to a muddle. To get at these answers, companies often engage in destination thinking. A simple process, destination thinking encourages us to start with the end in mind by writing down the business impact we are trying to achieve in short, clear sentences. The goal should be defined as specifically as possible because analytics require clear parameters.

Davenport encourages us to investigate any prior research that has been conducted addressing this challenge. How have these projects been designed in the past? How have they defined the problem? What types of data have been used to answer the question? How might we approach the question from a different angle that might generate new insight?

What other parameters are important for creating successful data and analytics solutions? Jesse Harriott, chief analytics officer for the online marketing company Constant Contact and Jean Paul Isson, global vice president of business intelligence and predictive analytics at the employment company, Monster Worldwide, Inc., have overseen many analytics challenges during the course of their careers. In their book, *Win With Advanced Business Analytics*, they provide simple and useful guidelines for translating business challenges into relevant and manageable analytics projects.

To offer parameters for creating successful analytics solutions, Harriott and Isson adapted the tried and true SMART framework,[19]

144

originally developed by management consultant George Doran. The adapted SMART framework for successful analytics solutions is:

- **S**pecific: Having a clear mandate and goal, defined by clear, expected benefits.
- **M**easurable: We can easily track performance.
- **A**ggressive and Actionable: A solution that could be quickly put into the organization and that leads to clear action.
- **R**ealistic: A solution that avoids overpromising or overestimating the value added of the outcome.
- **T**ime bounded: The solution should have a clear time line to deliver the business benefit to the organization.

Build the Model

Models are representations of the underlying challenge we are aiming to solve. Analytical models are essentially math equations that describe relationships among the variables that we are looking to evaluate. An art/science modeling also involves understanding which datasets and variables have a predictive influence on the challenge at hand and which analytical techniques are the most applicable. Modelers benefit from a solid understanding of data science and business as this combination of expertise helps modelers build successful models and solve the black box problem—business people not trusting or understanding the output of the model—because they can explain why the underlying model accurately addressing the business challenge at hand. Even when working with best modelers, marketers still need to satisfy our understanding of the model by inquiring about the assumptions, the causality between variables, and the data—its source, how it may have been enriched, and in the case of data fusion, the strength of the common characteristics between populations—in order to trust its output.

What types of analytical techniques are being used to address marketing-related business challenges? In their book *Win With Advanced Business Analytics*, Harriott and Isson created an Analytics Recipe Matrix, an adaptation of which appears in Figure 5.3, that

145

BUSINESS CHALLENGE	ANALYTICS SOLUTION	BENEFITS
Acquire new customers	Target response model	Bring in more customers for the same costs
Retain your profitable customers	Customer churn/ at-risk model	Increase customer wallet share and overall profitability
Up-sell and cross new and existing customers	Customer lifetime value model	Identify long-term profitability
Increase sales	Acquisition up-sell and retention models	Increase market share and customer profitability
Increase customer satisfaction	Market research and customer-profiling models	Deepening understanding of current and prospective customers through survey research
Increase customer satisfaction	Market research and customer-profiling models	Deepening understanding of current and prospective customers through survey research
Increase conversion	Seeker and visitors segmentation	Increase the usability and strategic value of web properties
Understand characteristics of customers	Customer profiling and segmentation	Improve customer profitability and CRM optimization
Streamline pricing	Pricing optimization models	Increase revenue and gross margin
Manage and anticipate competitors and gear up for competition coming from uncharted territories	Proactive competitive intelligence analytics	Win against the competition

Figure 5.3   Analytics Recipe Matrix

Source: **Jean Paul Isson and Jesse S. Harriott, *Win With Advanced Business Analytics* (Hoboken, NJ: John Wiley & Sons, 2013).**

provides a sampling of the types of challenges that can be tackled with analytics.

Find the Data

The next challenge to tackle is identifying what data sources will provide the necessary inputs and how we can access them. It may be hard to believe that given the amount of data that is out there, there may still be holes in our data; however, this is not uncommon. Sometimes data may exist, but we cannot get to it. An example might be the data generated by a new social new platform for which analytics have not yet been developed. Other times data may exist, but it is in a format that we are not yet able to manipulate.

Much of the data that our organizations have is proprietary—it comes from our own data streams. That does not necessarily mean that we have ready access to it, however. Data is often captured by business function; web analytics are often managed separately from customer-service metrics, marketing-campaign analysis, and sales-force productivity figures. Indeed, according to a survey conducted by the CMO Council, 52 percent of marketers list functional silos as top hindrances to customer-centric endeavors.[20] Further, systems often define terms and measure differently. Analytic modelers are necessary to collect, clean, standardize, and often enrich data so that it can be effectively analyzed. This is often the most time-consuming component of the entire analytic project because of the number of details. However, it is key to generating worthwhile insights: garbage in = garbage out.

Deploy the Model

If we have done the upfront work, deploying the model is relatively straightforward. To maximize the impact of any analytic effort, Davenport suggests that we operationalize the model. For example, a churn analysis can be turned into a daily dashboard for sales reps that flags customers who are displaying behaviors commonly associated with defection. Whenever we can, we should encourage our modelers to transform their work into user-friendly decision-making tools that can be readily employed by those who are charged with transforming analytic insights into action.

Put Insights to Work and Measure the Impact

The final steps in any analytics undertaking are to put the insights to work and measure the impact of the decision on business results. What have we learned? What will we do next as a result? Sharing our results with the broader enterprise facilitates learning and buy-in for further analytic endeavors. This can be accomplished through a variety of ways, including a formal communication plan, a knowledge

147

Find Actionable Insight in Big Data and Marketing Analytics

portal, and even Lunch-and-Learn discussions. Keeping the C-suite abreast of new learning is key to our ability to ultimately transform data into a strategic asset.

Develop a Marketing Data Analytics Capability

Developing a sophisticated data analytics capability in-house is fundamental to our ability to offer truly customer-centric experiences. While we can outsource this capability, it is in our best interest to grow this competency internally, to have it be part of our ongoing workflow as a way we routinely evaluate our business.

Companies' abilities in this realm currently run the gamut. Davenport devised a five-tier analytics pyramid to categorize organizations based upon their use of big data analytics to impact business results. As seen in Figure 5.4, the stages range from analytically impaired to analytical competitors.

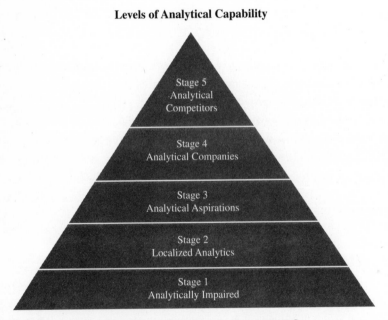

Levels of Analytical Capability

Stage 5
Analytical
Competitors

Stage 4
Analytical Companies

Stage 3
Analytical Aspirations

Stage 2
Localized Analytics

Stage 1
Analytically Impaired

Figure 5.4   How Analytical Is Your Company?

Source: Davenport, Thomas H. "Analytics at Work." PowerPoint Presentation. PBLS, Hong Kong. July 13, 2010. http://www.slideshare.net/sasindia/keynote-thomas-davenportanalyticsatwork.

In Davenport's experience, the majority of companies are currently in stage two, where impact remains localized, not yet shared across an ecosystem. Some highly analytical companies remain at the second tier of the pyramid because their analysis remains based on small datasets. A few companies, mostly smaller companies and a handful of large enterprises like P&G, GE, and Novartis, are at stage three, leading the way, defining what is possible. These companies blend data and analytics seamlessly and apply the insights into running their day-to-day businesses. Viewing data as a strategic asset, analytical tools are available at the point of decision, redefining agility, and applying insights at scale.[21]

Becoming a top-tier analytical competitor is complicated as it involves people with a range of understanding and commitment to data and analytics, complex and disparate systems, and myriad processes and policies. Several hurdles must be crossed in order for data and analytics to grab a hold and prove results. As complicated as finding insight in big data may be, it is not an impossible task. Bill Franks, chief analytics officer for Teradata and author of *Taming the Big Data Tidal Wave*, encourages us to keep perspective. Big data, according to Franks, is "simply a continuation of the struggle we've always had to incorporate ever-growing and ever more diverse data sources into analytics to enable better business decisions."[22] Besides we do not have to get there overnight. Companies are making progress by taking an incremental approach to adoption. Think big. Start small. Scale fast.

Big Data Means Big Responsibility

Given the sensitive nature of much of the data that we collect on our customers, we have to take great care to not turn this opportunity to deliver enhanced customer-centricity into a disaster.

Our customers trade off privacy for customized interactions. Although they are not always aware of the connection, our customers cannot have websites that greet them by name and offer personalized recommendations without small text files, or cookies, being left on their computers that facilitate this memory, e-mail addresses being captured, or having the content they are reading on their screens scanned.

How do our customers feel about their privacy? According to the research conducted by the Economist Intelligence Unit, 49 percent of consumers say they are "very concerned" about the threat of privacy online.[23] However, only 23 percent of marketers believe that their customers are concerned about privacy. The increase in apps that thwart location identifiers and interject random data into people's datastreams, along with the popularity of ephemeral social networks like SnapChat, where content disappears unless captured in a screenshot, suggest that people are increasingly concerned and taking matters into their own hands. If we are smart, we will proactively give our customers reason to trust us in this realm by making data governance an essential component of our customer experience. A new field, *data governance* focuses on how we can best manage data across enterprises and ecosystems. It's scope includes the technology that gathers, integrates, cleans, sorts, and analyzes data, as well as the people, policies, and processes that surround it. Data governance also includes preventing and managing security breaches. It helps our customers know that their data is safe with us and ensures that the data from which we derive our insights is trustworthy. Neither is trivial.

As we create data policies Bill Franks cautions us to consider the trifecta of what is legal, ethical, and acceptable to the public. In blog post published by the International Institute for Analytics, he warns that in this rapidly changing field, laws may lag our data collection and analytic capabilities and customer sensitivities may shift.[24] Franks recommends that we take a cautious approach, pursuing strategies that meet all three considerations simultaneously. Citing a large U.S. superstore chain's experience in predicting the early-stage pregnancy of its customers based on their purchase history, a summary of which follows, Franks cautions that what is legal and ethical may still not be acceptable to our customers.

Marketing Gets a Little Too Personal

One large data-savvy superstore chain has experienced success targeting its customers with offers based upon a number of behaviors including past purchases. A strong correlation was discovered between pregnancy and purchases of items such as unscented lotion and soap, vitamin supplements, and extra-big bags of cotton balls. So reliable were these predictions, that the company was able to estimate the mother's due date within a fairly small window. Operating on this finding, the retailer made it a practice to send coupons for baby items to customers who were flagged as potentiality pregnant.

One of the variables the company did not consider in their analysis was the age of the customers it was targeting. In one instance, the recipient of the coupon mailing happened to be a teenager who was living at her parents' home. When she received the coupons, the young woman's father became irate, stormed into their local superstore, and asked the manager, "Are you trying to encourage her to get pregnant?" The manager apologized profusely. Several days later the manager called the father again to apologize. This time the father had a different tone. "I had a talk with my daughter," he said. "It turns out there's been some activities in my house I haven't been completely aware of. She's due in August. I owe you an apology."[25] Despite the accuracy of its targeting and its good intentions, the superstore chain had crossed a boundary.

Taking Their Data Back

Recognizing the value of their data, coupled with concerns about their privacy, our prospects and customers may become more selective about what they will share with us in the future. To continue to have access to their digital footprint, companies will have to provide real value in return. Being radically transparent with our customers about the link between access to their data and our ability to provide them with a quick, easy, and personalized shopping experience is an important step.

As marketers we also need to be transparent about how we collect data and how we will and will not use it with our customers. Facebook is very clear about its view on privacy; it refers to it as a Data Usage Policy. Acxiom, which supplies marketing data to businesses, provides anyone with the opportunity to see what data is being collected about them and how it is being used by advertisers. Allowing customers who prefer anonymity to opt out of our marketing efforts will help them feel respected and more in control.

Find Actionable Insight in Big Data and Marketing Analytics

Offering tools that allow customers to proactively share additional data to further enhance their experience–such as Amazon's Improve Your Ratings feature–helps customers on the other end of the spectrum feel respected and in control.[26]

Doc Searls, author of *The Intention Economy: When Customers Take Charge*, envisions a future in which power shifts even more dramatically toward our customers.[27] He anticipates a time in the not-too-distant future when people actively control the flow and use of their personal data, dictate their own terms of service, and tell the marketplace what they want, how they want it, where and when they want it, and how much it should cost.

Under this scenario, an individual could send a Request for Proposal to a company or group of companies or the entire marketplace outlining the parameters upon which they would rent a car, purchase a house, or buy insurance. This announcement could take place anonymously or publicly and would specify the time frame for his or her willingness to receive information from the vendors—say July and August in anticipation of a late August purchase. This brings a whole new meaning to our notion of permission-based marketing!

Searls calls this the Intention Economy and believes that it will more efficiently link supply and demand than the system we currently have in place. Rather than customer relationship management systems, *vendor relationship management* (VRM) tools, technologies, and services will form that will allow people to manage their unique identities—imagine only having to input a change of address once and have it reach multiple vendors—as well as their demand. Vendors that make use of these tools will be able to build better relationships with their customers and close sales. Until such time as our customers are able to speak so clearly for themselves, we have data analytics to help us understand what makes them tick.

How do we make solid decisions in the absence of data, when the questions we are answering are not repetitive, or when there is not enough time to undertake a formal analytical project? In the next chapter we consider hallmarks of the entrepreneurial decision-making process that is helping marketers act quickly and with more confidence, even in the face of uncertainty.

QUESTIONS TO CONSIDER

- What stage of the five-tier analytics pyramid describes your company?
- What data is your company currently collecting? Who owns it, manages it, and is responsible for its security?
- What questions would you like to be able to answer if you were not limited by your current data capabilities?
- What is your next step?

RESOURCES

Influencers We Recommend

- *Matt Ariker*. As COO of McKinsey's Customer Marketing Analytics Center, Ariker works with customers to use advanced analytics to turn big data into practical insights. Explore the Center's work at www.mckinsey.com/client_service/marketing_and_sales /expertise/consumer_marketing_analytics_center and follow Ariker on Twitter @mattariker.

- *Thomas Davenport*. A thought leader in business-process reengineering, knowledge management, and big data and analytics, Davenport is also the author or coauthor of multiple books including *Keeping Up with the Quants: Your Guide to Understanding* and *Using Analytics*. To keep up on his blog contributions see www.tomdavenport.com/blogs-articles and follow his tweets @tdav.

- *Bill Franks*. Franks serves as chief analytics officer at Teradata, which provides data warehousing and ana-lytical applications to companies. He is the author of *Taming the Big Data Tidal Wave* and an avid blogger at www.iianalytics.com/category/faculty-blogs/bill-franks/. Learn

(continued)

Find Actionable Insight in Big Data and Marketing Analytics

(*continued*)

from Franks' insights at www.bill-franks.com and on Twitter @billfranksga.

- *Gartner.* As the world's leading information technology research and advisory company, Gartner produces great research for users and vendors on virtually any area of IT. In addition to publishing research, the company offers symposiums, conferences, and seminars around the world as well as consulting services. For more information see www.gartner.com or follow them on Twitter @Gartner_inc.

- *Jesse Harriott.* Harriott is chief analytics officer, Constant Contact, an online marketing company. Prior to joining Constant Contact, Harriott designed and built Monster Worldwide's global analytics business division. There are many insights to be had in the book he recently coauthored, *Win with Advanced Business Analytics.*

- *International Institute for Analytics.* The IIA is a "network of analytics experts who are committed to knowing and sharing the keys to success in an economy increasingly driven by data." Their extensive research library is supplemented by events, training, and advisory services. For more information see www.iianalytics.com or follow them on Twitter @iianalytics.

- *Rick Kash.* Kash serves as vice chair, The Nielsen Company. He is the coauthor (with Nielsen CEO David Calhoun) of *How Companies Win* and author of *The New Law of Demand and Supply: The Revolutionary New Demand Strategy for Faster Growth and Higher Profits.* Stay on top of his clear insights on Twitter @HowCompaniesWin.

- Blog.KISSmetrics.com. A blog about analytics, marketing, and testing, which is affiliated with KISSmetrics, a web analytics solution that helps businesses understand their prospects and customers for higher acquisition and retention rates and overall smarter decision-making. Read the blog and follow the company's thought-leaders @KISSmetrics.

- *Doc Searls*. Author of several books including *The Intention Economy* and coauthor of *The Cluetrain Manifesto*, Searls is the director of project VRM at Harvard's Berkman Center for Internet and Society. A lover of photography (he has 45,000+ photos posted on Flickr.com), geography, aviation, media, infrastructure, and understanding how things work. Find out more at www.searls.com, read his weblog at www.blogs.law.harvard.edu/doc/, and follow his tweets @dsearls.

- *Sri Sridharan*. A senior analyst at Forrester Research focusing on Customer Insights, follow Sridharan's thinking on Forrester's Customer Insights Blog and on Twitter @srividya.

- *Michael Wu*. Wu serves as chief scientist of analytics, Lithium Technologies, which creates customer experience management software. A former academic, Wu offers helpful insights on The Science of Social blog at www.lithosphere.lithium.com and in his two books, *The Science of Social: Beyond Hype, Likes & Followers* and *The Science of Social 2: Social Strategies for Long-Term Business Advantage and the Science Behind How They Work*. Voted an Influential Leader by *CRM Magazine*, you can follow him on Twitter @Mich8elwu.

Hashtags to Explore

- #analytics
- #attribution
- #bigdata
- #businsessanalytics
- #data
- #datascience

(*continued*)

Find Actionable Insight in Big Data and Marketing Analytics

(continued)

- #bloggeroutreach
- #emetrics
- #insights
- #IT
- #machinelearning
- #measure
- #ml (machine learning)
- #msure
- #predictiveanalytics

Chapter 6

Employ Entrepreneurial Thinking for Discernment and Agility

"Evidence is better than anyone's intuition."

—Scott Cook, founder of Intuit

When people ask Larry why he started his first company, he tells them about his wife, Dawn. The daughter of an entrepreneur, Dawn was not traumatized by the idea of leveraging their first condominium to the hilt so that Larry could launch a business in a new marketing category, technology public relations. In fact, she was all for it.

They were young and living in Boston at the time. Computing and software companies were popping up everywhere: Lotus, Digital Equipment Corporation (DEC), Wang Laboratories, and Cullinet among others. Marketing was challenging for these companies because their products were too complicated to be explained by advertising, which was the primary tool in our marketing toolkit at the time.

Larry will never forget sitting with Michael Dertouzos, the founder and head of MIT's Laboratory for Computer Science, back in 1989. Michael showed Larry a videotape of his 1980 appearance on the *Today* show where he discussed the future impact of the personal computer on society. The interviewer was unimpressed, dismissing the PC as a fad; however, Michael politely disagreed and went on to describe what seemed like science fiction. He spoke of a time when people around the world would be connected through personal computers. He described how they would be able to easily communicate, shop, and learn from each other. Unable to grasp what

Michael was describing, the interviewer shook his head and broke for a commercial.

Energized by the vision of these entrepreneurs and the potential impact of their products on the world, Larry wanted to help them tell their stories. The world needed to understand what they were envisioning in their labs. Having spent time teaching English literature, Larry understood the power of a good narrative and could see how storytelling could be a natural solution to the challenge of marketing technology companies. By educating the public about products that were difficult to grasp at the time, he believed that a market could be built for newfangled ideas such as personal computers, software, and even the World Wide Web. Drawing upon character development techniques and plot creation tools, he crafted stories that fostered an understanding and built an orbit around these emerging technologies. The approach was well received in the marketplace and over time Larry was able to build a highly profitable business for his employer.

Buoyed by the initial success and frustrated that he was not benefiting financially from it, after several clients agreed to follow him, Larry formed his first company, the Weber Group. Before doing so he did not complete a Five Forces industry analysis or project costs and potential returns, applying a large discount rate to reflect the uncertainty of starting a new venture in an emerging industry. Remember, he was an English Lit guy, not an MBA, but it would not have helped anyway as they were building a new market. Instead, he spotted an opportunity, spoke with myriad people in the industry, and did a few test runs with clients to prove the concept. Then he thanked his wife for her support, leveraged his home, bought a computer and printer, and was off to the races. Today that start-up is Weber Shandwick, one of the largest marketing service companies in the world.

We Are All Innovators

Whether we start our own companies or not, all of us are innovators. In fast-changing environments like the one we are operating in, marketers have to be professional creators,[1] continually improving our customers' experiences to stay relevant. To be effective stewards of our businesses, we have to be able to act quickly and smartly based on the continual flows of knowledge about our customers, the business environment, and the effectiveness of what we are doing. Sometimes that means altering our offers or copy based on customers' actions, other times it may require adjustments to our positioning or product and service offerings. As marketers' roles broaden, increasingly it may mean helping to redesign our business models altogether.

Often we are called upon to act in the face of tremendous uncertainty, with limited or no relevant data, when the best option is not readily apparent. This is the stuff that causes sleepless nights. Whatever we can do to increase our odds of making the right decisions is well worth our time. The default option for many of us in this situation is to dig in and think harder. If you talk to a serial entrepreneur, they will tell you to take action.

Entrepreneurial decision making is a way of thinking and acting that helps marketers (or anyone) take informed action even in rapidly changing environments characterized by high levels of uncertainty. It can also be used as a framework for managing complex processes. It is not the same thing as entrepreneurship, although the practices are based upon the behavior and mind-sets of serial entrepreneurs. Its mantra is: Think big. Start small. Scale fast. When practiced with focus, entrepreneurial decision making lubricates the flow of ideas, yields deeper thinking, and enhances organizational agility.

Learn By Doing

Perhaps the best-known feature of entrepreneurial decision making is its emphasis on continuous experimentation, measurement of results, and resets. We learn by doing as each iteration builds upon the findings of the last. Through this progression of experiments, we replace hypothetical discussions with evidence that reduces uncertainty, improving our ability to make decisions.

In their book *Just Start*, Len Schlesinger, the former president of Babson College, and Charles Kiefer, president of the consulting firm Innovation Associates, describe entrepreneurial decision making as creaction. A blend of *creation* and *action*, it captures entrepreneurs' inclination to "put their thinking into immediate action to see if they are right."[2]

Employ Entrepreneurial Thinking for Discernment and Agility

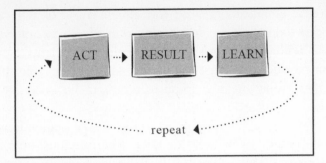

Figure 6.1   Creaction: How to Act When Facing Uncertainty

Source: **Adapted from Leonard Schlesinger, Charles Kiefer, and Paul Brown,** *Just Start* **(Boston: Harvard Business Review Press, 2012).**

Why is creation useful? When the future is likely to be similar to the past, using predictive analytical tools that are based on historical data can be highly useful. However, when operating in environments that are unfamiliar, such as new markets or industries, or in those that are rapidly changing, considering historical performance data may be comforting, but it is not always relevant. Faced with this scenario, entrepreneurs often opt to build evidence for an idea, not by generating models, but by testing the waters, developing real-life proof points. Each action they take generates new data until eventually they have the requisite data that they need. It is a straightforward process: act, learn, and repeat. This is distinctly different from the traditional way of making decisions, which takes the form of analyzing first, then doing, and learning.

Gather Our Own Data

Brian Chesky and Joe Gebbia are the designers that founded Airbnb.com. Back in the early days, when they were just beginning to build their digital accommodations marketplace, the New York market was having a hard time getting off the ground. As a new business in a nascent industry, there was not much in the way of historical data to help them understand what could be going wrong. Rather than overthinking the range of possibilities, the pair flew East from their headquarters in California, booking rooms with two dozen of their hosts—their name for the people who rent out a room or more of their homes to guests—to see for themselves what was going on.

In short order they determined that the problem centered on how the hosts were displaying their rental spaces online. The quality of the photos they were uploading left something to be desired; potential renters would not commit because they could not get a sense of the quality of the accommodations from the photos. The founders acted quickly, renting a high-resolution camera, taking pictures of as many of the host apartments as they could. Lo and behold, bookings at the properties that had the higher-quality photos rocketed. They took this insight and quickly applied it in other markets. "Rinse and repeat," Gebbia told *Fast Company*. "When we fixed the product in New York, it solved our problems in Paris, London, Vancouver, and Miami."[3]

As we can see, the two solved the problem through observation and action. They identified the problem by getting on the plane and flying across country to personally assess the situation and by testing the impact of higher-resolution photos on bookings. The marketplace reacted positively, revealing an important insight that they were able to spread across their other markets.

Connecting with customers, arranging an interview, building a prototype, testing ideas out on potential clients, are all examples of ways to generate data that can move an idea forward. These actions may reveal that an idea is not feasible or that substantial tweaking is necessary. These are highly valuable insights that help to focus our next iterations and perhaps give us an edge over the competition. It is the rare entrepreneur who gets it right on the first try.

By affirming the creaction process we are not declaring that traditional analytical thinking is no longer useful. As we discussed in the previous chapter, there is much value to be found in business analytics, especially when the underlying data is recent, relevant, and accessible. However, in the absence of pertinent data, or of our ability to create relevant synthetic data, we still have to be able to act. Creation allows us to generate enough data to move forward, one step at a time, with more confidence. To be highly effective, marketers need to know how and when to apply these complementary approaches.

Employ Entrepreneurial Thinking for Discernment and Agility

Experiment in Real Markets

One of the ways that marketers are acting their way into insight is through the testing and iteration of their marketing efforts by conducting A/B tests. Using this method, which is also known as split testing, one variable on a web or mobile site is tweaked, perhaps the wording of a headline or the call to action, the layout or images used, or the amount of text on a page, to determine its impact. Results are compared against a control group to ascertain which version more affectvely accomplishes the stated goal. One company tested the impact of a human photo versus a phone icon on a call-now trigger using this approach. The test revealed that replacing the icon of the phone with a human photo nearly doubled the conversion rate.[4] That is valuable learning. Multivariate or bucket testing involves tweaking multiple variables simultaneously.

Despite the robust learning opportunity, few marketers conduct formal testing on an ongoing basis. According to Hubspot's *2013 State of Inbound* report, less than one-third of inbound strategies were effectively tested in 2013, creating quite an advantage for those companies that do.[5] For access to a rich case study library of testing results, see whichtestwon.com.

Starbucks Experiments at Scale

Is this type of experimentation limited to small scale? Management at Starbucks, the world's largest coffeehouse chain, does not think so. The company rolls out huge-scale experiments with some regularity in order to move forward, fast. Whether it is running a Groupon offer that required extensive integration between Starbucks' eGift platform and the group-coupon site's system, or launching its mobile payments app, the company believes in bold action. As Adam Brotman, Starbucks' chief digital officer, explained to *Fast Company*, "We do not want to sit on our hands. If we feel excited about something, we'll get out there, learn our lessons, and correct the mistakes. It's not always the most stress-free way to launch, but it's the fastest."[6]

Mishaps happen when we innovate. The Starbucks Groupon deal was so successful that it crashed the site for hours, but it also amassed a quick $10 million before the deal expired at the end of the day.

The company's mobile-payment app had multiple challenges during its first six months; however, today Starbucks is the leader in mobile payments in the entire U.S. According to the research firm Berg Insight, the vast majority of the $500 million worth of mobile-payment transactions that took place in 2012 were made using Starbucks' mobile app.[7] That translates to over 10 percent of Starbucks in-store purchases in the United States.[8] Of course they could still be discussing their options and waiting for the market to evolve.

Forget Pro Formas

In support of their experimentation, entrepreneurs generally do not create pro forma reports that estimate financial potential. They know these financial statements are based on myriad assumptions and entrepreneurs prefer reality. They want to turn their hypothesis into evidence as soon as possible, by taking multiple actions, one at a time.

Saras Sarasvathy, who teaches strategy and entrepreneurship at the Darden School of Business, observes that entrepreneurs often evaluate the opportunities in front of them based upon what they can afford to lose and what they are willing to risk developing on the idea, rather than on a guesstimate of the potential profit to be realized. This creates the freedom necessary to iterate and learn.[9]

Schlesinger and Kiefer refer to this as determining an acceptable loss. To calculate acceptable loss, we consider what we can afford to risk and what we are willing to risk. Money is, of course, a key consideration, as are time, reputation, and the opportunity cost of forgoing other options. This calculation applies to individuals as well as organizations.

When Larry started the Weber Group, he had a fairly small acceptable loss in terms of finances: $20,000. (A quarter of his budget went to purchasing a printer, which cost $5,000 at the time!) The combination of having already ground-tested the validity of educative marketing for technology companies, having several clients that were willing to come along with him, and a supportive spouse, meant his total acceptable loss was quite low. As a result, he was able to act.

Similarly, a few years ago when social media was just catching the attention of marketers, wise senior managers created special budgets to fund experimentation with what was then a new and very different

163

form of communication. By quantifying their acceptable loss, they created space for marketers to learn by doing, without having to prove the return-on-investment of this new entity that they were yet to understand.

Don't Put All Your Eggs in One Basket

Another way entrepreneurs reduce uncertainty is by diversifying their options. Stanford strategy professor Kathleen Eisenhardt studied Silicon Valley firms and their ability to respond to major industry changes. From her interviews with CEOs, she found that those who were quickest to respond to change with relevant strategies were firms that regularly considered multiple alternatives simultaneously. By having several strategic options upon which to build, companies had a more complete understanding of the underlying issues and avoided backing themselves into a corner. Multitracking also prevented decision-makers from getting too psychologically committed to one alternative, making it easier for them to act on emerging negative information.[10] One caveat: The goal is not to maximize our options, but to at least consider two alternatives.

Share the Fun and the Risk

Hopefully it is becoming clear that in contrast to popular perception, entrepreneurs are not mavericks who have an unusually high appetite for risk. They know that risk comes with the territory of undertaking something new, but they work diligently to mitigate the risk. This is not just an interesting fact for us to consider; it means that we can act similarly. Like serial entrepreneurs, we can reduce risk by experimenting, multitracking options, and determining our acceptable loss. Another way we can emulate successful entrepreneurs is by establishing purposeful networks that allow us to tap into the knowledge base and capability of others, creating resource-rich and remarkably efficient enterprises.

This is not a new idea. Back in 1727, Ben Franklin organized a Junto Club as a means for mutual improvement. He invited 12 people from diverse backgrounds to join; among them were a printer, surveyor, cabinetmaker, bibliophile, astrologer, and a mathematician.

The Club convened on Friday evenings to debate moral, political, scientific, and business issues of the day. The debates were "conducted in the sincere spirit of inquiry after truth, without fondness for dispute or desire of victory," as he later described in his autobiography.[11] The list of the questions Franklin created as prompts for the gatherings are well worth a quick read.[12]

Social media allows us to create our own Junto clubs. As we described in Chapter 2, platforms like LinkedIn and Twitter allow us to learn directly and in real time with people and organizations both inside our personal networks and beyond.

Collaborative innovation networks, or CoINs, are another updated version of Benjamin's Junto club. Peter Gloor, a research scientist at MIT Sloan's Center for Collective Intelligence, coined the phrase and defines it as "a cyberteam of self-motivated people with a collective vision, enabled by the web to collaborate in achieving a common goal by sharing ideas, information, and work."[13] There is power in these networks. More than 300,000 users have helped to translate Facebook into 70 languages and over 91,000 authors have contributed to Wikipedia.[14]

Ask for feedback from our employees. One of the voices that companies can benefit from including in their decision-making loops is their employees. Sales reps, customer-service agents, call-center employees, and other front-line staff often have unique insight into our prospects and customers, and what impedes or inspires our ability to deliver remarkable customer experience. Capturing this insight can make a difference in our understanding of what drives value for our customers and how well we are delivering.

Involving our employees can also enhance their level of commitment to our organizations and our customer-centricity efforts. Feeling listened to is powerful. We cannot overestimate the importance of engaged employees in our ability to deliver valuable customer experiences. Time and time again, it has been shown that companies that excel in delivering exceptional customer experiences also excel in creating loyal employees.[15] The two are inexorably linked.

Toward this end, many companies are instituting Voice of the Employee programs. Designed to get around bottlenecks like the fear of repercussion or an unreceptive or incompetent boss—Michael Scott, the fictionalized boss played by Steve Carell on the television

Employ Entrepreneurial Thinking for Discernment and Agility

series *The Office* comes to mind—these communities often uncover what matters most to employees. Similarly, inviting employees from a variety of functions to participate in a customer journey analysis and in brainstorming of solutions is a winning strategy.

Connect directly with our customers. The value of having the voice of the customer as part of our company's decision-making network is obvious. Proactively capturing customer voices and behaviors across various touchpoints, synthesizing this knowledge into insight, and disseminating this insight across the organization where it can be readily acted upon, keeps us relevant.

There are myriad sources that we can tap. Traditionally we have reached out to customers through written surveys, interviews, and focus groups. These methods capture our customers' insights at a given point in time. As we saw with design thinking, ethnographic research provides a deeper context and understanding. Through web analytics, we can see what our customers are actually doing online. Social media has been a big breakthrough for marketers; it gives us ongoing access to our customers and the chance to crowd-source ideas. Social listening platforms gather our customers' chatter from across disparate platforms in real time, providing us with a good sense of what is being said in social media, on feedback pages, corporate websites, and in the blogsphere. We will eventually integrate and analyze these sources over time, offering us greater insight.

Some of the most fruitful conversations with customers are taking place in private digital communities. These conversations provide organizations with continuous access to prospects and customers rather than at one point in time. This allows companies to test big new ideas alongside everyday ideas, everything from new value propositions to content and advertising copy. The conversation that takes place in private online communities differs significantly from that in public spaces. People go to public brand-sponsored sites like Facebook Pages to hear from brands, but they prefer to talk to them in private online environments.[16] This has important implications for where deep insight is to be regularly found. We further explore private online communities in Chapter 8.

Tap broader innovation networks. Diversity is vital to the success of our resource network. Innovation is a team sport. Employees, customers, and business partners are essential components. Tapping unusual partners, especially players outside of our industries, often changes the conversation, generating creative and potentially disruptive solutions. Sometimes breakthroughs come from simply repurposing solutions that have already been proven in other environments.

Apple, Google, Facebook, and Amazon are perfecting the art of partnering to create new products offerings. Through application program interfaces, or APIs, they make it possible for external developers to create applications that dramatically expand their product offerings and usefulness to their end users. At last count there were over 900,000 apps available for the iPhone or iPad and 800,000 for the Android. ABI, the technology market research firm, estimates that more than 70 billion apps were downloaded in 2013 alone.[17] That is equivalent to 10 apps for every human on Earth. That simply would not be possible without collaboration.

The Kauffman Foundation, which focuses on entrepreneurship and tracks factors that are important to new firm success rates, recommends that when entering new markets, organizations try to partner with other firms that are also trying to enter that marketplace, but from a slightly different angle. One of their demonstration projects brings together entrepreneurs to improve patient health and to lower the cost of care. By combining the efforts of companies involved in personal health records, social media patient platforms, passive monitoring technology, mobile apps, and customer user interfaces, Kauffman believes that the value proposition to patients and the physicians will be greatly improved over what any of these entrepreneurs could bring to the table on their own.[18]

Look globally for innovative players. Disruptive change can be initiated anywhere and rearrange any industry. Apple was born in a garage. Google, Facebook, and Instagram were all created on college campuses. Vijay Govindarajan and Chris Trimble, in their book *Reverse Innovation*, provide numerous examples of how innovations created and adopted first in the developing world are impacting longtime industry leaders in mature markets.[19]

Consider the potential impact of India's Narayana Hrudaualaya Hospital (NHH) on the U.S. health-care market. NHH performs world-class quality open-heart surgery at one-tenth of the cost of its

Employ Entrepreneurial Thinking for Discernment and Agility

U.S. counterparts. What is more, it does so with better margins and outcomes. Lower labor costs are only partially responsible for the hospital's success; the lion's share stems from process improvements that dramatically reduce their cost per procedure.[20]

What does NHH's success have to do with the U.S. market? NHH is bringing their model to the West with the establishment a center of excellence in cardiac surgery, cardiology, and orthopedics in the Cayman Islands. Over the next decade, the Cayman Islands-based hospital will expand to 2,000 beds, offer neurology and oncology specialties, and include a medical university and an assisted-care living community.[21] Did we mention that Grand Cayman is easy to get to with regularly scheduled flights from many cities in the United States, Canada, and Central and South America?

Reverse innovation may be the most important growth opportunity for businesses operating in mature markets going forward. Rakesh Kapoor, CEO of Reckitt Benckiser, the Anglo-Dutch consumer products company, understands how reverse innovation can leave companies operating in mature markets vulnerable to lower-cost, higher-value players, especially as consumers continue to watch their budgets following the recent worldwide recession. Turning this potential threat into an opportunity, the company is testing product innovations in emerging economies for roll-out in mature markets. As Kapoor told attendees of the 2013 Reuters Global Consumer and Retail Summit, "At this point in time, people will think about value in a much more holistic way. They look at price points and benefits in combination. So you lower the price, improve benefits and it is very appealing for consumers."[22]

Nothing Happens without Desire

Many things contributed to the formation of Larry's first company, the Weber Group. A background in English literature, a terrific wife, supportive clients, a booming new industry, and some measure of talent top the list. Even with all these resources in place, without the *desire* to unearth, develop, and tell companies' stories, the Weber Group would never have come to be. It turns out that desire is a common reason that entrepreneurs start something. They *want* to.

Desire is essential to innovation. When desire is present, there is motivation, persistence, and creativity; new ideas are brought to life. In the absence of desire, odds are nothing will happen. It remains all talk, no action.

Schlesinger and Kiefer draw an important distinction between desire and passion. Desire is a wish for something; passion, on the other hand, is a strong and barely controllable emotion. Most entrepreneurs do not have a strong and barely controllable emotion about their business idea upfront. Indeed, if they had, it may have created blind spots that would have been destructive. What they have is inspiration, a desire to act, to create something. As they progress, proving their idea, desire often morphs into a useful, ground-in-truth passion.

What do these findings about entrepreneurs and desire imply for marketers? For us as individuals, it is a prompt for self-assessment: Do I have energy for what I am doing? If not, it may be a good time to get to work identifying where our desire lies. If we are lucky enough to be doing what we want to be doing, then our task is to continue to harness that desire and to inspire others to share the fun.

Facebook understands the power of desire in bringing out the best in its employees. In a recent *New York Times* article, Sheryl Sandberg, COO of Facebook, commented on the correlation between the success of a company and the number of employees who responded positively when asked, "Do you have the opportunity to do what you do best every day?" In terms of applying this metric to life at Facebook, Sandberg said, "We focus on what people's natural strengths are and spend our management time trying to figure out ways for them to use those strengths every day."[23]

Sprint. Evaluate. Repeat.

The iterative, incremental methods characteristic of entrepreneurial thinking can provide a framework for efficiently managing any process, including implementing marketing plans or project management. This application of entrepreneurial decision making is often referred to as *marketing agility*. The framework allows people to think big, while getting there through a series of smaller steps.

Employ Entrepreneurial Thinking for Discernment and Agility

Marketing agility has its roots in the software industry. For many years software companies followed a waterfall method of planning, in which project details were defined before a project began and completed projects were delivered in one piece. After being burned and burned out by multiple unanticipated customer changes to software requirements, software engineers decided that there must be a better alternative to the comprehensive method of upfront planning. Was there a way to break the behemoth project into smaller pieces that could build upon each other? Could decision making be shifted down to the level of self-organizing, cross-functional teams that would actually be responsible for the project? They found their answer in rugby.

Whenever a minor infraction takes place in a rugby match, the game is reset with a process known as the scrum.[24] Short for scrummage, scrums can take place multiple times during the course of a game.

How is the scrum related to marketing? The agility framework breaks down larger marketing plans or projects into small bites that allow for frequent evaluation and recalibration in the same way as a scrum breaks up and resets a rugby match. Also, like a rugby team that includes offensive and defensive players, a scrum team is cross functional, composed of all the players needed to start a project and bring it to fruition.

At the risk of over simplifying the process, let us briefly explain how a marketing scrum might work. Each of the small bites is known as a *sprint*; a typical sprint can last anywhere from a week to a month.

A sprint begins with a Sprint Planning Meeting, during which time the project team agrees on the work that is to be done, the time it is likely to take, and the deliverables. Each day during the sprint, the project team meets to review their progress in what is known as the daily scrum or the daily stand-up. Key players come prepared to address the following questions and then set out to make it happen:

1. What have you done since yesterday?
2. What are you planning to do today?
3. What, if any, impediments or stumbling blocks have you encountered?

This feedback allows for continual improvement and adaptation. A burn-down chart that records work completed to date against the goal developed during the original Sprint Planning Meeting is prominently displayed to keep momentum for the project up and to keep team members on task.

At the end of a sprint, a sprint review is conducted that addresses what was accomplished during the process. During this informal gathering, the project is reviewed against the upfront plan. The one- to two-hour review builds accountability and transparency into the process.

The last step in the process is the sprint retrospective, a short meeting, usually an hour or less, during which time the team discusses how things went during the sprint with an eye not to cast blame, but to improve. Mike Cohn, the founder of Mountain Goat Software, which helps companies adopt and improve their marketing-agility efforts, recommends that this meeting be conducted in a start-stop-continue format, in which teams focus on what they should start doing, stop doing, and continue doing.[25] After the brainstorming is complete, teams often vote on which of the recommendations they will follow in the next sprint. A list is created, which is reviewed in the next sprint planning meeting and retrospective.

The marketing department at HubSpot, the inbound-marketing company, uses monthly sprints to achieve their annual goals. As one HubSpot employee wrote in the company blog, "working on smaller monthly goals, be it a total leads number or a unique content piece, is much more manageable than chasing after a 12-month goal."[26] HubSpot has found that agile marketing brings focus to their efforts, enhances transparency, builds accountability, and helps the entire department prioritize more effectively. The process facilitates their ability to respond quickly to market opportunities, by collectively allocating new responsibilities and deciding which tasks can be delayed until the next sprint.

Stay Relevant

In rapidly changing environments, companies need to constantly improve the relevance of their business model: how they create, deliver, and capture value. In the past, most business leaders have not had to significantly alter their business model because markets remained relatively constant throughout their careers. Saul Kaplan, whom we met in Chapter 2, believes that going forward, all leaders will have to revamp their value propositions, multiple times throughout their careers. If they do not, Kaplan warns that they are likely to be disrupted by change, rather than being the one causing the disruption.

In his book *The Business Model Innovation Factory*, Kaplan argues that entrepreneurial thinking is crucial to our success. Collaboration is key; we must look to engage with usual and unusual suspects including our customers. Design talent enables us to more fully explore what is possible. Ideas must be developed, prototyped, and tested in the real world. Desire helps us exceed our expectations and take risks with confidence.

To successfully explore and test new value propositions, however, Kaplan also recommends establishing a *business innovation factory*, an adjacent-innovation platform that is separate from, but connected to, our present operations. This platform allows us to explore and test new value propositions while we continue to execute on our existing model.

When he was president of Babson College, Len Schlesinger worked with Kaplan to form an adjacent-innovation platform, the Babson Entrepreneur Experience Lab. The goal of the platform is to create a real-world laboratory to design, develop, and test new entrepreneurship-support solutions and systems.[27]

Why is a separate platform necessary? After all, Babson is consistently ranked number one for entrepreneurship. Kaplan will tell you that game-changing innovation starts with the customer in mind and considers new ways of creating value for the end-user. This is distinctly different than starting with the way our organizations currently create and deliver value today. In fact, this starting point is so potentially disruptive to our current business model that it can only thrive if it can be nurtured in a platform that is adjacent to our present organization.

While senior managers talk a lot about innovation, and have even formed corporate-innovation departments, in Kaplan's experience, these efforts usually result in tweaks to the current business model. They are strategies for taking market share, not for making markets, because they start with the goal of improving a current business model. This is not a waste of time—it fine-tunes our existing operations—but it does not lead to sustainable competitive advantage. In Kaplan's experience, that comes from combining, recombining, and perhaps adding to our existing capabilities in a way that helps us meet our customers' emerging and latent needs. We have to be willing to disrupt our current model, to pull this off.

Adjacent platforms create the space needed to disrupt. Supported by their own leadership and resources, these teams have the freedom to explore new approaches, especially those that may threaten today's model, and to test ideas in the marketplace. However, to be successful, they also need to remain connected to, and informed by, the core business. Without the support of its senior leadership, the platforms will fail. Transparency and open communication between the two entities fosters cross-pollination, and enables the ongoing stream of customer-inspired ideas from which the next core business model will emerge.

Rethink Failure

When he was president of Babson College, Schlesinger used to tell potential parents that their children would have more chances to fail at Babson than anywhere else. Not surprisingly, this did not always come across as a major selling point for most parents, who hoped college would be about learning how to stack up successes and avoid failure. When he described the same process to parents using phrases like "learning to pivot" or "iterate," the message was better received.

Failure has been a four-letter word in our culture for some time. However, a rebranding is now taking place. Opinion leaders such as Arianna Huffington of the *Huffington Post* are challenging us to rethink failure. She encourages us to consider that "failure is not the opposite of success; it's a stepping stone to success."[28] Jeff Stibel, the chairman and CEO of Dun & Bradstreet Credibility Corp., publicly described why he hires people who fail in a recent *Harvard Business Review* blog.[29] What is going on here?

Living in a time of rapid change and innovation, we have to create room for new questions, connections, ways of discovering, and methods for evaluating potential solutions. Any time we are operating in ways we have not done before, we have to create space;

173

generous space that makes room for learning. If we play it too safe, afraid of making mistakes, we will only allow ourselves to envision incremental change, not birth new ideas or disruptive solutions. And that is not good enough. Failure is better.

Let us be clear. Creating space for failure is not a license to be sloppy or to be anything less than razor sharp in our thinking. Rather, it is permission to push beyond the frameworks that have worked well in the past, to consider new connections, limits, and possibilities using our most honed disciplines alongside emerging skills. It is the challenge to think, act, learn, and repeat, in order to move forward. It has been done before; imagine what it was like to reconstruct perspectives and practices after it was determined that the world was not flat.

So will failure disappear from our lexicon? Absolutely not. Failure still exists, especially in the realm of repetitive tasks such as pilots flying planes or doctors conducting colonoscopies. And it exists in the realm of entrepreneurial decision making, too. One can fail to bring adequate resources to the table, to consider multiple priorities or perspectives, to be disciplined about testing assumptions, or to implement appropriate solutions. One can fail to learn. But when it comes to testing new ideas, our organizations can take a page from the entrepreneur's playbook: fail early, learn from it, and create value in the process.

In the next chapter we focus our attention on customer engagement skills and how we can develop a content experience strategy that delivers.

RESOURCES

Influencers We Recommend

- *Kathleen Eisenhardt.* A professor of strategy and organization at Stanford University, Eisenhardt is widely known for her work on strategy, strategic decision-making, and innovation in high velocity, competitive markets. She is also the coauthor of *Competing on the Edge: Strategy as Structured Chaos.* Eisenhardt is a favorite at Stanford, having been named one of the Top 8 Professors. For more information see www.stanford.edu/~kme/.

- *Benjamin Franklin*. Although not currently active on social networks, Franklin's writings endure. To browse the complete works of Franklin see www.franklinpapers.org.

- *Vijay Govindarajan*. Vijay is a professor of International Business at Tuck and an expert on strategy and innovation. He served as GE's first chief innovation consultant and professor in resident which jumpstarted GE's "spend less and innovate" approach. Govindarajan is a regular contributor to Harvard Business Review blog and is the coauthor, along with colleague Chris Trimble, of *Reverse Innovation: Create Far From Home, Win Everywhere* and *How Stella Saved the Farm*. He was recently rated the #3 business thinker in the world by Thinkers 50. Follow his blog at www.tuck.dartmouth.edu/people/vg/blog and on Twitter @vgovindarajan.

- *Saul Kaplan*. Cofounder and chief catalyst of The Business Innovation Factory (BIF), Kaplan authored *The Business Model Innovation Factory*, in which he describes how to create an innovation platform. A regular contributor to *Harvard Business Review*, *Fortune*, and *Bloomberg BusinessWeek*, Kaplan muses about innovation on Twitter @skap5 and on his blog, "It's Saul Connected," at www.itssaulconnected.com.

- *Eric Ries*. Author of *The Lean Startup: How Today's Entrepreneurs Use Continuous Innovation to Create Radically Successful Businesses*, Ries is credited with founding the lean startup movement. Ries argues for capital-efficient enterprises that create minimally viable products that can be taken to market quickly, tested in the field, and rapidly interated upon, to best meet customer demand. Consider Reis' thoughts at www.theleanstartup.com, www.startuplessonslearned.com, and @ericries and @theleanstartup.

- *Saras Sarasvathy*. An associate professor of business administration at the Daren School of Business and a professor in entrepreneurship at the Indian Institute of Management

(continued)

(continued)

in Bangalore, Sarasvathy was named one of the top 18 entrepreneurship professors by *Fortune Small Business* in 2007. Her book *Effectuation: Elements of Entrepreneurial Expertise* describes a framework for understanding the creation and growth of new organizations and markets. To learn more, see www.effectuation.org or follow the movement on Twitter @effectuation.

- *Leonard Schlesinger*. An entrepreneur, professor, consultant, and former university president, all wrapped into one, Schlesinger is the coauthor of 11 books, including *Just Start*: *Take Action, Embrace Uncertainty, Create the Future*. After serving as president of Babson College, which is consistently ranked number one in entrepreneurship, he recently returned to Harvard Business School where he serves as a professor of business administration. Follow him on Twitter @lschlesinger and learn more about the Just Start model at www.just-start.com/.

- *Phil Simon*. A speaker and journalist, Simon writes about management, social media, publishing, disruption, and information management. He authored five management books including *The Age of the Platform* and *Too Big to Ignore: The Business Case for Big Data*. He is a frequent contributor on *Huffington Post*, the American Express Open Forum, the *New York Times*, *Fast Company*, *ReadWriteWeb*, and more. Keep up on his thinking at www.philsimon.com or on Twitter @philsimon.

Hashtags to Explore
- #agile (agile marketing)
- #entrepreneurs
- #firestarters
- #innovation
- #leanplanning (agile marketing)
- #startups

Chapter 7

Create a Content Experience Strategy That Delivers

"… The aim of marketing is to make selling superfluous. The aim of marketing is to know and understand the customer so well that the product or service fits him or her and sells itself. Ideally, marketing should result in a customer who is ready to buy. All that should be needed then is to make the product or service available."

—Peter Drucker, management consultant, educator, and author

Small and medium-sized companies generally do not have the luxury of a large IT staff. As a result, when they evaluate potential IT solutions, they often look to trusted advisors, business partners, and industry analysts to help evaluate, recommend, and deploy their IT decisions. Understanding this dynamic customer experience journey, IBM developed Midsize Insider, a lightly branded customer community where conversation about the tech needs and concerns of the group flows. Through Midsize Insider, community members are able to educate themselves about a rapidly changing and complex market while IBM continually takes the pulse of its prospects and existing customers.

Midsize Insider operates like a newsroom, with over 60 bloggers and journalists contributing a steady flow of content on topics that are on the minds of business owners and IT folks—topics such as smarter computing, security and resilience, cloud computing, CRM, and business analytics. Each of the writers is carefully chosen and possesses a deep understanding of midmarket challenges, offering

177

a unique and informed perspective on industry trends. News stories and trending topics complement the articles, creating a vibrant and up-to-the-minute resource for members.

Recognizing the quality of the site's content, Google News, which aggregates content from a variety of high-quality sources, taps Midsize Insider's content for distribution to its readers. By syndicating its content through this news site, Midsize Insider reaches a broader base of interested parties and is able to direct them back to its site, where they can access additional expert content. A robust discussion group on LinkedIn provides a forum for members to connect directly with each other.

By aligning its marketing efforts with how current and prospective customers gather information in support of potential IT purchases, IBM offers real value, positioning itself as an expert and trusted advisor for small and medium-sized businesses. Serving as the connective tissue between IT decision makers and IBM, Midsize Insider's informative content keeps a steady and relevant conversation going and ensures that IBM is continually in touch with the marketplace.

Prospects and customers are enthusiastic about the community, as evidenced by engagement and response rates that are consistently above industry averages. The community enjoys a 1.8 percent click-through rate from MidsizeInsider.com to solution pages on IBM.com, which is 36 times the average .05 percent click-through rate of banner ads. Community members share content regularly; the site has a 20.8 percent social-sharing rate of program content versus Facebook's social-sharing average of 1.4 percent. Midsize Insider is also attracting a global audience, with visitors from 209 countries. The publishing platform has won numerous awards including being named one of "5 Brands that have Mastered Publishing," by iMedia Connection.

Who Signs Our Paycheck?

Ann Handley, the chief content officer of Marketing Profs, a professional development resource for marketers, issued the following challenge at a recent Content Marketing Conference: "Ask yourself: If my customer signed my paycheck, what would marketing look like?" The irony of her comment is that our customers do, and always have, signed our paychecks, albeit indirectly. It makes sense that we create experiences that serve their needs. While this may seem obvious, Hanley's comment reflects a seismic shift in perspective, a move away from a product focus where we harnessed advertising to persuade our people to buy our products, toward a more customer-centric orientation, where we develop useful and engaging content that addresses our customers' needs and establishes us as a trusted resource. Marketing consultant Jay Baer summarized the distinction between these perspectives, "The difference between helping and selling is just two letters. But those two letters now make all the difference."[1]

It Was Not Always This Way

Remember the old Burger King jingle: "Hold the pickles, hold the lettuce, special orders don't upset us, all we ask is that you let us serve it *your* way"? Back in the days of *push* marketing, when advertising was the leading lever in our marketing mix, we caught our customers' attention primarily though catchy tag lines, creative commercials, and small amounts of product personalization: Do you want pickles or lettuce on your hamburger?

As marketers, we pushed our messages out to relatively passive customers through a handful of channels—television, radio, print, direct mail, and phone calls—to convince them to purchase whatever we were hired to sell. Our strategy was to saturate the market with carefully crafted ads that would push consumers through the sales funnel from awareness to purchase. Much of what we created was clever—think of the "Mean Joe Greene" commercial for Coke[2] and catchy phrases like "mmm good" and "the quicker picker upper"— branding that continues to evoke emotion and brand recall but whose effectiveness in driving sales is still uncertain. We were often entertaining and imaginative. However, we were not customer-centric; we were still pushing our own goods and telling our own story.

In addition to marketers telling the story of our companies' products, marketing communications managed our corporate reputation. Through press releases and annual reports, we described our companies, our achievements, and our contributions to shape and maintain a positive image. We spoke with a singular voice, that of the official

Create a Content Experience Strategy That Delivers

spokesman for the company, which was often formal and faceless. Steeped in a one-way communications tradition, we talked; we did not interact. "No comment" was an appropriate response.

Over the years our constituents grew tired of our producer orientation, our sales pitches, our perceived indifference, and of being viewed predominantly as transactions, even being labeled as consumers. Bombarded with advertising directed *at* them—Yankelovich estimates that the average consumer was exposed to 5,000 brand messages daily—people began to turn a deaf ear to our messaging with TiVo, satellite radio, caller ID, spam blockers, and by throwing our carefully crafted print pieces in the garbage. They wanted to get on to latest episode of *Seinfeld*, the Top 40 countdown, or a *Newsweek* article, and not be interrupted by our latest promotion. As a result, the effectiveness of our marketing efforts was diminished. Our producer-based marketing had actually moved us farther away from achieving our stated goal of customer-centricity.

Content Marketing Focuses on Our Customers' Agenda

In recent years, companies have recaptured the attention of their prospects and customers through content marketing. The Content Marketing Institute defines *content marketing* as "a marketing technique of creating and distributing relevant and valuable content to attract, acquire, and engage a clearly defined and understood target audience—with the objective of driving profitable customer action."[3]

Through its Midsize Insider community, IBM successfully employs a content marketing strategy. Similarly, Home Depot shows its customers how they can use the company's products and services to solve their current challenges with its home-improvement videos. Did you know that cayenne pepper can prevent rodents? If not check out Home Depot's animated video on Vine.

Designer Tory Burch uses content to more fully build out her brand and engage her prospects and customers. The Tory Blog offers value by highlighting Burch's style as evidenced in entertaining, beauty, culture, and music. Her City Guides describe her favorite places to "eat, sleep, shop, and see around the world."[4] While reading the blog, viewers can click on an embedded hyperlink to research or purchase items.

How does content marketing differ from our previous push-based strategy? Content marketing achieves its goal of driving profitable customer action by focusing on meeting the needs and desires of our prospects and customers rather than by selling them on our products and services. A customer-centric strategy, content marketing looks to educate, advise, and engage our constituencies.

Unlike advertising, content marketing is non-interrupting. Rather than directing advertising *at* our prospects and customers, this form of "pull" marketing creates ways for people to find out about our products and services in the course of their daily lives by acting as resources *for* them. Our prospects and customers seek us out. If our content is compelling enough, it draws people to us. Then *they* can then decide for themselves whether we are able to help them. There is no hard sell.

Following a content strategy, marketers blog about subjects that are of interest to our prospects and customers and comment on blogs that they read. We tweet, host webinars, publish white papers, produce videos, and curate Pinterest boards to offer information and experiences that our customers will find useful. When carried out correctly, our organizations become more approachable and trustworthy.

Content marketing can be interactive; when activated through social media channels, it promotes dialogue with our constituents, inviting them to tell their stories and to share, review, and comment on ours. This builds important word of mouth and fosters community—customers and prospects connecting with each other.

What Is Old Is New

Content creation is not a new strategy. As early as 1900 the tire manufacturer Michelin employed content marketing to stimulate demand for cars, and therefore, for car tires. The company published the *Michelin Guide* to France to encourage people to explore the wonders of the French countryside by automobile. The Guide included maps, lists of restaurants, hotels, car mechanics, and gas stations, as well as instructions for changing and repairing tires. Provided free of charge, the Guide increased people's motivation to purchase cars by opening their eyes to new travel possibilities. The Guide also reduced the risk of taking a trip by identifying resources to meet people's travel needs while on the road. Good content is enduring. Over a hundred years later, Michelin is still publishing the guides.

The web has increased demand for content marketing. As we have seen, today's customers are do it yourself-ers, people who actively search out information to meet their needs. Great content meets our customers' need for self-serve access to information and brings us into the conversation in a trustworthy way. It also maintains a consistent dialogue that can steward our prospects and customers through the customer journey, before, during, and after a sale. As a result, successful content marketing often tees up new, repeat, and cross- and up-sell opportunities and fosters advocacy and co-creation. It puts marketers in the position of *directly* contributing to revenue generation, increasingly our value to our organizations.

How Do You Create Useful Content If You Sell Clothes Dryers?

With a little imagination and a lot of understanding of our customers' needs, desires, motivations, and existing beliefs, compelling content can be created for any product or service. Here is an example of useful content—if you are in the market for a clothes dryer (see Figure 7.1). A search for clothes dryers reveals multiple results including a link to About.com's landing page, titled "Before You Buy a Dryer." (A landing page is the page of a website that viewers are directed to when they click on the search link.)

Intrigued, viewers click through to the landing page and find all kinds of information about gas versus electric dryers, dryer capacity, energy-saving trips, must-have features, and even pricing considerations. Notably there are no sales pitches in the body of the content. Links to vendors appear on the side of the page, clearly marked under the heading Ads, which the viewer can choose to click through. If viewers are looking for dryers and the range of options seems overwhelming, this is indeed compelling content. Even more useful content might include a simple questionnaire that helps potential purchasers prioritize features and a tool that generates a list of models that best match their specified criteria. Links to local vendors that sell the selected models and their current pricing and inventory would further increase the site's usefulness.

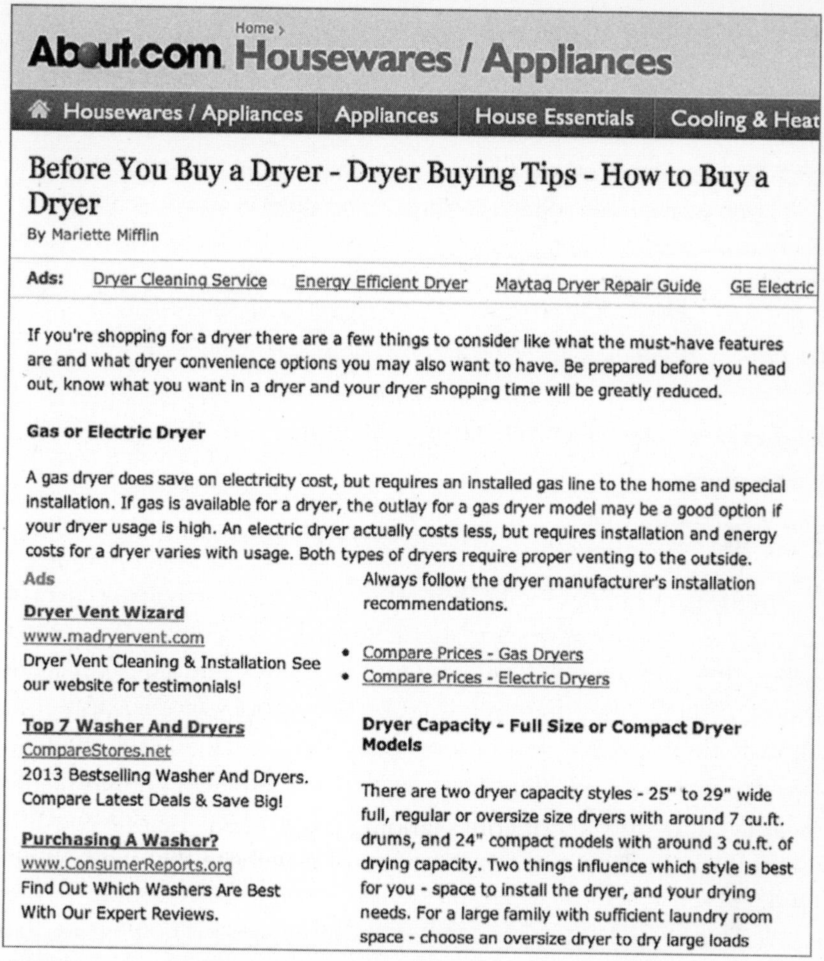

Home >

About.com Housewares / Appliances

Housewares / Appliances | Appliances | House Essentials | Cooling & Heat

Before You Buy a Dryer - Dryer Buying Tips - How to Buy a Dryer

By Mariette Mifflin

Ads: Dryer Cleaning Service Energy Efficient Dryer Maytag Dryer Repair Guide GE Electric

If you're shopping for a dryer there are a few things to consider like what the must-have features are and what dryer convenience options you may also want to have. Be prepared before you head out, know what you want in a dryer and your dryer shopping time will be greatly reduced.

Gas or Electric Dryer

A gas dryer does save on electricity cost, but requires an installed gas line to the home and special installation. If gas is available for a dryer, the outlay for a gas dryer model may be a good option if your dryer usage is high. An electric dryer actually costs less, but requires installation and energy costs for a dryer varies with usage. Both types of dryers require proper venting to the outside. Always follow the dryer manufacturer's installation recommendations.

- Compare Prices - Gas Dryers
- Compare Prices - Electric Dryers

Dryer Capacity - Full Size or Compact Dryer Models

There are two dryer capacity styles - 25" to 29" wide full, regular or oversize size dryers with around 7 cu.ft. drums, and 24" compact models with around 3 cu.ft. of drying capacity. Two things influence which style is best for you - space to install the dryer, and your drying needs. For a large family with sufficient laundry room space - choose an oversize dryer to dry large loads

Ads

Dryer Vent Wizard
www.madryervent.com
Dryer Vent Cleaning & Installation See our website for testimonials!

Top 7 Washer And Dryers
CompareStores.net
2013 Bestselling Washer And Dryers. Compare Latest Deals & Save Big!

Purchasing A Washer?
www.ConsumerReports.org
Find Out Which Washers Are Best With Our Expert Reviews.

Figure 7.1 Content Marketing Aims to Be Useful

Source: **Mariette Mufflin, "Before You Buy a Dryer," About.com.**

Content Marketing Works Throughout the Journey

Once potential customers have found our blog postings, videos, white papers, or tweets via search engines, social media, or an embedded link in an article or blog post, we invite them to further engage with us by directing them to our website, landing pages, or other digital environments through a compelling trigger, or call to action (see Figure 7.2).

Figure 7.2   An Effective Trigger Reaches and Engages Customers

Source: **Skyword.com.**

In the case of our clothes dryer shoppers, the call to action may be the link on About.com's page that takes them to CompareStores.net, where they can then click through to Whirlpool's landing page. While they are there, they may read about Whirlpool's mobile apps that allow them to assign laundry jobs to family members and to manage laundry remotely, ancillary features that just might seal the deal for Whirlpool. For business-to-business (B2B) prospects, a call to action could invite prospects to download a white paper, sign up for an RSS feed, view a video, or request a demo among other options.

If prospects take us up on our call-to-action, a conversion has taken place; awareness has been built and a lead has been nurtured. That is not to say that they are ready to make a purchase, however, especially for high involvement purchases characterized by a long sales cycle. Brian Carroll, CEO of inTouch and author of *Lead Generation for the Complex Sale*, observes that up to 95 percent of prospects that make it to our websites are in research mode. Seventy-five percent will eventually buy a product from us—or our competitors—so we want to make sure that we continue to develop these relationships.[5]

We nurture these leads with additional content that becomes increasingly focused based upon our prospect's actions. By noting the pages that they visit and the topics they explore, we can refine our content to reflect their interests. As prospects get closer to making a purchase, the nature of our content changes. Case studies, testimonials, product descriptions, and surveys that help identify the most appropriate solution and describe our products' value replace more general information. If our prospects continue to download these materials, we may offer another trigger, perhaps a free trial if appropriate, that will keep them moving forward.

The Progressive Company's content highlights this progression. Flo, the upbeat, fictional character who sports heavy makeup and a retro hairstyle, represents the car insurance company in television commercials. Her persona is sincere and helpful; she is able to make something as complex as insurance seem easy. These light and memorable commercials build brand awareness and draw people to the company's other digital properties, where in addition to viewing all of Flo's commercials, they can access more hard-core content including auto quotes and the specifics of Progressive policies.[6]

Our engagement efforts continue after a sale is made, with content that is focused around frequently asked questions (FAQs) and best practices, information that can help new customers get the most out of their recent purchase. Thoughtful, ongoing engagement through challenges, contests, text messages, webinars, mobile apps, and social communities like IBM Midsize go a long way toward retaining customers, facilitating cross-sells and up-sells, and fostering engagement, customer advocacy, and co-creation.

Where Is the Content Engine Heading?

Content-based marketing is quickly becoming mainstream. Some 91 percent of B2B marketers and 86 percent of business-to-consumer (B2C) marketers use content marketing and their content marketing budgets are increasing.[7] Organizations like IBM, Red Bull, and Coca-Cola have become content-media producers in addition to their other lines of business. The purchase of the *Washington Post* by Jeff Bezos, the founder and CEO of Amazon, suggests that the future for digital content is bright. However, there is evidence that

Create a Content Experience Strategy That Delivers

our customers are becoming overwhelmed by the amount of content that is out there, reminiscent of the way they felt when advertising was bombarding them.

#Unplug, #Filter, #Spam

When Baratunde Thurston, the author of the *New York Times* bestseller *How to Be Black* and CEO of the comedy and technology agency Cultivated Wit, decided to unplug for 25 days, he made the cover of *Fast Company* magazine. The headline read: #UNPLUG: BARATUNDE THURSTON LEFT THE INTERNET FOR 25 DAYS, AND YOU SHOULD, TOO. Why was this big news?

People are finding life in the connected lane to be rather overwhelming. In a recent blog post titled, "Burnout: The Disease of Our Civilization," author Arianna Huffington described our culture as being "enraptured with technology to the point that tools meant to give us greater control over our lives have, instead, taken control of our lives."[8]

Many of us are inundated with content from work, friends, family, and brands. Often these messages appear in the same information streams on e-mail, Twitter, or Facebook. A photo of a college friend's recent trip appears just below a message from a local non-profit describing its upcoming gala, which is just below an invitation to participate in a contest for a soft drink company, which is below a blog post from a favorite columnist, which is just south of a comment left by our mother inquiring as to why we never call. Phew. And that might only reflect updates received in the last three minutes. A recent study by Jack Morton Worldwide found that 39 percent of people are also information frustrated, confused by conflicting messages and reports.[9]

New ways to filter content are appearing to reduce the noise. Robust RSS Readers, like the ones we described in Chapter 2, are being used to actively avoid information sources to which people have not intentionally subscribed. Google's Priority Inbox and Tab features automatically sort incoming e-mails by priority and type (social, primary, promotions) to make it easier to consume—or not. What's a marketer to do in an environment inundated with content? Distinguish ourselves by only offering the most relevant content possible.

Commit to Relevance

The key to being heard in a noisy world is relevance. Rather than unleashing more content in the hope of connecting with more prospects, our goal is to create smarter, more relevant experiences, that appeal to our customers and reflect our organizational priorities.

How do we accomplish this? Our prospects and customers want to see themselves in our content. To see themselves, our content must be personalized, reflecting each individual person's motivations, attitudes, preferences, needs, desires, and past behavior. More and more, our content must also reflect the setting in which our prospect or customer is experiencing it. Sometimes these *contextualized experiences* are also predictive, anticipating the future needs and buying behavior of prospects and customers by providing relevant recommendations. Amazon is a prime example, as is L.L. Bean, which was tied with Amazon for first in customer satisfaction during the 2013 holiday season.[10] When customers visit L.L. Bean's site, in addition to receiving personalized product recommendations, the company also offers them suggestions for seasonal outdoor adventures available in their geographic area.[11]

While not every piece of content needs to be contextualized, we should aim to build out our most pivotal interactions. Most contextualized experiences are currently experienced through smartphones as they accompany people throughout their days and they generate the necessary situational data. A lean-forward medium, mobile also allows us to create richer experiences because we can engage customers though touching, swiping, voice recognition, cameras, and GPS technology.

Mobile Is Essential

Mobile has become an essential component of today's customer experience. People have adopted mobile faster than any previous technology; it has rapidly become the remote controls for running people's lives. Fogg explained, "In my book, you don't adopt mobile, you marry it."

People are not just using their phones to talk and text. Mobile has become a key search and discovery tool. The number of people

187

accessing the Internet via a mobile phone has increased by 60.3 percent to 818.4 million in the past two years.[12] Already more Chinese Internet users access the web via their mobile phones than they do their desktops.

Most mobile interactions lead to a cross-channel experience; 75 percent of mobile searches trigger a follow-up activity on a desktop or a phone and more than half of those follow-up activities take place within an hour.[13] As a result, our content must be coordinated across channels, creating a cohesive story and customer experience.

Consider the case of the data-savvy online retailer Rue-La-La. Its data analytic efforts revealed that its most profitable customers shop across multiple devices. (It is unclear if these customers spend more because the cross-channel shopping experience is better, or if bigger spenders prefer shopping in multiple environments.) Further, Rue-La-La has uncovered consistent patterns in device use among members of its shopping community. During the day, shoppers prefer to purchase via their desktop; during the evenings and weekends, those same shoppers use the company's mobile app. To offer its customers the experience they want and have come to expect, Rue-La-La's shopping experience must be comparable, consistent, and coordinated across screens. And it is.

Optimize Mobile Engagement

To provide an omnichannel experience, our content must be optimized for each channel and for each device. Google found that 61 percent of consumers are likely to leave a site if it is not mobile optimized.[14] What is more, they also found that sites that do not render properly can harm a company's reputation as 48 percent of people said if a site didn't work well on their smartphones, it made them feel as if the company didn't care about their business.[15]

Responsive web design (RWD) facilitates optimization across devices as it automatically adapts content to the screen size of the users' viewing device. This is a key consideration in emerging markets, where access to the web often takes place exclusively on mobile devices, and for e-mail communications, as much as half are now opened on mobile devices.[16] RWD also improves search results as traffic from all devices are routed to a single web address.

There are instances when RWD does not make sense, however. Sometimes we may want to vary our content by device because our customers use their devices differently. NZ Kiwibank redesigned its mobile when it realized that its customers were only using a fraction of the features. Supplementary content remains available on its website. This approach would not work for Rue-La-La, however, as its customers want access to the same content wherever they are and on whatever device they choose.

A word of caution: Do not assume that mobile devices are all the same. While tablets and mobile phones are often used for on-the-go browsing, they have different demographics and are generally not used in the same way. Tablets tend to be employed more like desktops than mobile phones; as a result, the user experience should be designed accordingly.

Mobile Apps Offer a Unique Opportunity

In addition to optimizing their mobile websites, many companies with well-developed customer bases are also choosing to create their own mobile apps. People seem to have an insatiable appetite for apps. Mobile-app downloads have almost doubled in the last year from 64 billion in 2012 to 102 billion in 2013.[17] Do not let the numbers wow you. Only a fraction of apps remain active over time. An app has to be highly compelling to remain permanent real estate on users' devices.

Mobile applications can deliver remarkable customer experiences. Take the app created for the Guatemalan athletic shoe store, Meat Pack, for example. Through its app, Meat Pack sends discount-based offers to its customers when they enter a competitor's store. The feature is known as Hijack because it is designed to stop, steal, and redirect Meat Pack's customers away from competitors' stores. The deal offers them a generous 99 percent discount; however, a timer accompanies the offer, which reduces the percentage discount by 1 percent for every second that passes from the time customers receive the offer, until they enter a Meat Pack store. A novel approach, this Hijack feature is made possible by real-time data, a location-enabled device, and Meat Pack stores that are located within running distance of competitors' retail presences. Does the

Create a Content Experience Strategy That Delivers

app work? In one week over 600 people were hijacked away from competitors, with one speedy customer earning a hefty 89 percent discount on his new sneaks.[18]

An app does not have to have hijack features to be useful, however. Some of the most active apps simply make it easy to renew a prescription, pay for a coffee, or sign up for a spin class. In terms of the Fogg Behavior Model, they enhance customers' ability to scratch the itch or get the job done.

Develop a Content Experience Strategy

Sun Tzu was a Chinese military general, philosopher, and strategist during the Zhou dynasty. Although he lived more than 2,500 years ago, his words about strategy remain relevant to marketers: "Strategy without tactics is the slowest route to victory. Tactics without strategy is noise before defeat."

Knowing where our businesses are headed and how we want to get there remains essential. Developing a content strategy keeps us focused on creating experiences that are results-driven and meet both our customer' goals and objectives and our own.

Our content experience strategy describes our vision for the type of customer experiences we want to offer. This vision sets the course for how we will create, deliver, manage, and evaluate content experiences for all of our personas, at each stage in the customer experience journey, across all of our channels and devices. While it sounds like a laborious process, developing our content experience strategy does not have to be unnecessarily grueling. Our goal is not to preplan our every move; that is a futile task in rapidly changing environments. Rather, we set out to develop a vision and point-of-reference that allows us to act now and next quarter, to be thoughtful and spontaneous.

Aim for a Brand Journalism Platform

As we set out to design our content experience strategy, it is helpful to remember Horace Greeley and Jim Bellows. Rather than following the traditional marketing model of executing discrete campaigns to generate short up-ticks, our goal is to build relationships with customers

190

over the course of a customer journey. To do so we have to act more like these respected newspaper editors, generating a steady, but not overwhelming flow of useful and increasingly contextualized content to keep customers tuning in regularly.

Following this approach, corporations are turning their websites into publishing platforms. GE, for example, has a digital storytelling platform, *The GE Show*, which builds a broader awareness of the challenges the company is addressing with the technology it creates. The content is fascinating even to the non-technically inclined. An episode from the Future Flight series takes us on an insider's tour of airports from the Congo to Iceland. Another episode from the Solar series uses weather balloons, hydrogen, and helium to simulate the sun's power.[19]

Similarly, Coca-Cola has launched Coca-Cola Journey™ through which it is "Refreshing the world, one story at a time."[20] The dynamic digital magazine, which replaces its traditional corporate website, focuses on news, opinions, and stories in a variety of areas. (A food section was added after web analytics revealed that most common search term that brought people to the site was "Coca-Cola cake.") The site has been quite successful, managing to engage Coke customers and keep them coming back. Several localized versions of the Coca-Cola Journey are being launched around the world—in Germany, Morocco, Japan, New Zealand, and Australia to name a few.

Keep Your Brand Promise in Mind

Effective content meets the needs of our customers while remaining consistent with our brand promise. People want their brands to be creative, but they also want them to be trustworthy and consistent, something they can understand and count on. Inconsistent brand messaging, is confusing and erodes our brands.

To ensure that we are on-brand, it is important to develop design identity guidelines for our content and touchpoints that reflect our brands' essential identity including their values, personality, attributes, promise, and purpose. What tone, style, topography, page layout, and colors reflect our brands? What type of visual imagery accurately and adequately captures our brand's essence? What interactive qualities define our brands? These parameters ensure that our brands are

191

instantly recognizable and that the experiences we create reinforce our brands in the eyes of our prospects and customers, rather than confuse.

Identify Themes, Events, and Opportunities

The experiences that we bring to life reflect the themes that are on our customers' minds, our organizations' top objectives, promotional events as product launches or major sales events that we want to highlight, as well as ideas and interactions that we believe will encourage the conversation and move our customer relationships forward. In addition, our content calendar is flexible enough to incorporate real-time events, chatter, and trends. Oreo's brilliant tweet when the Superdome lights went dark during Super Bowl XLX—"You can still dunk in the dark"—is a prime example. To take advantage of these moments, we need to have people and policies in place to craft and approve quality messaging in real time.

Real-time engagement also refers to creating messaging and experiences around seemingly unexpected events. J.P. Maheu, the CEO of Bluefin Labs, a social analytics company now owned by Twitter, explains that conversations about many topics in social media are fairly predictable. Surprisingly, tweets about ice cream or running take place in patterns that can be anticipated. As a result, in many cases it is possible to plan ahead for spontaneous engagement. Through Twitter's paid media products, brands can schedule and promote content during these proven peak discussion times.

Create or Curate?

We are often asked, "How original does our content need to be? Is it enough to curate other's work?" The bottom line is this: To put our name on it, the content we publish has to be useful.

Remember, people are not inherently interested in our products and services. They interact with us because they perceive that the content we are providing, or the community that congregates around us in social environments, is going to improve their lives in some way. We may provide information that helps them make better decisions. Or offer entertainment that makes them smile or produces a deep guttural laugh. Or inspire them with the opportunity to be a part of something bigger than themselves. Sometimes we can accomplish this by curating others' content, but more often than not, it requires us to generate stories and create experiences that are unique to our brands. If we are always regurgitating, people will bypass us and go directly to the sources from which we are drawing.

An exception to this is curating our customers' content. According to Mass Relevance, which specializes in social experience content marketing, 62 percent of people are more likely to engage with brands that integrate social media content into their brands' properties.[21] This makes sense. Our prospects and customers are looking to understand how our products and services will meet their needs. How better to illustrate our potential impact than by having our own customers advocate for us?

Patagonia has curating down to a science. Customers' stories and photographs of rock climbing and hiking adventures fill their catalogues and digital sites. Compelling stories of achieving the goal and missing the mark capture the outdoor enthusiasts' experience. Product descriptions and photos are interspersed among these inspiring tales and images, making it easy to follow through with a purchase if inspired. We, too, can actively curate or crowdsource a given theme, run a contest in which we ask for user submissions, or reproduce commentary provided we are not violating any privacy policies.

Conduct a Content Audit and Review

Before we commit ourselves to creating too much new content, it is a good idea to take stock of our existing content assets. A potentially time-consuming process, an audit can actually end up saving us time if we discover content that can be refreshed or repurposed. Can a slide deck morph into a short blog post or perhaps an infographic? Can we update a blog post with a year-later perspective? Can we edit a long video down to six seconds to distribute through Vine? After undertaking this process, some brands find that they have ample content. Rather than create more, their content strategy is editorial in nature. Simplifying, organizing, and tagging content assets for search may better engage their prospects and customers, and, therefore, be a better use of their resources.

Create a Content Experience Strategy That Delivers

To get the most out of the audit process, it is helpful to catalog and tag our assets as we go. A word of advice about cataloging: Only collect information that is essential to keep from getting bogged down in the process. Suggestions include the name of asset, location, type (webinar, video), content owner, date last updated, and perhaps a scoring mechanism of some type. Each asset should also have a unique ID number and be tagged with short descriptive keywords that can facilitate search. To keep our records current, new content should also catalogued as it is created.

Map Our Content across the Experience Journey

As we conduct an audit of our existing assets and add new content to the mix, it is useful to map out the content that each of our personas may interact with as they progress along the customer journey. Creating a simple matrix, which lists our personas on one axis and the stages of our customer-experience journey on the other, provides a useful structure to help us uncover any content gaps and redundancies. Applying the results of our content audit, in each quadrant we list the asset, the questions it answers, and the form it takes (see Figure 7.3). Looking across the entire persona's experience journey, we can evaluate whether each piece of content builds upon earlier messaging. Is there variety in the type of content used? Is our content leading to action? How might we enhance our customer experience?

Tips for Creating Relevant Content

Strategic thinking extends to each piece of content. As we set out to create content it is useful to consider the following questions.

To Whom Is This Targeted?

To create relevant content, we need to know for whom we are developing the experience and where they are in the customer experience journey. With this information in hand, we can design content that will effectively address our target persona's needs, desires, motivations, and beliefs at a given point in time. Personas can help us focus

	Persona 1	Persona 2	Persona 3
Awareness			
Research			
Evaluate			
Select			
Engage Advocate Cocreate			

Figure 7.3 Map and Develop Content for Each Persona across the Customer Journey

our efforts by giving us a clear picture of whom we are directing our efforts.

Adele Revella, the president of Buyer Persona Institute, defines personas as "an example of the real person who buys, or might buy, products like the ones you market, based on what you've learned from direct interviews with real buyers."[22] These mini snapshots of our customers often include representative names, demographics, job titles, and even pictures. They describe our constituents' different needs, goals, motivations, income levels, influencers, and communications preferences. They give market segments personalities like "Pampering Parents" and "Performance Fuelists."

While persona development may seem like a natural fit for B2C companies, it can be equally as helpful for organizations pursuing

Create a Content Experience Strategy That Delivers

a B2B strategy as well. In a B2B setting, these profiles can help us better understand our prospects. We can develop personas for entire companies and for each member of the buying team. Hubspot views these marketing tools as so critical to their marketing efforts that its office is physically organized according to these personalities.

Is This Content Useful?

Remember Jay Baer's advice from Chapter 1: Create marketing experiences that are so valuable people would pay for them. This is our goal. Is this content that useful? Is it interesting? Is it surprising? Does it bring something new to the conversation? Is it up to date? Does it answer the questions our personas may have at this stage? What action are we hoping to inspire with this content? Does it have an effective trigger? Is it contextualized as best it can be? Does it reflect our most recent learning about this customer?

Is This the Right Time?

Timing of the content matters as well. Does it come at the right time of day and the right time in our customers' journey? Is it sensitive to events taking place in the news? Who can forget the day of the tragic Aurora, Colorado, movie theater shooting, when the National Rifle Association's *American Rifleman* tweeted, "Good morning, shooters. Happy Friday! Weekend plans?"[23] Awareness of what is currently happening can help avoid similarly unfortunate communications.

Is It Short and Sweet?

Our customers are busy and distracted. To sustain our constituents' attention our content should be bite-sized. It is just too easy for them to click away. Think small and effective. Chunk it down. Use bullet points. Create lists. Break long messaging down into a series of episodes. Use the inverted-pyramid style for writing.

Seem impossible? Consider for a moment what Harold Schwartz, the founder of Starbucks, did back in 2008 when faced with a stock price that had declined by almost 50 percent. He articulated his entire vision, strategy, and key steps for transforming the coffee store chain in a one-page memo.[24] (A brief Q&A was also attached.) His ideas were more fully fleshed out in 15 follow-up memos over the course of the next four months after he returned to the company as CEO. It is possible and potent.

Brevity applies to our triggers as well. Contact forms, the information that we ask people to fill out about themselves to download a white paper or view a video, that require a lot of personal information are a major disincentive to further engagement with us. Research conducted by *Gleanster* found that after five fields, the drop-off rate increases by up to 15 percent for every additional field.[25] As we create contact forms, we need to consider what is absolutely essential. To enhance our customer knowledge, we can practice progressive profiling in which we ask additional questions in future interactions as we earn our prospects' engagement and trust.

Are We Using the Most Appropriate Type of Content?

The type of content we create reflects the underlying purpose of the communication and our target customers' preferences. Digital content takes many forms. It can be text based, like a blog, a blog comment, or a white paper; visual like a photograph, a video, or an infographic; or audio based such as a playlist or a podcast. It can be a digital event like a webinar or a Twitter Chat. It can be in long form, such as an e-book, article, case study, or movie, or it can be short form—a 140-character tweet or a six-second video on Vine. Whatever the form, our customers should be able to access content via the device of their choice: mobile phone, tablet, or desktop.

In general, B2C companies tend to use more mobile content, apps, and print. B2B companies create more case studies, white papers, webinars, webcasts, and retail reports.[26] It is a good idea to mix up the types of content regularly to keep things interesting. Offering an infographic between white papers, or an educational video series instead of an e-book, creates a refreshing rhythm.

Is It Appropriate?

Social media has blurred the lines between what is considered personal and what is considered professional. Transparency has redrawn

Create a Content Experience Strategy That Delivers

the line between what we share broadly and what remains confidential. Partnering has reconfigured corporate boundaries. In a time when our sense of boundaries is in flux, it is important to stand back and ask ourselves if our content is appropriate. Are we inadvertently releasing proprietary information? Will publishing this piece impact any of our partners or other stakeholders? If so, have we made them aware of the initiative and the timing?

Is It Better Expressed with Pictures?

Text is the most common form of storytelling on the web; however, it is not always the most engaging form. People generally scan written content, reading only 20 to 28 percent of the words on a page.[27] Keeping things short, well organized, and easy on the eye can increase the effectiveness of text.

Visual communication tends to be more effective, as long as the material is relevant. Forty percent of people respond better to visual information than plain text.[28] Visual content also drives engagement. Posts with videos attract three times more inbound links than all-text posts and those that combine videos, images, and lists attract almost six times as many.[29] Photos generate more likes, comments, and shares on Facebook than text, video, and links.[30] When it comes to local search, 60 percent of people are more likely to consider or contact a business when a relevant image accompanies search results.[31] Getting the picture?

Remember Warby Parker, the purveyor of eyewear that we highlighted in Chapter 4? Its blog is primarily visual, incorporating the work of fashion photographer Danielle Levitt to show its story. Every year the company publishes a visual annual report, chock full of interesting infographics. Take a look and see how you respond to the presentation.[32]

Eloqua, which offers a marketing automation platform, has an informative and entertaining video that describes the underlying needs that this technology addresses. The interactive video invites viewers to participate, tailoring the content to the viewers' needs. Take a few moments to see what can be done.[33] Interested in trying your hand at creating animated video or presentation? A free and easy-to-use tool for creating professional-looking videos is available on www.PowToon.com. You may also want to explore Prezi.com's presentation software that creates a dynamic virtual whiteboard for collaboration and storytelling.

Infographics present complex data in a way that is often more easily absorbed and interpreted than a paragraph. To see how they are being used, check out www.Visual.ly.com, www.DailyInfographic .com, or the Marketing Infographics gallery on Pinterest.[34] To create infographics and other visualizations, check out Visual.ly.com. Watch the first video-based infographic creator coming soon at Infogr.am.

One of our favorite visual effects is the *cinemagraph*, which blends a still photo and video. A partially animated photograph, the cinemagraph captures people's attention by their uniqueness and their subtlety. If you have not seen one before, do a quick search and be delighted.

Do not overlook the power of music. Burberry showcases the work of emerging British musicians through its online videos, Burberry Acoustics. Recognizing the importance of music to its marketing efforts, the brand has its own full-time music team.[35] Oreo recently released its Wonderfilled anthem, a 90-second music video in which it asks the question, "I wonder what would happen if you gave an Oreo to…?" Download it for free at www.oreo.com/wonderfilled.

Is the Content Placement Right?

In addition to considering the form our content will take, thoughtful consideration of where that content will be distributed is essential. To maximize the effectiveness of our content and create a unified experience for our prospects and customers, our content should be optimized for each channel and for each device and build cohesive story across touchpoints.

One of the most used distribution channels is e-mail. With over 294 billion e-mails sent daily, it is not surprising that click-through rates on mass e-mail campaigns are often as low as 0.3 to 0.5 percent. When e-mail is personalized, however, response rates dramatically improve. Crafting e-mail communications to reflect activity in another channel—an e-mail that focuses on content viewed on a website—increases its relevance. Williams Sonoma realized a tenfold increase in response rates when it incorporated customers' online and catalogue behaviors into its e-mail messaging.[36]

E-mail remains a relatively vanilla platform compared to the rich experiences that we have become accustomed to in social media, but there are few other options for private communications. Redbox is creating a richer e-mail experience by embedding video trailers of its featured movies in its e-mails. An alternative to e-mails, Post-wire's has created software that makes it easy for marketers and salespeople to share videos, photos, links, and documents with their customers via private webpages. Creators of the webpages can edit their page, choose who can view and contribute to it, and create discussion spaces within the space so there is no need for follow-up e-mails.[37]

Can We Socialize Our Content?

Social media is a vital component of our communication strategy. It amplifies our content as it is shared across networks. On average, companies are active on six social media platforms. LinkedIn has been an important distribution vehicle for B2B companies jumped from 51 percent to 71 percent.[38]

In addition to reaching out to our existing prospects and customers via social media, we can augment our efforts by developing relationships with influential individuals and organizations that can impact our target market. Influencer marketing is a proven strategy; 80 percent of the top performers interviewed in a *Gleanster* research study said that active engagement with an influential customer was a "top three value driver for social media marketing."[39]

Developing this influencer base takes some effort. It requires establishing criteria for influencers with whom we want to be associated, identification of potential influencers (social network analysis and social listening), and ongoing cultivation of these relationships. For B2C companies, these influencers are typically other customers or professional bloggers, whereas for B2B companies, they may also be business leaders, bloggers, journalists, industry analysts, regulators, and our own business partners. Don't overlook international influencers.

Is It Sharable?

We know we have created great content when it is shared. What is more, when content is distributed through the networks of our prospects and customers, it has been vetted; it has the sharers' stamp of approval. This is potent. As Jonah Peretti, the CEO of *BuzzFeed*, which keeps us up to date on the hottest social content on the web, explains, "You'd rather get something from your friend sharing it than you would get it from a headline or have it pushed to you through the industrial media apparatus of broadcast pipes and printing presses."[40] People like to share. Facebook reports that people like and comment on content a remarkable 3.2 billion times each day.

Creating content that is worthy of being passed along gets the ball rolling. Adding relevant hashtags (#) pulls our content into broader conversation streams related to the topic. Embedding share widgets for social networks like LinkedIn, Facebook, Twitter, and Pinterest into every piece of content facilitates sharing. We can also directly ask our viewers to share the content if they like it. Some companies ask their employees to share relevant company content through their networks and provide pre-scripted tweets for their use.

Is It Searchable?

In addition to distributing our content via e-mail, blogs, and social media, our content must be able to be found on the web. Ninety-three percent of online experiences begin with a search engine.[41] Knowing that 75 percent of searchers do not move past the first page of the search-engine results, getting our content to show up near the top of the search engine results page (SERP) is important.

There are two forms of search: organic and paid. Organic-search results appear on the SERP because of their relevance to the search terms used; paid-search results are advertising that appears because of a media buy. Figure 7.4 is a snapshot of the search results for SkinCeuticals Vitamin C. Organic search results show up in the box at the bottom left side of the page. Ads appear on the top of the page and along the side. Prime real estate for SERPS is considered to be above the fold because the content is visible without having to scroll down the page.

Create a Content Experience Strategy That Delivers

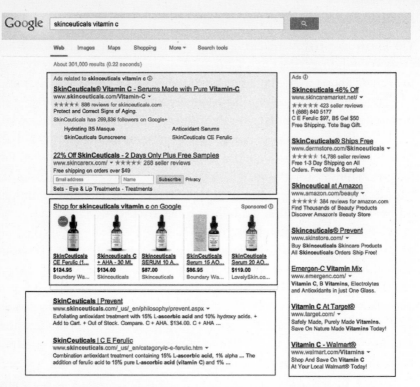

Figure 7.4 Google Paid and Organic Search Results for SkinCeuticals Vitamin C

The economics of organic and paid search differ greatly. Paid-search results are a function of the dollar amount spent and a quality score. The price is often cost prohibitive for many brands. Organic results are free and can be improved by search engine optimization (SEO); however, it does require content creation and specialized SEO knowledge.

How do organic and paid search results compare? According to Wordstream, which creates software to optimize search results, paid search performs better for high-commercial intent search terms such as "front-loading clothes dryer." On the other hand, organic performs better in generic searches for information such as, "Who is Benjamin Franklin?" It is unclear which performs better in cases of branded key words such as "Whirlpool driers" or local searches.[42]

Is There a Quick Way to SEO?

The most effective way to improve organic search results is by creating great content. People share worthy content and link back to it in their posts and blogs, both of which enhance search-engine rankings. Creating great titles that concisely describe the content, and include a few keywords, can also improve search results. Remember, these titles are actually displayed in search results so make sure that prospects will find them interesting.

In Figure 7.4, the title for the first organic search result is SkinCeuticals Prevent. (Not exactly riveting.) The description that follows the title is called a metadescription—essentially data about data. In this case the meta description starts with "Exfoliating antioxidant treatment..." These descriptions should be short, less than 150 characters, and compelling.

Embedding targeted keywords into our content, images, and metadata also increases the opportunity for our content to be found in a web search. Do not overdo it just make sure it is mentioned in the first 50 words and a couple of times in the pages that follow. Creating keyword lists for our industries that reflect how our prospects and customers might search for us, and testing these terms with tools like Google's Keyword Planner that shows traffic for each term can help us identify the most relevant and highest-trafficked phrases to use.

Finally, tagging images enhances SEO. In addition to crawling the keywords in our text, search engines note the names of our image files and image searches direct people to our digital properties. To get the most out of tagging, create descriptive, keyword-rich file names, not just "Image 145." Checking web analytics to see what phrases our customers might be using is useful fodder for photo naming. Using *img ALT tags*, in addition to the image name, can further enhance results. Technically these tags specify alternative text to display if an image cannot be rendered; however, these details of the image—who is in the photo or what products are being shown—offer rich opportunities to improve a search result.

Whatever we do, we should not try and game the system, because the system knows. The practices mentioned above are clean. *Black hat SEO* is the term that describes unethical practices designed to fool the search engines into awarding higher results than is warranted

Create a Content Experience Strategy That Delivers

according to their algorithms. It is only a matter of time until black hatters get busted; having a site removed from the index altogether is not an uncommon result.

Would Paid Media Expand the Reach?

Paid media, or advertising, can be successfully combined with content to reach beyond an organization's own database, fans, and followers to gain the attention of new audiences and to remarket content to existing customers in different channels or venues. Drawing from their enormous amount of customer data, some social networks are able to narrowly target content in ways that have not been previously possible. We will discuss these converged strategies in more depth in Chapter 9.

How Will This Play in Dubai?

In this day of borderless communication and commerce, content knows no boundaries; it can show up everywhere. As a result, we must consider how our content will be perceived and distributed across cultures as sensibilities and preferences vary. The condom manufacturer Durex experienced a social media snafu when it asked its Facebook fans to vote on a city to receive its SOS service, which rushes delivery of condoms to the point of need, and a town located in a conservative Muslim province in Turkey was selected.[43] It is also useful to consider early on how our branding, distribution, trademarks, and patents will transfer across borders.[44]

A global perspective is essential even in our own backyards as Nielsen predicts that in the next five years, multicultural clients will drive 86 percent of the total growth on spending in retail in the United States.[45] If we are not intentionally cultivating multicultural relationships through our marketing, Nielsen warns that we are limiting ourselves to 10 percent of forecasted U.S. growth.[46]

What about Global Search?

If we embrace global content opportunities, it is a good idea to explore local search options. Although Google is the most-used search engine in the world, there are others to consider if we want to make sure our content is found in local markets. According to ComScore, the Chinese search engine Baidu has the second-largest worldwide share of searches (8.2 percent),[47] but is the number one provider within China (78.6 percent of Chinese market).[48] Yahoo! comes in third on a worldwide basis (4.9 percent), followed by the Russian search engine Yandex, which holds 2.8 percent of worldwide market, but over 60 percent of the Russian market.[49] The bottom line: Check out who the players are in the markets in which we are interested in playing.

Is Our Content Working?

A *2014 B2B Content Marketing Benchmark Report* by the Content Marketing Institute and Marketing Profs, found that only 42 percent of B2B businesses believe that their content is effective.[50] A similar study of B2C companies conducted by the same parties found that only 34 percent of B2C companies believe their content works.[51]

That is a hard place to be when content is such an essential part of the customer experience. How do we know if our content is working?

Many content metrics exist; the challenge is picking the right ones. Metrics should reflect what is important to our organization and ultimately help answer the question, "Are we any closer to our business goals?" They also need to be understandable, actionable, and able to be consistently measured. While each company will have to determine the specific metrics that are most relevant for its business, there are five general areas to consider: awareness, engagement, sharing, lead generation, and conversion. The latter metrics demonstrate marketing's contribution to revenue and are particularly interesting to other members of the C-suite. It speaks their language.

> **Awareness.** Are we exposing new people to our brand, product, or service? How many unique visitors are we seeing? What is our audience growth rate? What is our share of voice relative to our competitors? What is our ranking in SERPs? What are our traffic sources?

Engagement. What is the impact of our content? Are we inspiring people to interact with us? What do our prospects and customers do with our content? Do they simply click through or vote, comment, endorse (like), or favorite it? What degree of involvement does this reveal? What is our abandonment rate? Is this changing?

Where is it being shared and who is reacting? What are they saying? What are we doing that is getting their attention?

Lead Generation. Is our content drawing people closer to us? Are they finding themselves in our solutions? What is our rate of return visits and how long are they spending on our site? What questions are they asking that our content is answering? Are there other questions we should be addressing? Which channels are recruiting the most new leads? How big is our pipeline?

Conversion. Are our experiences creating customers? What is our conversion rate? Do we have content that effectively nurtures them through the customer-experience journey? How long is our cycle time from lead generation to sale? How often do our marketing-qualified leads (MQL) become sales-qualified leads (SQL)? Marketing-automation technology, which we will discuss in Chapter 10, makes it possible to capture the data necessary to answer these questions accurately.

Can We Lengthen the Life of This Content?

Creating a resource center on our website creates a long-term home for our content. By making it easy for people to find and share our content, we can enhance our resourcefulness, increase the stickiness of our websites, and lengthen the life of our content. To reap the benefits, content must remain relevant, up-to-date, and be easy to locate on our site. Great examples of content creators and maintainers are Marketo, HubSpot, Kissmetrics, and Kaiser Permanente Share.

Who Is Going to Create All This Content?

Content creation takes time, people, and technology. An important question to consider is whether we have access to the creative talent that we need to generate great content internally or if we need to look outside of our organizations. Content needs are growing; 72 percent of B2C marketers and 73 percent of their B2B counterparts are producing more content than they did a year ago.[52] How do they manage the content load? B2B marketers outsource content more often than their B2B counterparts (49 percent vs. 44 percent). Writing and design are the activities most likely to be outsourced.[53]

Tap Internal Sources

Internal content creators can be found outside of our marketing organizations. Front-line employees or product developers often have the inside scoop and understanding for which our customers may be looking. Who are the valuable sources of content within our organizations and what is the best way to tap their knowledge and individual social-media activities?

To equip brands with the education, programming, policies, and customized strategies their employees need to confidently serve as brand ambassadors across social media channels, Larry's company created the Digital Influence Group Spark™. Using proprietary survey technology they access individual employees' social-media behaviors across eight dimensions of Social-Indicator Types. With these results, they create customized media-engagement plans that are unique to every participant and reflect each companies' corporate media policies. Programs like Spark quickly and consistently educate employees on how to participate in social media on behalf of the brand and in the changing social landscape, thereby multiplying the number of content creators or contributors available.

Get the C-Suite Involved

More than 75 percent of executives worldwide believe that CEOs should be active in social media, according to research conducted by public relations firm Weber Shandwick and KRC Research.[54] Reasons cited include enhancing "information-sharing throughout the business, improve company reputation, demonstrates innovation, humanizes the company, and improves business results."[55]

A profile of the most social CEOs shows that they are quite knowledgeable about social media, making use of a variety of platforms

Create a Content Experience Strategy That Delivers

in well-crafted, strategic ways to connect with multiple stakeholders. Many keep a blog that they write themselves and understand the significance of the website as their anchor and home base. Their interactions have an appropriate tone—not too formal and not to loose—and they are responsive to the questions and comments of their readers.

Draw from Our Broader Ecosystems

Tapping our broader ecosystems is another useful strategy for developing and distributing content. The nonprofit United Way of America, for example, has two fulltime staff members working with more than 1,200 local offices throughout the country.[56] Each of these local offices has partnerships with schools, government agencies, businesses, financial institutions, development organizations, community groups, and faith institutions in their communities. United Way is able to magnify its marketing efforts with the help of these local partners.

For example, through its Alternative Spring Break program, United Way provides opportunities for college students and corporate employees to volunteer their time working in areas devastated by natural disasters or with students in at-risk communities. The nonprofit works with sponsoring organizations to deliver these volunteer experiences and to cocreate related content that is distributed through their partners' preferred marketing channels and their own.[57]

The practice of cocreating and scaling distribution with partner networks is known as *brandscaping*. In his book *Brandscaping*, Andrew Davis describes how unconventional partnerships can be used to create and distribute content. Brandscaping works because the customers with whom we are interested in engaging are likely to already be fans, followers, and subscribers of other brands. If we can create symbiotic marketing relationships with those companies, we will be able to expand our customer base one network at a time, rather than one customer at a time.

Using External Technology Providers and Agencies

Many journalists are filling content-related roles in companies and agencies as content budgets grow. Some companies and agencies are bringing this writing talent in-house, while others are augmenting their capabilities through strategic partnerships.

Racepoint Global's content partner, Skyword.com, has a content platform that automates the entire content-marketing process from writer management to content creation, editorial review, social promotion, and measurement and analytics. Brands and agencies use the platform to simplify and improve content creation and publication and to analyze how their content is performing in real time. Brands also take advantage of Skyword's content strategists to facilitate development of content strategy, as well as their network of more than 20,000 professional writers who have a broad range of domain expertise to produce content. Racepoint partnered with IBM and Skyword to create Midsize Insider. Other potential content partners include Scripted.com, Contently.com, WriterAccess.com, and Zerys.com.

How are brands using social media to create remarkable customer experiences? We will explore that question in the chapter that follows.

QUESTIONS FOR CONSIDERATION

- What portion of your current marketing budget do you invest in content creation?
- How rich are your customer experiences?
- How close are you to being able to provide contextualized experiences to your prospects and customers? What is getting in the way?
- Are you able to coordinate your customer experiences across channels?
- How do you create your content experience strategy?
- Have you conducted a content audit and mapped your assets across the customer experience journey by persona?
- Are you running your content creation efforts like a newsroom?
- What resources do you have for content creation?
- What is your next step?

Create a Content Experience Strategy That Delivers

RESOURCES

Influencers We Recommend

- *Jay Baer*. Baer is an author, speaker, and marketing consultant. His latest book is *Youtility: Why Smart Marketing Is about Help Not Hype* sheds light on how to create useful marketing. His blog, *Convince & Convert*, is one of the highest ranked content blogs around. Keep up with his latest thinking at www.jaybaer.com and follow him on Twitter @JayBaer.

- *Andrew Davis*. Davis is an author, speaker, and marketer who has also spent some time wrangling for *The Muppets*. The author of *Brandscaping*, Davis has a lot to say about creating new partnerships to accomplish marketing goals. Learn more about Davis and the book at www.brandscapingbook.com and by following him on Twitter @TPLDrew.

- *Tom Gerace*. Gerace is the founder, CEO, and director of Skyword, a content production platform. A plethora of resources regarding content marketing is available on *The Content Standard* (www.contentstandard.com), Skyword's newsletter, and on www.Skyword.com. Follow Gerace on Twitter @Tom_Gerace or @tomgerace.

- *Ann Handley*. The chief content officer of Marketing Profs, a professional development resource for marketers, Handley is also the coauthor of *Content Rules*. She cofounded ClickZ.com, a source of interactive marketing news and commentary. Follow Handley @MarketingProfs and be sure to check out their website as well: www.marketingprofs.com.

- *Joe Pulizzi*. The founder of the Content Marketing Institute (formerly Junta42) and a leading evangelist for content marketing, Pulizzi is also a prolific author. He has written *Epic Content Marketing*, *Get Content, Get Customers*, and *Managing*

Content Marketing. The Content Marketing Institute publishes *Chief Content Officer* magazine, runs Content Marketing World, and has a wealth of resources available on the subject at www.ContentMarketingInstitute.com. To have your finger on the pulse of where content marketing is heading see www.joepulizzi.com or follow him on Twitter @joepulizzi.

- *David Meerman Scott.* An online-marketing strategist who has authored several books including *The New Rules of Marketing and PR*, Meerman Scott was one of the folks who got social media and content marketing early on. Read his blog at www.davidmeermanscott.com and follow him on Twitter @dmscott.

- *Brian Solis.* A principal analyst at Altimeter Group, which focuses on disruptive technology and its impact on businesses, Solis is also a speaker and writer. Solis' latest book, *What's the Future of Business?*, explores how business and customer relationships are changing. Connect with Solis on Twitter @briansolis and read his blog at www.briansolis.com.

Hashtags to Explore

- #blogger
- #content
- #contentmarketing
- #contentstrategy
- #emailmarketing
- #mobile
- #mobilemarketing
- #mobileweb

(continued)

(continued)

- #omnichannel
- #seo
- #sew (search engine watch)
- #share
- #socialmediamarking

Chapter 8

Engage Customers via Social Communities

"The unexpected connection is more powerful than the one that is obvious."

—Heraclitus, Greek philosopher

When you are a respected thought leader and provider in an industry that is prime for disruptive change, being part of the conversations that will shape the future of the industry is essential. Recognizing this imperative, Kaiser Permanente (KP), one of America's leading health-care providers and managed-care organizations, is actively creating environments for its multiple constituents—members, employees, policy makers, other members of the industry, and the press—to discuss and influence the future of health care.

Being an innovator and thought leader is not a new role for KP. The company's pioneering roots reach back over 65 years when, as part of its efforts to provide medical care for workers on the Colorado River Aqueduct Project, it started one of the first prepaid health-care plans. Taking a fresh look at the way in which health care is delivered remains a high priority for KP and is part of the reason that the company is continually recognized as a top performer and a leader in providing quality care.[1]

To continually foster new approaches, KP formed an internal Innovation Consultancy—born out of work with the design firm IDEO—that focuses on better ways to deliver health care.[2] The Innovation Consultancy makes its services available to the entire organization and jumpstarted the Innovation Learning Network, a consortium of 10 health-care organizations to expand

213

the conversation beyond its own organization. The group meets regularly to share ideas and results.

The Center for Total Health, KP's learning space in Washington, DC, brings additional voices into the conversation. The vision for this unique conference center is to be "a place for the nation to discuss the future of health care."[3] Interactive touchscreen exhibits about wellness and meeting rooms equipped with Cisco Telepresence, which enables local and virtual meeting participation, encourage ongoing discussion.

To engage the company's constituent community and the general public in conversation about wellness and health policy, KP has a new, robust digital presence: Kaiser Permanente Share. A brand journalism platform where all the company's communications and marketing efforts can live, the site offers both thought leadership and news content. It replaces 15,000 pages of content that were previously scattered around the web on two websites, seven corporate blogs, and numerous social channels, simplifying access and improving the visibility of the content so that it can reach a broader audience. By publishing all content to one destination, it also maximizes opportunities for the organization to stand out as a leader in the health-care space from an SEO perspective.

A sophisticated, backend content management system, combined with a simple interface, allows for greater participation in content creation from employees across the organization and brings more voices into the conversation. Members of the KP community can hear their CEO discuss health policy, in the same space where they receive messages from their doctors, make appointments, read about breaking health-care news, and receive online coaching about healthy lifestyles. Between all of its forums, only a fraction of which are captured here, KP is getting more people talking about total health.

Community Matters

Kaiser Permanente understands the importance of community in providing the necessary support and education that encourages people to take care of their health. Community provides the fodder for innovation and forms the coalitions that make large social change possible. The need for community is not new, but

214

in the last decade social media has created digital communities that can overlay, augment and, in some cases, replace physical communities.

Looking for Connection, Information, and Fun?

Two types of entities comprise social media: social networks and social communities. As we saw in Chapter 3, a network is the social structure made up of people connected to an individual. Each of us has our own social network that includes our family, friends, work colleagues, classmates, neighbors, and more; we are the glue that brings these people together. Popular online social networks include Facebook, LinkedIn, Google+, Pinterest, Instagram, and Twitter.

Although motivations for participation vary from person to person, the primary reason people join social networks is to connect with others, to maintain existing relationships and meet new people, be they personal or professional. Sharing content creates connection and can take the form of status updates, uploaded photos and videos, presentations posted through SlideShare, likes and comments, and even retweeting of brand content if it is compelling enough. The most active sharers on social media are from Saudi Arabia; more than 60 percent of Saudi respondents indicated that they share everything or most things online. This compares with 50 percent in India, 24 percent worldwide, and 16 percent in the United States.[4]

People also look to their social networks to provide them with vetted information, whether it is discovery or search oriented. These trusted sources simplify people's lives and help them to make better decisions. According to the Generation C Study conducted by IBM, 85 percent of users say social networks help them to decide what to purchase.[5] Combing newsfeeds, following hashtag-designed discussions, and actively querying friends and colleagues through social search features like Facebook's Graph Search, Google's Search plus Your World, Bing Social, or Quora expand their personal resources.

People also enjoy social networks because they can be fun. Profile surfing is enjoyable for many, as are the myriad contests, games, and creative challenges that social media offer. They also provide a popular public platform for self-expression.

Engage Customers via Social Communities

Have an Interest to Further Explore?

Social communities are vehicles for connection around an interest (fitness) or event (#Super-Bowl), a place (work), a sense of shared purpose (health-care reform), or a common set of needs (marketing tips). Social communities may be public or private (password protected), branded (owned by an organization) or independent (established by users or trade association).

People join social communities to learn, find others that share their interests, and for self-expression. They join branded social communities to be able to collaborate with brands. People may or may not know each other when they join the group and can be involved in multiple communities depending upon their interest, time, and qualifications. In contrast to social environments characterized by passive observation or anonymous contributions, in social communities people are known. They share ideas and feel connected. Some groups also connect offline, using tools like Meetup.com to facilitate gatherings.

Social networks and communities are often intertwined because community can take root anywhere. Groups form on LinkedIn. People form networks of followers around their Instagram uploads and Pinterest pins. Like most everything these days, the boundaries are blurring.

Social Media Has Taken the World by Storm

It is hard to believe that these pervasive communication tools have only been around for a decade. People and organizations everywhere have adopted tools that once were the domain of academics at CERN (the Organisation Europeenne pour la Recherche Nucleaire) in Switzerland or college students at Harvard. A lot of statistics follow on the next page or two, but bear with us, because they tell a fascinating and important story for marketers.

Social media has become a fundamental component of today's marketing toolkit; 93 percent of marketers say they use social media.[6] Big companies, small companies, nonprofits, and even governments are tweeting, posting, pinning, and uploading. Social media is maturing as organizations become increasingly sophisticated about its use.

A recent study by the public relations firm Burston-Marsteller found that companies are using social media to engage with their constituents, not to just broadcast information.[7] Fifty-seven percent of companies on Facebook and 67 percent on Twitter actively connect with their fans and followers by responding to comments on their walls and timelines or with @mentions.[8]

YouTube is no longer just a place for posting funny videos; 79 percent of companies have a branded YouTube channel and many are successfully using it for educational purposes and branding.[9] Customers have also moved beyond status updates; more than 10.4 million conversations about Fortune Global 100 companies that take place monthly in social spaces.[10]

Social Media Has a Global Reach

People are active on social networks around the world and their time commitment is significant; social media accounts for roughly 20 percent of people's total time online on computers and 30 percent of their time online via mobile.[11] Facebook alone has over 1.3 billion monthly active users. Of those, 60 percent log in daily and average of 130 friends with whom they connect.[12] Forty-eight percent of 18- to 34-year-olds check Facebook when they wake up.[13] But Facebook is not just a young people's playground. In recent months, its fastest-growing age demographic was 45- to 54-year-olds.[14] Facebook remains the biggest player, but it is by no means the only player.

Twitter is the fastest-growing social network in the world in terms of active users; 21 percent of the world's Internet population use Twitter every month. Twitter's fastest-growing age demographic is slightly older than Facebook's: 55- to 64-year-olds.[15]

LinkedIn remains the largest professional network, with two new users joining every second. Google+ is growing substantially, revealing just how quickly companies are getting up to speed on new platforms. It took only 16 days for Google+ to reach 10 million users. That compares with 780 days for Twitter and 852 days for Facebook.[16]

Social media use is by no means an American phenomenon. The majority of Facebook, LinkedIn, and YouTube users are from outside the United States. These numbers would be larger if Twitter and Facebook were freely available in China. The country is not lacking

Engage Customers via Social Communities

for social media, however. Nine of the top 15 social networks in the world are based in China (see Figure 8.1).

Social Media Differs Around the Globe

There are many variations on the social media theme around the world reflecting the nuances of each market. In China, for example, Guan.Xi focuses on mobile social discovery, helping introduce people to each other, enhancing opportunities for face-to-face contact. Its founder, Alvin Graylin, who also serves as CEO of mInfo, the leading mobile search service in China, explains why these features are popular: "It makes it a lot easier for people to start conversations—social is still an issue for a lot of the younger generation because they don't have brothers/sisters/cousins."[17] Key features of Guan.Xi include a recommendation engine that identifies people in the vicinity who may be interesting—whether for business, social, or dating purposes—based upon predetermined criteria, and the ability to push a button and instantly begin chatting with that person.

Social media tend to be quite integrated in China. Tencent's Weixin (We Chat), for example, is a mobile platform that combines instant messaging, video calls, group chatting, photo sharing, and status updates.[18] The microblogging site Sina Weibo combines the capabilities of Twitter and Facebook and incorporates rich media. Infrastructure challenges temporarily limit adoption, however. According to Graylin, the majority of the 500 million China Mobile subscribers are still working on a 2G network despite the fact that they have 3G/4G phones. (As a reference, G stands for the generation of the mobile network. The higher the number, the more efficient the network.) This is likely to be a temporary challenge. The other Chinese carriers, Unicom and Telecom, already operate on 3G; Graylin expects China Mobile to jump directly from 2G to 4G in the near future.

In South Africa, the largest social network is Mxit.[19] With over 10 million users, the network has a broader reach throughout the country than Facebook (6 million users) and Twitter (1.1 million subscribers). Mobile is key in South Africa. It has made it possible for a continent that previously had very little communications technology to be able to connect almost all of its citizens.

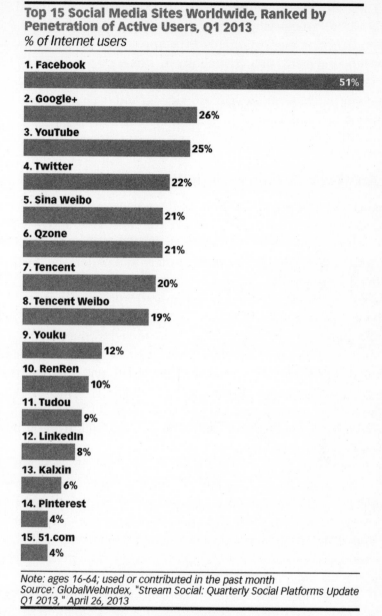

Top 15 Social Media Sites Worldwide, Ranked by Penetration of Active Users, Q1 2013
% of Internet users

1. Facebook — 51%
2. Google+ — 26%
3. YouTube — 25%
4. Twitter — 22%
5. Sina Weibo — 21%
6. Qzone — 21%
7. Tencent — 20%
8. Tencent Weibo — 19%
9. Youku — 12%
10. RenRen — 10%
11. Tudou — 9%
12. LinkedIn — 8%
13. Kaixin — 6%
14. Pinterest — 4%
15. 51.com — 4%

Note: ages 16-64; used or contributed in the past month
Source: GlobalWebIndex, "Stream Social: Quarterly Social Platforms Update Q1 2013," April 26, 2013

Figure 8.1   Top 15 Social Media Sites Worldwide

Source: www.emarketer.com/Article/Which-Social-Networks-Growing-Fastest-Worldwide/1009884

Engage Customers via Social Communities

There are several features that make Mxit work well for the African market. Its text messaging pricing is a fraction of the cost of SMS texts, making adoption more affordable. The app serves as a mobile wallet, facilitating payments in a community in which people may not have access to traditional banking services. Its mobile marketplace allows people to purchase music, games, videos, and wallpaper, providing sources of entertainment for people who may not have iPads, PCs, TVs, or Xboxes.

Social Media Is Increasingly Visual

Some of the most popular players on the scene are visual platforms—Pinterest, Snapchat, Instagram, Tumblr, YouTube, Vine, and Facebook. When you consider that Facebook purchased Instagram for $2 billion, Yahoo! acquired Tumblr for approximately $1.1 billion, and Snapchat declined a reported $3 billion offer from Facebook, it appears as if a picture is worth even more than a thousand words these days.

Pinterest is a visual content sharing service that is organized around pinboards to which users "pin" their favorite images, infographics, and videos. In its first three years of operation, Pinterest amassed 70 million users representing 20 percent of women who use the Internet in the United States. Tumblr is a microblogging platform that allows users to post multimedia to their dashboard. The company currently hosts 158 million blogs with over 70 billion posts. The ephemeral messaging platform Snapchat allows users to take photos and videos up to 10 seconds in length, add text and drawings, send them to the people they choose, and have them disappear from the recipients' phone and the Snapchat server after a designated period. Over 350 million photos are shared through the app daily. Instagram, the photo taking, enhancing, and sharing app we discussed in Chapter 4, also allows users to create videos of up to 15 seconds in length. YouTube remains a favorite, with over 100 hours of video uploaded to the platform per minute.[20] In 2013, Twitter introduced Vine, a mobile app that allows people to create and share short (6 seconds or less) looping videos. It has caught on like wildfire, becoming the most-downloaded free app within the Apple store in just over three months. According to the 7th Chamber, a social video agency, five tweets a second contain a Vine link.[21]

Niche Is the Future

Despite the fact that Facebook now has over 1.3 billion active members, in the next few years we will see a proliferation of smaller, interest-based networks and communities. Once again, our customers are driving this change. Niche networks can be a more efficient way of gaining the information for which our customers are looking than larger one-size-fits-all networks. In addition to search, they facilitate discovery. Smaller communities means less time spent filtering through streams of photos, updates, and advertising. Niche networks also offer the opportunity for deeper engagement with like-minded colleagues; it's hard for 1.3 billion people to enjoy each other.

Since 2011, approximately 3 million teens (ages 13–17) have left Facebook, many of which are opting for smaller networks.[22] A new image-based social network, WeHeartIt.com, has over 25 million users, 80 percent of which are under the age of 24, and is adding 1 million users monthly. Its distinctively young feel is prompted by a platform that, according to CEO Ranah Edelin, prohibits comments so as to prevent verbal bullying or negativity.[23] Over 23 million people have joined Care2.com to be part of an environment in which people are actively making make a difference on issues about which they care. The network facilitates connection, knowledge sharing, and job finding.

Who Is Not Using Social Media?

Not everyone is the world is active on social media or the Internet. Of the world's 7.1 billion people, an estimated 61 percent are not presently using the Internet according to the International Telecommunications Union (ITU).[24] The majority of users (77 percent) are in what ITU defines as the developed world. The least-penetrated regions are Africa and Asia and the Pacific. Lack of connectivity is partially responsible as are Internet *black holes*, areas of the world where news is not free to circulate due to government policy.[25]

Some people within developed markets remain unconnected. According to a recent study conducted by the Pew Foundation, 15 percent of American adults ages 18 and older do not use the Internet or e-mail.[26] When asked why, over a third said they did not think the Internet was relevant to them. Just under a third said that they found it too difficult to go online, either because they were physically unable or because they were worried about spam, spyware, and hackers. (This latter represents a significant increase over earlier years.) Others (19 percent) found the cost of owning or paying for access to a computer to be prohibitive or they simply did not have access (7 percent).

What Have We Learned?

When marketers made their first steps into social media, there were some casualties. We did not fully understand why our customers where there, but knowing they were there was enough of a reason to pique our interest in being there, too.

We learned over time that social media was not another broadcast medium. Many times we entered these communities with a sales orientation, talking about ourselves and peddling what we had to offer. This approach was not well received. Our formerly passive audiences had evolved into active social networks and communities. People were not congregating online to hear our sales pitches. They were there to connect and to learn, not to be sold. We had to adopt a humble stance of learning with, rather than selling to, of being participants, not peddlers.

We also learned that social media is about conversation and mutuality—give and take. To have our fingers on the pulse of our consumers' sentiments, we needed to listen as well as to speak. To be responsive we have to live on the network, not just check in occasionally, because discussion is immediate and can take place often. Because social media is a dialogue, engagement meant that we could not dictate the terms of our interactions; we had to be prepared to lose control of the conversation. This was a hard pill to swallow for many of us who were trained in the no-surprises school of marketing—and our corporate lawyers.

As new channels and devices emerged, we learned that people's preferences can change overnight. If we wanted to be where they were, we had to follow their lead. In short order it became clear that each of these channels has a different purpose and personality. We needed to get to know each before jumping in, so we could have an appropriate presence.

As our customers became always connected, we came to understand that we would need an omnichannel experience to match their media consumption habits. To create a seamless and consistent customer experience, our social media efforts would need to be coordinated, driven by our overall experience strategy, rather than by specific channel strategies.

We learned that if our customers were pleased with us, they would share their experiences broadly. They would help us manage our reputations, augment our customer service efforts, and optimize our marketing and innovation efforts. On the other hand, if our customers were not getting the responses they needed from our other channels—sales or customer service—they would take to the airways and make their needs known there. We are still learning to manage customer issues quickly and publicly and coordinate our efforts internally to resolve problems before asking for a higher level of involvement from our customers.

We also learned that engagement requires that our brands be accessible and have a point of view to which people can relate. We needed to drop the formality and speak personally. Today, we are empowering people throughout our organizations to connect directly with our customers, balancing broader connection with simplicity and multiple voices with a unified brand message.

We learned the hard way about transparency, about being honest, open, and empathetic. We now know that where we manufacture our products, how we treat our employees and suppliers, what we pay our top executives, and how our activities impact the environment all matter. Whereas only a handful of years ago we balked about transparency, today our concern is whether we are being transparent enough.[27]

What Are Marketers Doing with Social Media?

Having learned a lot over the past decade, what are marketers now able to accomplish with social media? Plenty. Social networks and communities are robust digital vehicles through which we can interact directly with our prospects and customers across the entire customer experience journey. Social networks and communities serve different purposes, however.

Through social networks we can successfully build awareness, encourage simple engagement, and garner feedback. Conversation among these loose networks follows the pattern of comment and response, with social media managers largely fostering engagement. Communities, on the other hand, are more conducive to achieving more complex goals such as capturing insight, encouraging collaboration, and fostering advocacy. Conversation in these more stable and connected communities is multidirectional; when well nurtured by experienced community managers, these discussions deepen over time, creating shared value.

Build Awareness and Generate Sales

Social media is successfully being used for brand building. To build a following for its brand, the teen-oriented fashion retailer Wet Seal hired the highly popular 16-year old influencer, Miss MeghanMakeup, to create a SnapChat story—a collection of pictures—documenting her life the weekend before Christmas. Clad in Wet Seal gear, she snapped images of herself making cookies, hanging out, and playing with her dog. The result: 9,000 new followers for the company—it had 2,000 before the weekend—and 6,000 views of the video.[28] Social is also being used to tee-up sales.

According to HubSpot's *2013 Inbound Marketing* report, social networks produce almost double the amount of leads of traditional advertising, telemarketing, and paid search. Of the 3,000 marketers HubSpot surveyed globally, 52 percent had sourced a lead from Facebook, 43 percent of companies acquired a customer via LinkedIn or a company blog, and 36 percent from Twitter.[29] Every social network is getting savvy about sales generation. Observing that when pinners find something they like on Pinterest, they are often ready to act—a trigger—Pinterest has created rich pins to make it easier for them to do so. Product pins include real-time pricing, availability, and information on where the item can be purchased. Alerts let pinners know when items have gone on sale. Of people with Pinterest accounts, 21 percent have purchased an item after viewing it on Pinterest.[30]

Break News in Real-Time

Organizations are using social media to disseminate news. NASA broke the news "We have ice on Mars" and @NYTimes announced the appointment of an Argentinian Cardinal as Pope on Twitter. We learned of the death of Michael Jackson and the engagement of Prince William on Twitter. The Boston Marathon bombing was first described on Twitter; traditional news sources quoted tweets in their coverage. Twitter announced its SEC filing for its initial public offering and marked the moment when its stock—TWTR—began trading on the Stock Exchange with the tweet: #Ring![31]

Enhance the Product Experience

Social media can augment our brand experience. To engage with its viewers, the producers of MTV's television series *Teen Wolf* launched an eight-week game on Facebook that ran in parallel with the show's second season. Players set out to solve a murder mystery using clues revealed by the show's characters that players "friended" on Facebook. As they unlocked exclusive photos and video, fans gained a sense of intimacy with the characters and more in-depth knowledge of the show. The game engaged the show's existing viewers and attracted new fans. It's success directly contributed to the show's renewal for a third season.[32]

Similarly, social media can put real names, faces, and Twitter handles on our brands to create a refreshing and authentic presence. The Washington Nationals baseball team (the Nats) posts every player's Twitter handle on the Jumbotron when he comes up to bat, encouraging fans to connect with players. The Nats also encourage fans to place themselves in the Nats' story by uploading photos of the #Nationals to its Instagram site and to tag themselves in the official panoramic game photos.

In celebration of the 100th anniversary of the favorite Tin Pan Alley song, "Take Me Out to The Ball Game," the Nats ran an

Engage Customers via Social Communities

American Idol–style contest in which they invited fans to vote for their favorite local singing group to lead the crowd in a rip-roaring rendition of the song during the seventh-inning stretch. They also invited fans to create a Nationals-themed video of themselves and their friends singing what has become the unofficial anthem of American baseball.

Improve Our Customer Service

Companies use social networks and communities to augment their customer service efforts. Apple has myriad customer support communities that are organized around products. As Figure 8.2 illustrates, people are encouraged to their share tips and solutions with fellow Apple product users from all around the world in these social spaces.[33] Similarly, the software company Intuit has a customer-service forum for its QuickBooks finance product. Members of the online community answer about 80 percent of user's questions.[34] User comments have been the source of numerous significant changes to its software.[35]

Many companies (32 percent) have established dedicated Twitter accounts to manage customer inquiries and complaints.[36] Within the

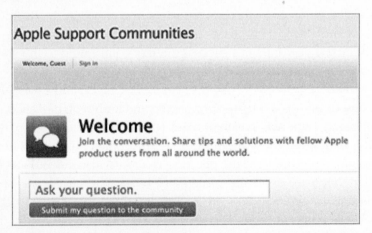

Figure 8.2   Customers Share Tips and Solutions in Social Communities
Source: https://discussions.apple.com/index.jspa

last year, 17 percent of Americans have used social media to resolve a customer-service issue.[37] Expectations are high for responsiveness for companies on Twitter; 72 percent of customers expect a response to their complaint within an hour. If companies do not meet those expectations, 38 percent feel more negative about the company and 60 percent initiate "unpleasant actions" to express their discontent.[38]

How are companies doing? The average response time is 4.6 hours, although times vary considerably.[39] Needless to say, given the responsive nature of social media, these delayed reactions do not go over well with customers. The tweets below tell the story of a disappointed customer's experience after receiving a half-filled taco at Taco Bell.

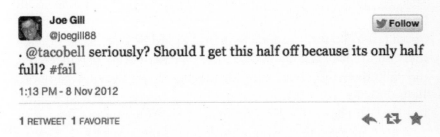

Joe Gill
@joegill88   Follow

. @tacobell seriously? Should I get this half off because its only half full? #fail

1:13 PM - 8 Nov 2012

1 RETWEET 1 FAVORITE

Figure 8.3   Joe Tweets About His Disappointment

Two weeks later, when he still had not received a response, he tweeted once again:

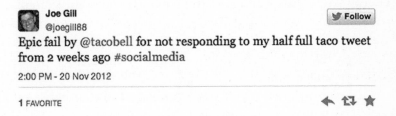

Joe Gill
@joegill88   Follow

Epic fail by @tacobell for not responding to my half full taco tweet from 2 weeks ago #socialmedia

2:00 PM - 20 Nov 2012

1 FAVORITE

Figure 8.4   In the Absence of a Response, Joe Tweets Again

Joe has not been back since and he is not alone; 55 percent of people walk away from an intended purchase because of a poor customer experience. If we are going to have a social media presence,

Engage Customers via Social Communities

we have to be responsive. To see how it is done when it is done well, follow Nike Support, JetBlue, Chase Support, or Nokia Care, voted the most responsive companies on Twitter.[40]

Crowdsource Ideas

Social media is terrific for engaging our customers and crowdsourcing content. Anyone who has watched the commercials during the Super Bowl in recent years has seen what can happen when we spark our customers' energy, creativity, and insight. Over 20,000 people have submitted ads to Doritos' "Crash the Bowl" contest during the past six years—that is a lot of engagement. The creativity evident in the submissions has been remarkable, and fun, resulting in some of the best ads aired during this top-dollar media event.[41] Through its Be The Buyer program, Modcloth.com invites its customers to serve as virtual fashion buyers for the company. Would be buyers can preview items on the site, cast their vote for which should be manufactured, and rally their friends to vote for their favorites as items garnering the most votes are available for sale within weeks. Take a look at the You Made It Happen section on their site to see the favorites.

The Canadian television series *Continuum* invited its viewers to influence the final outcome of the series. The storyline of the science-fiction series features time travel and political struggle between two opposing groups wanting to influence the community's future. Viewers were brought into the story and influenced its arc by choosing one of the opposing views—law enforcers or liberators—and then voting, sharing related videos, pictures, and comments on Facebook and Twitter to convince others of their point of view. Dedicated hashtags facilitated a robust political discussion and videos released periodically on Vine by the show's producers fueled the conversation.[42]

The American rock band, Pearl Jam asked one of its superfans, who had seen them in concert more than 100 times, to determine the band's set list for an upcoming concert. The devotee came though. After approximately 40 iterations, he created what some fans are calling the greatest Pearl Jam set list of all time. Check our notes to see a copy of the set list.[43]

Amplify Our Content via Influencers

The impact of word of mouth referrals is well documented. Our prospects and customers look to their friends, family, industry experts, and people they respect or admire (bloggers) to discover new things, educate themselves, and make decisions. Being able to tap into this influence network magnifies our marketing efforts. Influencers have successfully assisted in new product and service launches, event promotion, brand advocacy, and crisis management. They often help with content creation, product development, and competitive analysis as well.

When Cindy Gorden, vice president of new media and marketing partnerships at Universal Orlando Resort, was charged with announcing the launch of a new themed environment, The Wizarding World of Harry Potter, her entire marketing plan consisted of reaching out to seven bloggers. The lucky seven were able to interact with the set designer of the Harry Potter movies to get a sense of what the park would bring to life—Hogwarts, Hogsmeade, and even Butterbeer—and were then asked to blog about it. Within 24 hours, Universal's site had more than 1.5 million visitors as a result of these seven blog postings. Over 350 million people from around the world eventually learned about the new attraction through supplemental news coverage.[44] The story was compelling, and the bloggers influential, so that was all she needed.

Some companies are using *referral-marketing* programs to encourage customers to promote their brands to friends. Successful programs provide customers with a generous incentive to share and offer their friends an opportunity that they cannot get anywhere else. These offers are balanced to maintain a sense of equality among advocates and their friends. Testing and optimizing ensure the best results.

Extole, for example, develops end-to-end customer referral programs that can be shared via channels such as e-mail, social media, or a website. Personalized landing pages enhance the referral experiences for friends. For example, a brightly colored landing page may say, "Your friend, Larry, loves our brand! Any friend of Larry's is a friend of ours, so join today and get $10 off your first order."[45] The company also provides dashboards to advocates that summarize the effectiveness of their sharing.

Listen to the Market

One of the key benefits of social media does not require us to speak at all; it involves listening, continuously monitoring what is being said online about our products, services, and experiences. Several companies have set up war rooms to be able to track feedback, run sentiment analyses, and feed insight back into the organization. Through their listening efforts, companies have gleaned important product and marketing insights. Social conversations have tipped off companies to potentially negative publicity as well as to grateful customers.

Remember Everlane, the company that creates great quality tees, shirts, sweaters, and accessories that we introduced in Chapter 1? The tweet below captured the sentiment of one of Everlane's happy customers.[46] This is the kind of tweet that will make our day as marketers—and maybe sell a lot of T-shirts as well.

> *Oh my goodness - this Everlane t-shirt feels like I'm wearing a warm breeze. #gift*

Figure 8.5 Everlane Customers Tweet Their Satisfaction

Fish Where the Fish Are

Social media can be enticing, but it can also be overwhelming. Before jumping in, it is important to determine where the opportunities really are for our individual organizations. What are the key market issues in our industries and who is discussing them? Where are the people with whom we want to connect congregating? Of those networks and communities, where does it make sense *for us* to be? This is not a question to ask only once. Life on the social web is fluid. Preferences change.

On average companies are active in six social environments. More often than not, companies are involved in the big networks, but there are plenty of others that may better meet their goals. At Racepoint

Global, we regularly explore the social media landscape to identify the best fits for our customers. We have identified, investigated, and developed metrics for over 150 different platforms.

In the past few years companies have been rushing to establish their own social communities. Unfortunately, Gartner the technology research firm, has found that there is about a 10 percent success rate for these collaborative initiatives.[47] Why don't these communities thrive?

Many times communities fail because they lack a clear purpose. Gartner refers to this as the "provide-and-pray" approach, in which organizations provide their customers with access to a social collaboration technology and pray that something good comes out of it.[48] (This approach is a cousin of the "spray-and-pray" broadcast tactics marketers used for many years.) Needless to say, customers rarely find these communities compelling.

Other times communities fail because their host companies have been too self-serving. Collaboration requires trusted relationships that take time, interaction, and a smaller and more stable community to develop. In an attempt to garner as much market insight as possible, companies can neglect building the community. Running their communities like a focus group, they ask questions and look for answers, without taking the time to get to know their members in a way that really promotes ongoing collaboration.[49]

Sometimes, particularly in the case of customer care communities, companies assume that the communities can run themselves or be managed by social media marketers. It is difficult to build productive communities without community managers.[50] Professional community managers who are experts in managing relationships, implementing collaborative processes, and fostering community spirit. They generate compelling content to sustain members' interest, moderate discussions, and re-engage lapsed users. Working on a shared-value basis for brands and the community, community managers are essential to cocreation. They invite members to help improve brands and translate relevant insight back into the business where it can be incorporated into strategy. In the absence of community managers, there is not enough value in the community to sustain member involvement.

Engage Customers via Social Communities

Finally, communities often fail because they are asked to produce something that they simply cannot. One of the primary reasons that companies participate in social media is to glean insight from prospects and customers. Research shows, however, that people go to public social spaces, such as Facebook, to *hear* from brands, but to *share* their thoughts, our customers often prefer a private setting away from the influence and ears of their friends.[51] To successfully collaborate, many brands are forming *private online communities* to supplement their public social media presence.

Dig Deeper with Private Customer Communities

"Online customer communities are a 24/7 strategic marketing asset that ensures that customers are at the center of marketing and communications planning, innovation and strategies for growth," explains Diane Hessan, CEO of Communispace, which creates private-brand communities. Over the last decade Communispace has partnered with 200 of the world's most admired brands to create 700+ online communities, with members in more than 96 countries.

What is the secret to a successful private-customer community? "When we create environments that are conducive to collaboration, and help brands really listen to their customers, asking for their input on material business issues, they deliver," Hessan explains. "Building trust is absolutely critical—and you get that often by creating a relatively intimate environment in which customers feel that they truly have a voice. As participants become more connected to the company through the online community, they trust the company more and provide more thoughtful and detailed feedback." They also recommend the company's products to people. This is the highly sought-after place where customers become co-creators and co-marketers. "There is a huge difference between treating consumers as respondents and feedback-givers versus really making them feel like partners—and the distinction plays out in the value you get in return."

Consider the impact that members of Godiva Chocolatier's customer community had on the company. Since 1926, Godiva Chocolatier (Godiva) has been known as the premier maker of fine

Belgian chocolate. To keep its finger on the pulse of today's customers, Godiva worked with Communispace to develop and manage a private, invitation-only online customer community, aptly named, Chocolate Talk. Member-to-member conversations accessed daily provide the company with powerful insights into how chocolate fits into their lives.[52]

During the last U.S. economic downturn, Godiva turned to community members to understand their changing purchasing behavior. Through insights gathered from a variety of exercises and assignments that members undertook, the company uncovered critical recession-induced patterns that were adversely impacting their sales. They also discovered a great opportunity.

While members loved Godiva chocolates, in an effort to cut back on spending, many were making fewer visits to the mall, where the majority of Godiva boutiques are located. Instead they were purchasing more affordable premium brands available at grocery and drug stores. Competitors also offered chocolate gift boxes, which customers purchased as casual gifts for teachers, coworkers, and mail carriers, saving the signature Godiva gold ballotin for highly special occasions. As the conversation unfolded, community members described another important preference: They did not always like to share unwrapped chocolates—like those found in the Godiva gold boxes—with people that they do not know well.

Acting on these insights, and after the community validated the idea, the company developed the Godiva Gems line—quality chocolates that are individually packaged in colorful wrappers with a sprinkling of Godiva's signature gold—sold at a more-value oriented price point. Today, Godiva Gems can be purchased in boutiques, department stores, and grocery and drug stores, making the chocolates more readily accessible. The young brand is a significant new source of revenue for the brand globally.

"The community provides us with the ability to continuously tap into our members' minds to be sure we are meeting their desire for Godiva chocolate," explains Rick Keller, global business director for the Everyday Godiva Platform. "In addition, it was instrumental in getting Gems to market fast so we can stay competitive in the Premium Chocolate category. Our members' input was crucial to the success of the Gems platform every step of the way."[53]

What to Look for in a Partner

When thinking about establishing a private online customer community, finding the right partner is essential. Hessan offers these questions to ascertain fit:

1. How many communities have they built? Get several references and check them.

2. Ask to see a sample report from a community manager. How do they deliver insights? How actionable are the insights?

3. What is the length of involvement of members in a typical community? How do they keep members engaged?

4. How active is a typical community? What is the level of participation? How many activities does a community manager initiate weekly?

5. How are members are chosen for each community?

6. What are the backgrounds of your community managers?

7. What are examples of the impact your communities have had on the companies that support them?

8. What is the best way for us to use the community? (If they say "Everything," run!)

Are Our Social Media Efforts Working?

As with everything, the key to effective social media engagement is being clear about what we are hoping to achieve. Many organizations plunge into the social media space without a clear sense of what they are hoping to accomplish. Are we trying to drive brand awareness? Close a deal? Tap customer insight? Retain customers? Our goal brings focus to our engagement efforts and determines the types of metrics that will be the most useful to us.

If our goals are oriented around increased brand awareness we may consider the following metrics:

- Share of voice, which captures the percentage of mentions within our industry in which we are cited, gives us a sense of how often our brands are discussed in our categories. A free tool available from SocialMention.com makes it easy to measure our mentions relative to our competition.

- Engagement reflects how many people interact with our content by sharing, liking, commenting, favoriting, clicking-through, and visiting our site.
- Sentiment metrics record how people feel about their experiences with our brands.

If our primary focus is on sales, we may want to calculate:

- Leads generated through social media and leads generated through social media that convert to sales.
- The impact of social media engagement on the length of the time between awareness and sale. Are our social media efforts accelerating the process?
- Cross-sells and up-sells that can be linked to social media engagement.

If on the other hand, our goals are around customer service we might ask ourselves:

- How many customer complaints were we able to solve via social media?
- How long is our average response time?
- How many customers have we retained who had threatened to leave?
- How have we reduced our customer service costs as a result of our efforts?

If our goal is to crowdsource innovation, we can monitor:

- The number of ideas that we generate from our community and how it makes sense for us to adapt.

Engage Customers via Social Communities

- The increase in positive commentary and referrals that come from soliciting and responding to our customers.

The bottom line: Once we articulate our goals, the metrics become clearer.

Assess the Health of Our Communities

Knowing that social communities can be valuable corporate assets, we may want to assess the health of our social community. Communispace, for example, focuses on two key metrics to assess the health of its communities.

1. How many members are actually participating, not just enrolled?
2. If members are participating, how much work are they willing to do?

Communispace communities routinely have participation rates of 70 to 80 percent—to put that in perspective consider that most communities' participation rates are between 1 and 10 percent. Communispace members often go mystery shopping, take field trips, make collages, create videos of their home, and take pictures of their pantries on behalf of the sponsoring companies. They are healthy communities.

Lithium Technologies, which provides social customer-experience management software for companies, developed the Community Health Index to measure community well-being. Derived from data from 15 billion actions and 6 million users, and normalized for community purpose, size, and age, the Index measures whether the community is growing, useful, popular, responsive, interactive, and lively. The Index generates suggestions for how to improve each of these areas.[54]

The Community Roundtable, which also works with companies to build and grow successful communities, offers its Community Maturity Model that helps organizations plan for and track the performance of their social communities. It defines eight competencies that they identify as keys to success: strategy, leadership, culture, community management, content and programming, policies and governance, tools, metrics, and measurements. The framework also maps how these competencies morph as companies evolve. It has successfully been used as a management checklist and a road map.[55]

In the following chapter we turn our attention to convergence media strategies, where we combine social engagement with owned and paid media to maximize our impact.

QUESTIONS

- What is your company's social media narrative? How have you been involved and what have you learned?
- Where are your customers most active on social media? How do you know? Are any niche players?
- Are you active in the social environments that are important to your customers? Are there any communities that may no longer be worth your effort?
- In what ways are you using social media across your customers' experience journey?
- How successful are these efforts? How do you define and measure success?
- What other ways can social media work for your business?
- Could your business benefit from a private online community?
- What is your next step?

RESOURCES

Influencers We Recommend

- *Chris Brogan*. Marketing consultant, CEO of Human Business Works, and author of several books including *The Impact*

(*continued*)

(continued)

Equation, Brogan writes about business, marketing, and sales, with a bit of personal development thrown in. Connect with him at www.humanbusinessworks.com and on Twitter @chrisbrogan.

- *Jeff Bullas*. Bullas is a blogger, author, and strategist specializing in digital marketing. Recently named a Forbes Top 50 Social Media Power Influencer, Bullas is the author of *Blogging the Smart Way*. Stay up to date on all things social on his blog at www.jeffbullas.com and by following him on Twitter @Jeffbullas.

- *The Community Roundtable*. Founded by Jim Storer and Rachel Happe (www.thesocialorganization.com), the group's mission is to advance the business of community. The Community Roundtable (www.communityroundtable.com) conducts research on the field, offers professional development, and provides research and advisory services. Read their blog, join the CRNetwork, and follow them on Twitter @TheCR.

- *Diane Hessan*. As president and CEO of Communispace, one of the fastest-growing social networking companies in the United States, Hessan has her finger on the pulse of social communities. Author of *Customer-Centered Growth: Five Strategies for Building Competitive Advantage*, Hessan has received numerous awards including Ernst & Young's Regional Entrepreneur of the Year, and the Greater Boston Chamber of Commerce Entrepreneur of the Year. Follow her on Twitter @CommunispaceCEO or at http://blog.communispace.com.

- *Guy Kawasaki*. The former chief evangelist of Apple, Kawasaki now serves as a special advisor to the Motorola business unit of Google. The author of *APE, What the Plus!, Enchantment*, and nine other books, and the cofounder of Alltop.com, Kawasaki has plenty of wisdom to share. Learn with him at www.guykawasaki.com and on Twitter @GuyKawasaki.

- *Charlene Li*. Coauthor of *Groundswell*, author of *Open Leadership*, and founder of Altimeter Group, a research-based advisory firm that helps companies and industries leverage disruption to their advantage, Li is an expert on social media and technology. She was named one of the 100 most creative people in business by *Fast Company* in 2010 and one of the most influential women in technology in 2009. Explore her thoughts at www.charleneli.com and on Twitter @Charleneli.

- *Michael Stelzner*. Founder and CEO of *Social Media Examiner*, an online social media magazine, whose mission is to help companies navigate the constantly changing social media jungle, Stelzner authored *Launch* and *Writing White Papers* and created the Social Media Marketing World event. Follow him on Twitter @Mike_Stelzner, listen to him on Social Media Marketing Podcast, and keep up to speed on what is happening in the jungle at www.Socialmediaexaminer.com.

- *SocialMedia.org*. A community for social media folks working on large brands, SocialMedia.org is a forum for sharing best practices and solutions to social-media-related challenges. SocialMedia.org sponsors BlogWell, regular brands-only summits where case studies are presented and peer-to-peer discussions take place. For more information on Blogwell, see www.socialmedia.org/blogwell. Follow them on Twitter @SocialMediaOrg.

Hashtags to Explore

- #cmgrchat
- #communitymanager
- #share
- #smdata (social media data)

(continued)

(continued)

- #smm (social media marketing)
- #smo (social media optimization)
- #social
- #socialchat
- #socialmedia
- #socialmediaexperts

Chapter 9

Maximize Marketing Impact with Converged Media

"Reward comes in creation and re-creation, not just in the consumption of the world around us."[1]

—Tim Brown, CEO and president, IDEO

If you have ever wanted to spruce up a room, but find the process of picking paint colors to be overwhelming, Glidden has the solution for you. With roots that extend back to 1875, Glidden has years of experience with paints and color and a time-tested appreciation of how challenging color selection can be.

To make this process easier, Glidden launched MyColortopia .com, a microsite that features DIY-oriented bloggers, an advice column, and multiple color discovery tools to build people's confidence in their color choices. People are moving beyond being color-fuddled—that is, emotionally and physically paralyzed when making the life-altering commitment to a paint color—by using My Colortopia. They are making headway with their projects, creating the rooms of their dreams, buying Glidden paint, and having fun in the process.

My Colortopia is not about pushing Glidden paints—you have to look hard to find their name on the site—it is about self-expression. Several engaging tools on the site help people identify their individual style. The multiple choice quiz, My Life, My Colors, generates customized-color palettes based upon individuals' personalities, styles, and preferences. My Image Inspiration allows people to upload a photo of an object they like—a couch, rug, or fabric—from which it will identify paint colors that both match and coordinate with it.

To visualize how colors will look on the walls in people's homes, My Colortopia offers Color My Room. After selecting paint colors and uploading a picture of the room, people are only a click away from seeing how their own space can be transformed. A picture of the refreshed room can be shared on a variety of social platforms to gather friends' feedback. If it is a winner, Color My Room will calculate how much paint is needed for the space, identify the closest store, and generate a shopping list to take along. Could it be any easier? People love the tool. *BuzzFeed* featured Color My Room in an article titled, "31 Home Décor Hacks That Are Borderline Genius."[2] Imagine having your marketing content be considered borderline genius.

Ten influencers write weekly posts for the My Colortopia blog on topics such as painting and decorating tips and myriad do-it-yourself projects. Recognizing the underlying emotions that often accompany tasks like picking out paint colors, the writers reflect from time to time on their experiences undertaking tasks that have made them feel uncomfortable, building a deeper sense of connection with readers. Customers are encouraged to submit questions, which the bloggers answer, and to post before-and-after pictures of their projects. This content is distributed beyond the site through My Colortopia's social media presences on Pinterest, Facebook, Twitter, and YouTube, via media partners that share the same audience, and by customers who enjoy what they find.

Although Glidden no longer purchases television advertising, the company did recently place an interactive ad for My Colortopia in *House Beautiful*. The piece, which appeared on the second page of the magazine, was written by their bloggers and guided people through the painting process. Bloggers were introduced on tabs, that when lifted, described where the writers found color inspiration. The information provided was so useful that readers experienced the ad as if it were magazine content.

The My Colortopia experience, right down to the digitally generated shopping list, builds brand preference and insistence for Glidden products in a competitive marketplace. After a little more than four months in market, the site enjoyed over 170,000 visits, and 1.2 million minutes of customer engagement. Forty percent of site visitors are repeat visitors, a testament to its value. How is the site impacting Glidden's sales? After visiting My Colortopia, people were 70 percent more likely to consider Glidden Paint for their next project.

Pursue a Converged-Media Strategy

We are often asked if content marketing can scale to effectively drive organizations' marketing efforts, or if it needs to be combined with advertising to realize its full impact. As was the case with My Colortopia, the best strategy is the one that most effectively reaches our prospects and customers and addresses the itch they are trying to scratch, regardless of whether its components are owned, earned, or paid. Indeed, some of today's most effective customer experiences are a combination of media types. When done well, the mixture creates something more than the sum of its individual parts.

When we tell one story through two or more integrated channels—owned, earned, or paid—we are applying a converged-media strategy (see Figure 9.1). Public relations and digital media agencies have been utilizing this strategy for some time, amplifying our clients' content through social media and incorporating their customers' and influencers' comments into their owned content. The practice is going mainstream, with many brands creating rich integrated-media experiences that break through the clutter and capture people's attention.

Native advertising, which, at a minimum, combines paid and owned media to create commercial-content experiences that appear native to the environment in which they appear, is one of the fastest-growing applications. In this case, paid media plays a supporting role. Owned content remains the primary basis for engagement with our prospects and customers. Recognizing the impact of these hybrid experiences, the Altimeter Group recently issued a Converged Media Imperative, stating that given changing consumer behavior, brands *must* combine paid, earned, and owned media in order to be effective.[3]

Maximize Marketing Impact with Converged Media

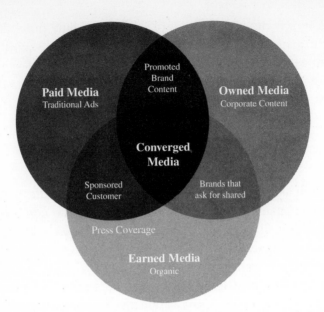

Figure 9.1   The Convergence of Paid, Earned, and Owned Medi

Source: "The Converged Media Imparative," Altimeter Group, (July 19, 2012).

A Closer Look at Paid, Earned, and Owned Media

Convergence strategies blur the distinction among paid, earned, and owned media, because they exist in their intersection. These distinctions among media, which developed because of the way our companies and agencies have traditionally been organized, are not relevant to our prospects and customers. They do not see them, nor do they care. They just interact—hopefully with us. That having been said, to truly understand converged strategy, it is helpful to briefly examine its component parts.

Paid Media Is Advertising

Often referred to as push or outbound marketing, *paid media* is advertising. It can be used in service of brand building or direct-response strategies. What tools comprise the paid media category? As Figure 9.2 illustrates, paid media includes traditional forms of advertising and

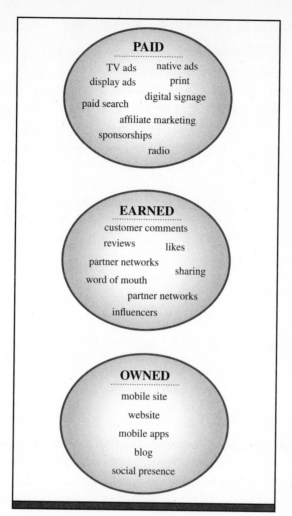

PAID

TV ads   native ads

display ads   print

paid search   digital signage

affiliate marketing

sponsorships

radio

EARNED

customer comments

reviews   likes

partner networks

word of mouth   sharing

partner networks

influencers

OWNED

mobile site

website

mobile apps

blog

social presence

Figure 9.2   What Comprises Paid, Earned, and Owned Media?

digital offshoots including online display ads, paid search, native advertising, paid blogging, and in-store media.

Paid media involves a media buy and therefore has higher direct costs than owned or earned media. Brands control the messaging and, as a result, people have historically been skeptical of its trustworthiness; however, incorporating customer comments and influencer content into advertising is altering that perception.

245

Owned Media Is Everything We Create

Owned media includes our traditional print and retail assets as well as our digital properties: websites, branded blogs, YouTube channels, microsites, videos, social media pages, mobile apps, and branded-social communities. Following a content strategy, owned media captures the attention of prospects that have searched us out—a key point of distinction from paid media—and *accompanies* them through the customer-experience journey.

Owned media–derived leads are considered to be warmer than those delivered via paid media as prospects have initiated engagement with us. In general, owned media tends to have a lower-cost-per-lead than paid media, but it also has a more limited reach and takes time. While companies create owned media content, the tone is consultative and educational rather than persuasive, enhancing its credibility among potential customers.

Earned Media Is the Voice of the Market

Earned media refers to anything that our users, viewers, or customers have created or shared and includes reviews, blogs and blog comments, photos, videos, social media comments, and customer forums. It also includes bloggers and our traditional coverage in newspapers, magazines, radio, and television. Earned media, particularly if it is customer-created, is generally considered to be the most trustworthy content source.

Earned media is often generated in social spaces. We can influence these conversations, but we cannot control them. These conversations can be powerful, both positively and negatively. Actively listening to the conversations taking place in these environments keeps us in touch with our customers, uncovers potential issues, and provides important insights into the themes we may want to further develop in our content.

Converged Media Mixes It Up

Successful converged strategies are like a bowl of spaghetti. Media are combined to create experiences that in turn create more interactions that generate more content, which can then be incorporated into still another experience. A few examples of successful applications of converged media follow.

MyColortopia.com: Colorful Living Made Easy

Think back for a moment to the MyColortopia.com experience. Or better yet, take a moment to explore the site for yourself. My Colortopia successfully combines owned, earned, and paid media to make it easier for people to tackle makeover projects and add color to their homes. The microsite itself is owned media even though the Glidden brand does not dominate the site. An intentional branding decision, MyColortopia.com looks and feels like a community created for its users, rather than one made to advertise the sponsoring brand.

Influencers are paid to create a steady stream of engaging content for the site (paid media) that address customers' questions and challenges and provide inspiration. This paid content is amplified as it is shared across customer networks, prompting people back to My Colortopia's owned properties to explore the tools and content for themselves. Content is similarly amplified though My Colortopia's social channels (owned) and shared by its fans and followers (earned). The foldout in *House Beautiful* (paid) extends My Colortopia tools and content to new audiences, directs them back to their owned channels, and facilitates sharing among their networks (earned). Customers upload before-and-after pictures to the site, which combines earned and owned. Complex, yes—and it works.

Pepsi Pulse: Keeping a Finger on Pop Culture

Pepsi is also on the frontier of converged media. This strategy puts the brand right where it wants to be: in the center of social media conversations. "Brand wars are being fought in news feeds and streams," explains Shiv Singh, head of digital for PepsiCo Beverages, in a recent *Mashable* article.[4] To insert its brand into the center of the conversation, Pepsi created Pepsi Pulse, an interactive dashboard that Singh describes as a "cheat sheet for pop culture."

Through the social media–driven platform, the company curates global conversations about trending pop culture, music, and sports. Housed on Pepsi.com, Pepsi Pulse interjects brand messages in the center of its customers' news feeds and streams by providing engaging and easily sharable content.

Viewers are encouraged to "live at the speed of now" and to share what is going on in their world by tweeting pictures and comments marked with #LiveForNow. Sharers are rewarded for their efforts with Pepsi Experience Points, which can be redeemed for items like Beyoncé Pop Art Travel Bags and autographed sports jerseys. Pepsi offers its Twitter followers free music downloads, music videos, and even access to pop-up concerts if they include the hashtag #PepsiforNOW on their tweets. Take a quick look so you too can have your finger on the pulse.

Here is a simplified breakdown of the PepsiPulse converged mix. People all over the world create much of the content (earned) for the Pulse dashboard (owned) as they live their lives on social media. Pepsi catalyzes additional content creation in social spaces through its contests and conversations that are identified by Pulse-related hashtags: #LiveforNow, #Now, #Celebs (owned and earned). Portions of these conversations and images reappear on Pepsi's website (owned), social properties (owned), and in TV, radio, cinema, and outdoor advertising (paid). Complex, yes—and it works.

Paid Media Supports Owned Media

How does paid media enhance our content distribution efforts? Paid media can reach beyond an organization's own database, fans, and followers to gain the attention of new audiences. If successful, it directs them to the company's owned media sites where a relationship can be formed or a transaction completed.

For example, through its Lookalike program, Facebook can identify prospects from its base of 1.3 members that share key characteristics and behaviors of our preferred customers. This is a thought-provoking proposition as this target group has a high probability of being interested in our organizations. Facebook can also target individuals based upon their age, education, interests, and even relationship status. Although operating on a smaller base of members,

Twitter can also target people who are similar to our followers, as well as or those who have used certain keywords in recent tweets. Targeting by location, interest, type of device, or peak discussion times for given topics are also possible. LinkedIn can target members of specific LinkedIn Groups as well as by criteria such as job title and function, industry, geography, and company size.

Paid media can also be used to engage existing customers, loyalty members, or lapsed users. Why is this necessary? Our organic reach can be spotty. Facebook estimates that only 16 percent of our fans see our content in newsfeeds organically[5] and the half life of a post or a tweet is just over a couple of hours. A targeted social media-based advertising strategy can reach a broader base of our own followers by making our posts or tweets more visible on their newsfeeds. Facebook can also help us connect with our customers with whom we are not yet engaging on the social media platform through its Custom Audiences targeting tool. By matching our customer e-mail and phone lists to Facebook accounts, we are able to reach out to targeted customers on a new channel, and one that is designed for engagement.

Native Advertising Is Converged Media

A subset of paid media, native advertising is by definition a converged-media strategy because it integrates paid media with owned media, often with the goal of generating earned media. Although the category is still evolving, the premise of native advertising is to be useful and nonintrusive—native ads look, feel, and function like the content that appears organically in the environments in which they are placed. As such, they function as a cross between content marketing and traditional advertising.

Jay Rosen, who teaches journalism at New York University, defines native advertising as "advertising that is as worth reading as the editorial into which it is mixed, from which it is distinguished."[6] As such, native advertising is meant to be distinctly different from traditional *display advertising*. An umbrella category, display advertising includes banner ads (offers placed along the edges of websites), prerolls (the short videos that often appear before we get to the content we want to see), and popup ads (messaging that blocks our content for several seconds).

Consensus is yet to be built around native advertising's structure and parameters, however. The U.S. Federal Trade Commission is examining the young industry and the Interactive Advertising Bureau recently put forth its own recommendations. In the absense of clear guidelines, many interations are appearing as brands look to engage and social networks and publishers seek new ways to monetize their digital operations. Some native ads are direct-response offers that look similar to traditional display ads, but have been formulated to blend into the digital environment in which they appear. As marketers, it is a good idea to keep our eyes on this rapidly evolving space.

Recognize Native Advertising

Native advertising appears in a variety of digital and analogue forms. It would take an entire book, and one that would be quickly outdated, to fully explore the options, so we will only provide a snapshot here.

In social environments native ads often appear as in-stream content, examples of which include Promoted Tweets on Twitter, Promoted Videos on YouTube, Slideshare Content Ads on LinkedIn, Sponsored Check-Ins on Foursquare. Promoted Tweets are ordinary tweets that can be purchased to reach a wider swath of prospects or to engage existing customers. These Tweets behave like ordinary tweets but are targeted to specific persons and are placed in prominent positions on the site, increasing their visibility.

How might a brand use a Promoted Tweet? In connection with Inventor's Day, which takes place every year on Thomas Edison's birthday (February 11), General Electric (GE) used Promoted Tweets to spark conversation about imagination and invention in social environments. In the days leading up to Inventor's Day, GE launched the #IWantToInvent initiative in which it shared quotes and Vine videos highlighting accomplishments of various inventors. On the actual day, GE used Promoted Tweets to encourage people to tweet about their own invention ideas. Designers created 70 customized sketches of these crowdsourced that day, which were shared on

Twitter throughout the day. The result: #IWantToInvent helped spark creativity and increased brand conversations over four times the daily average.[7]

Similarly, *Sesame Street* made a huge splash on Twitter using Promoted Tweets to tell an updated version of its classic children's book, *The Monster at the End of This Book, Starring Loveable, Furry Old Grover*. The digital version of the story was told in 29 Promoted Tweets. Knowing they were on to something, an hour before the first Promoted Tweet appeared, Dan Lewis, director of New Media communications for Sesame Workshop tweeted, "Let's win the Internet today. In an hour or so,"[8] And they did. It is well worth a peak.[9]

Figure 9.3 captures both a Promoted Account (Samsung Mobile US) and a Promoted Trend (#mixingbeats), which are designated as promoted via words, an icon, and a unique color. Part of Twitter's Who to Follow feature, Promoted Accounts allows brands to reach out to people who do not yet follow them. Twitter's algorithm makes recommendations based upon the user's public list of people they follow and their similarity to the brand's existing followers. For example, Twitter may recommend @SamsungMobileUS to people who follow several mobile-technology related accounts, but not Samsung.

In the case of a Promoted Trend, a brand pays to have its name, event, or related subject matter appear at the top of the trend list, which highlights the most popular topics under discussion on the network at a given point in time. In Figure 9.3, the Promoted Trend is #mixingbeats, referring to a 2-day musical experience sponsored by Hewlett Packard.[10] Twitter's research shows that Promoted Trends help boost conversation about brands, increase purchase considerations, and have a long-term impact on customer conversation about brands.[11]

On a publishing site, in-stream native advertising looks and acts much like a news story, with a headline, image, description, and some indication that it is paid content. Figure 9.4 captures a page from *BuzzFeed* in which native advertising is embedded. *BuzzFeed* works with advertisers to develop content that resembles its own editorial pieces. Following a cross-channel strategy, it also buys ad space on Facebook, YouTube, Twitter, and other publishing sites, to generate additional brand lift.

251

Maximize Marketing Impact with Converged Media

Figure 9.3   Facebook's Sponsored Stories Appear as Native Content

Source: Facebook.com/help/162317430499238.

Native advertising can also take the form of paid search results and Promoted Listings, which as we saw in Figure 7.4, appear on the same search engine results page as their organic counterparts. Promoted Listings, which appear in response to a search for a specific

Figure 9.4   Twitter's Promoted Trends Expand Content's Reach

product, are marked as sponsored and include a photo, price, and location in which the item can be purchased.

Other popular native advertising formats include recommendation widgets that serve up paid content to users from content discovery platforms such as Taboola or Outbrain. Appearing on websites like CNN.com, FastCompany.com, Time.com, and Rolling Stone.com, this content is often labeled as "You May Also Like," or "We Recommend," or "Elsewhere Around the Web." Another fun variation is branded playlists from the digital music service, Spotify. In a recent campaign, Carnival Cruise Lines offered to "bring the Caribbean" to people who did not have time for a cruise, through its fun, tropical playlist. The campaign attracted over 450 followers, who spent 20 minutes on average with their brand.

Does Native Advertising Deliver?

Do people pay attention to native advertising? To answer this question, Sharethrough and the IPG Media Lab tracked eye movements of

Maximize Marketing Impact with Converged Media

viewers as they looked at native ads and owned content. They found that people view native ads as editorial content; content and native ads have equivalent engagement.[12]

This does not mean that all native advertising works—just as not all of our content works. There are a variety of native advertising types and each is designed to deliver value in a different way. Matching the social platform and type of ad to the marketing goal is key. Twitter, for example, is often used effectively for lead generation; Slideshare works well for nurturing relationships with existing customers. Presentation makes a difference. As is the case with organic content, photos and videos have been shown to provide a lift in impressions for native ads.

How are people measuring the effectiveness of native advertising? Because native advertising is designed to look like content, most types are being measured in terms of the exposure, engagement, and sharing they generate. Companies that are able to create closed-loop marketing systems, which we will discuss in more detail in Chapter 10, can actually determine whether these ads ultimately convert to leads and sales.

How do native ads compare with digital display ads? According to the Sharethrough and IPG study, native ads perform differently from banner ads. Viewers are 25 percent more likely to look at a native ad than a banner ad and they look at them 53 percent more frequently. They are also more likely to share native ads (32 percent versus 19 percent) and show 18 percent higher purchase intent after viewing them. However, banner ads significantly outperformed native ads in brand recall, where display ads enjoyed a 38 percent to 25 percent advantage. This is not surprising as company logos are often featured prominently in banner ads.

Looking at results like these, many publishers, platforms, and marketers are embracing native advertising. Nearly three-fourths of polled U.S. publishers said that they offer native advertising on their sites and another 17 percent are considering offering it this year.[13] Some publishers, like *BuzzFeed*, only allow native ads on their sites.[14] CMOs are also getting into the game. Thirty-two percent of CMOs say they have bought native video advertising or will buy in the next six months.[15]

254

Don't Ruin a Good Thing

To play in the native advertising game requires caution. If our constituents feel as if they have been tricked into thinking that advertising is organic content, we will end up damaging our brands and moving the customer-centricity dial backward.

We also have to be mindful of how we use our customers' data. Faced with a class-action suit, Facebook recently announced that it will no long offer Sponsored Stories, which tapped into the power of peer influence by sharing details of an action that a person may have taken with their brand with a broader audience. In Figure 9.5, the advertiser Jasper's Market, reposted its content about smoothies, adding that one of its followers, Courtney Cronin, had liked the link; the ad appeared prominently in the newsfeeds of her friends. Many Facebook fans were shocked when the ads appeared and felt taken advantage of; reflecting this sentiment, the law suit claimed that Facebook unlawfully used people's information to sell products without their consent.

 Courtney Cronin likes a link on **Jasper's Market.**

 Jasper's Spotlight: healthy, delicious smoothies
www.jaspersmarket.com
Learn how to make healthy and delicious smoothies. Just in time for summer!

Like · Comment · Share · 👍 10,345 💬 460 📤 332 · ⚙ · Sponsored

Figure 9.5　Native Ads Blend in with Content on Publisher Sites

Similarly, if our native ads begin to look too much like advertising and not organic content, they are likely to perform more like display ads, which have a click-through rate of less than 0.02 percent. Remember why people engage in social environments—it is not to hear us promote our products. The more engaging the content, the better performing the ad.

The New Kid on the Block: Mobile Advertising

Mobile advertising is in its infancy, but growing quickly. Given the spectacular rates of mobile adoption and the types of experiences

Maximize Marketing Impact with Converged Media

that can be designed around it, this is no great surprise. As brands build multiscreen-advertising strategies, mobile is often seen as the channel that knits the overall experience together.

Native ads comprise the majority of mobile ads; they work well with the smaller-size screens. SMS-text offers are common. An opt-in form, customers sign up to receive messages via their phone numbers. SMS campaigns can target multiple features including interest, time, and location, which increases their relevance to customers and makes them cost-effective and easy to scale. Responses found that 64 percent of subscribers have made a purchase as a result of a highly relevant mobile message.[16] Display ads have also found their way onto mobile phones in the form of banner ads and interstitial ads, the latter cover the screen while we are waiting for an app to load or take the form of a background jingle that plays while we are on hold.

Recognizing that 87 percent of U.S. smartphone users spend time in apps, advertisers also place ads within games and applications. These ads are thought to be especially salient as people tend to be more focused when they are playing a game or using an app. What is more, rich media and gaming technology take advantage of mobile's touchscreen and GPS features, heightening the appeal of these ads.

For example, in connection with the launch of its performance-enhancing Boost shoe, Adidas Philippines recently ran an ad within lifestyle and sporting mobile apps and sites. When people clicked through, they were taken to Nike's Facebook page where they could play a mobile game using their fingers to simulate running in Boost shoes. Rich media displayed a variety of terrains and conditions that the new shoes was designed to endure. Location-based technology allowed players to compare their scores against others playing nearby. Taking advantage of the Facebook platform, players were encouraged to share the ad and like the brand's Facebook page.[17]

Programmed Advertising Is Making Its Mark

Approximately 20 percent of today's digital advertising is sold through automated interactions, machine to machine. Programmatic buying has traditionally been used with remnant inventory—that is, advertising space that a publishing site has not been able to sell. Sold at a deep discount, this practice can stretch a company's ad budget and create incremental revenue for the publisher. Increasingly we are seeing this technology applied more widely, suggesting that it may ultimately transform how we buy and sell advertising.

Here is a simplified example of how it works. A customer visits a website on the device of his or her choice. Within fractions of a second, a request is sent by that website to an ad server for an appropriate ad to show the customer. That ad server redirects the request to an ad exchange that sends the request to real-time bidders. The winner of the bid serves the ad to the website, and within milliseconds, the ad appears in front of the customer.

The system targets buyers by analyzing the content they are consuming on the website and/or their previous behavior. In the case of the former, when the customer arrives on the website, keywords are scanned, alerting the ad server of the topic that is capturing his or her attention. Almost instantaneously, a related ad appears on the webpage. For example, if he or she was reading about cycling in the Santa Ynez wine country of California, an advertisement for a bicycle touring company, which offers great cycling trips in the region, might automatically appear on the same page's border.

The next generation of contextual marketing, semantic targeting, aims to further improve the relevance of ads by broadening the context around the scan. Recognizing that the English language has many polysemous words—words like *apple* that could refer to a type of fruit or to Apple, the maker of the iPhone—semantic marketing goes beyond keyword analysis, to examine all the words on a given page to try and get a deeper understanding of the content. *Sentiment analysis* takes semantic targeting one step further to try and decipher the tone of the content. If the sentiment is positive, an ad will be placed; if it is negative, it will not. For example, if the viewer were reading an article about the health benefits of cycling, an advertisement for the bicycle touring company would appear. If, on the other hand, he or she were reading about life-threatening bike injuries, the ad would not appear.

Rather than scanning the content of a give page, *behavioral targeting* taps customer profiles and historical behavioral data to determine which ads to display. Beyond this, the rest of the process is the same. Using this information, ad exchanges are alerted and ads served up within milliseconds.

Figure 9.6   A Remarketed Web Ad for the Broadway Show
Kinky Boots
Source: http://www.wikihow.com/Add-Your-Site-to-Google-News

Whether an ad is matched up via context or behavior, if a purchase is not made, ads may be remarketed to that customer on subsequent website visits. For example, if the aforementioned customer did not click through to the biking site while reading about the Santa Ynez wine country, the bike company can arrange for them to see similar ads as they browse the web in the coming days. *Remarketing* allows companies to stay engaged with their target audience, remaining top of mind should their prospect choose to act.

What does a remarketed ad look like? Figure 9.6 shows a remarketed ad for *Kinky Boots*, the 2013 Tony Award–winning Broadway show. The simple display ad appeared on multiple unrelated sites across the web for days after Lisa inquired about ticket purchases, including this site focusing on How to Add Your Site to Google News.

Second Screening Enhances Brand Touches

Increasingly our customers are engaging with content across a variety of screens simultaneously, creating a multiscreen-viewing experience. Any combination of screens can be paired; often a TV screen is combined with a mobile device or computer. Disney's latest rerelease of the movie, *The Little Mermaid*, came with the invitation to bring an iPad along to the theater. Moviegoers were encouraged to download

The Digital Marketer

the accompanying iPad app and play digital games with others in the theater while singing along and–oh yes–enjoying the film.

Recognizing this behavior, companies are working to create complementary mobile experiences, making the rather passive experience of watching television or a movie more interactive. IntoNow, for example, offers supplemental program information for television viewers. Using SoundPrint recognition technology, it identifies the show, season, and episode and then tees up related information, including cast tweets, actor bios, and links to related sites. Shazam, the song recognition software that makes it easy to figure out what song is being played on the radio, can now do the same for music that is played on television shows.

Second screening allows for interesting advertising opportunities. It is quite common for people to tweet or post comments on Facebook about the shows they are viewing. In 2012, 32 million people in the United States tweeted about TV programming. Through its recent purchase of BlueFin Labs, Twitter is able to measure social conversations about programs and commercials, in much the same way as Nielsen ratings capture TV viewership. As a result, brands can use Twitter's Promoted Tweets to directly engage those viewers who have been exposed to their TV ads—within 24 hours of the time when the ad was initially shown. This combination extends the life of the TV spot, making it more interactive and measureable. Is it working? Studies show that viewers who have dual exposure demonstrate 95 percent stronger message association and 58 percent higher purchase intent compared to those viewers who were exposed to TV alone.[18]

What About Print?

In the digital age, print advertising is often the stepsister. There is no question that newspaper and magazine ad revenues are declining. As a result, some magazines have transitioned to exclusively digital versions. Other magazines and newspapers have created adjacent digital platforms and are employing them to define what digital journalism can be. The *New York Times'* interactive piece, *Snow Fall*, for example, won a Pulitzer Prize and a Webby, an international award that recognizes excellence on the Internet.[19]

Yet print remains key to many brands. Converged-media strategies, like the one MyColortopia.com used, can be highly successful, leading prospects and customers to our digital properties for further engagement. One of the most successful print ads that we have seen was recently created by Nivea to promote its sun-protection products. The theme of the ad was simple: When you are on the beach, you do not want to leave for any reason, especially not to charge your cell phone. To help you stay put, their ad includes a solar-powered charger to power your cell phone while you are sunning, so that you do not have to go home until the sun goes down. Brilliant.

Direct mail is still making a difference for many brands. Ironically the popularity of digital messaging has made the direct-mail pieces stand out. According to Epsilon's *2012 Channel Preference Survey*, 73 percent of consumers say they prefer direct mail for brand communications because they can read the information at their convenience.[20]

Several attempts have been made to turn print into an interactive experience via QR codes, two-dimensional barcodes that are scanned to connect people to digital properties. Although brands continue to adopt QR codes, only 7 percent of people say they are a valuable source of information about brands.[21] New technology by Digimarc may change the game, however. Their technology lets content creators embed content into images via watermarks, invisible patterns that appear under certain conditions. Magazine readers can quickly access online content—websites, e-commerce sites, and social spaces where they can enter contests, share content, watch videos, explore merchandise, and make purchases—with a simple scan of an object or article. This creates a dynamic reading experience similar to that available via a tablet. The patented watermark technology is not limited to print. Brands can also embed watermarks in audio, video, and packaging and at every touchpoint in the customer-experience journey.

Digital Signage Captures People's Attention

Digital signage is being used indoors and outdoors to engage prospects and customers. They can be found in taxis, bars, health clubs, restaurants, gas stations, and retail stores—almost anywhere.

China is currently leading the pack in terms of the number of digital sign displays, but there is no shortage in other markets. Nielsen estimates that U.S. adults are exposed to over 237 million ad exposures through this fourth-screen experience—TV, Internet, and mobile comprise the first three screens.[22]

What is the appeal? Digital screens can create a richer shopping experience. Fourth screens in retail stores demonstrate how outfits can be created by mixing and matching items available in the store. At Burberry's flagship store on London's Regent Street, this fourth-screen experience is taken one step further. RFID sensors embedded in selected clothing and accessories personalize the shopping experience. When customers take the tagged merchandise to areas like the dressing room, sensors activate product-specific videos on nearby screens.

In Korea, QR codes embedded in displays are turning everyday experiences into events. Tesco Home Plus, a leading supermarket chain, is using QR codes to turn subway stations into virtual shopping experiences.[23] Walls of train stations are lined with displays resembling grocery store aisles. While waiting for the train, shoppers can walk up and down aisles just as they would in their local stores, browsing simulated shelves stocked with products. The difference, however, is that rather than putting items in a physical grocery cart, shoppers scan QR codes on the displays, which places items in virtual shopping carts. Groceries delivered to their home before the end of the day. These displays also allow Tesco to expand its footprint without incurring the expense of building and managing additional stores.[24]

Not to be outdone, Tesco's main rival, Emart, uses outdoor three-dimensional QR codes to create a unique lunchtime shopping experience.[25] These are not typical QR codes, however. They are shadow-based codes that can only be scanned during midday sun, when the sun is at a specific angle. When shoppers scan the codes, they are directed to Emart's mobile site, where there are special noontime-only offers. Purchased items are conveniently delivered to purchasers' homes later that day. The solar feature creates an added dimension of surprise for users and engages them during what is generally a slow time of day for Emart. During the first month

Maximize Marketing Impact with Converged Media

that the Sunny Sale campaign was in place, membership increased 58 percent over the previous month and sales during the lunch hour lifted by 25 percent.[26]

Britain's National Centre for Domestic Violence (NCDV) used multiple interactive billboards at Euston Staton in London to raise awareness about domestic violence and to prompt viewers to act. An angry man is shown yelling at a young woman, who is clearly frightened. A notice on a second billboard encourages viewers to use their smartphone to protect her. Using their fingers on the touchscreen, viewers can literlly drag the man across multiple screens to the other side of the station, putting distance between them, modeling the type of action that people can take in real-life.[27]

Events Are Immersive Customer Experiences

Events can engage our prospects and customers in multisensory ways, immersing them in a total-brand experience. According to the *Customer Attainment from Event Engagement* study, nearly 90 percent of brand marketers surveyed say events hold some level of importance and value for their organization, with 31 percent considering them to be essential.[28] We can design events to raise brand awareness, facilitate demand generation, help close deals, and engage prospects and customers. To be effective, events must be memorable and, like all of our marketing efforts, they must be useful. When held during nonbusiness hours, events must offer equivalent value to alternative entertainment options.

Events include digital occasions like webinars and live streaming of events, as well as tradeshows, conferences, seminars, and in-store events. Live tweeting and streaming and specially designed apps transform physical events into enhanced hybrid experiences, often expanding their life and the number of potential participants.

As retail stores become increasingly experiential—think Burberry, Apple, Niketown, REI (the latter sports in-store climbing walls)—shopping itself is becoming an event. Pop-up stores that appear for short periods of time create alluring limited-time engagements. Intel, for example, is using the pop-up store model to create an Intel Experience Store for the holiday season. Free coffee and movie screenings are offered to lure prospects and customers into their store, away from the nearby, permanent Apple, Samsung, and Microsoft retail spaces.

Coca-Cola Stages Small World Experiences

Reflecting the Coca-Cola Company's mission of refreshing the world and inspiring moments of optimism and happiness, the company recently created Small World machines. Although they look like simple vending machines that might bring forth a soda, the Small World machines are a live-communications portal that allow people to see and interact with each other.

In an attempt to "dissolve difference and create a simple moment of connection," Coca-Cola installed machines in both India and Pakistan so that residents of the two countries, which have "historically delicate relations, but a shared history, common language and similarities in culture,"[29] could connect with each other. The machines went live for one evening and people from both counties embraced the opportunity to reach across their borders. They greeted each other warmly, danced together (virtually), and sent a message of tolerance by tracing a heart or peace sign together on an interactive screen.

An inspiring video captures moments from the evening, including one participant's reaction, "[Tensions between the two countries' people exist] mainly because there's no communication—they're near us but we have no access to them. And it's sad, because together I think we could do wonders."[30] One member of the Pakistani team that brought the Small World machines to life later reflected in a blog post, "What I remember from that evening is that moment when these people weren't Pakistanis or Indians. For that one moment, they were simply human beings. Connecting. Sharing. Smiling."[31]

Working with Agencies in a Converged World

Today, most marketing departments and agencies are organized by channel, which impedes our ability to create and implement a converged model of customer engagement. This is changing, albeit slowly, and there are still many questions to be answered. Can companies better serve their customers with the help of agencies

Maximize Marketing Impact with Converged Media

that combine all competencies under one roof? Or will best-of-breed models that focus on expertise in one market or one skillset continue to flourish?

At Racepoint Global, we are banking on the full-service approach. Larry recently merged two of his companies, Racepoint Group (Racepoint) and Digital Influence Group (DIG) to facilitate this convergence for our clients. Racepoint's specialty is public relations; DIG's is digital marketing. While the synergies have always been clear, when he formed these sister companies a decade ago, the buyers for these services were two separate groups within companies: marketing and corporate communications.

Today the walls are coming down as companies are reorganizing to be customer-centric and remain relevant. Although for some time now we have been designing converged solutions for our Racepoint and DIG clients, it has necessitated coordination across two different companies. As we have seen over and over again, magic happens when the usual and unusual suspects come together at the same table.

QUESTIONS FOR CONSIDERATION

- How are you currently applying a converged strategy?
- What channels have you found to have synergy?
- What types of paid media has proven to be the most effective for your content?
- Do your agency partners approach communications from a customer-centric or channel-based perspective?
- What is your next step?

RESOURCES

Influencers We Recommend

- *Lauren Drell*. Branded content editor at *Mashable*, Drell spends a lot of time thinking about and creating native advertising. Follow her on Twitter @drelly.

- *Dan Greenberg*. The CEO and cofounder of Sharethrough, a leading native advertising platform, Greenberg is on the forefront of native. (He also did research for BJ Fogg when he was studying at Stanford.) Stay abreast of his thinking at @dgreenberg and www.sharethrough.com/blog.

- *Tessa Gould*. Director of the HuffPost Partner Studio, the in-house content studio that works with brands to create sponsored content. You can follow Gould @TessG_Tweets. See the latest branded content coming out of HuffPost on Twitter @HuffPostPartner.

- *Jay Rosen*. A media critic, writer, professor of journalism, director of the Studio 20 program at New York University, and advisor to First Look Media, Pierre Omidyar's new journalism platform, Rosen keeps his eye on new media developments. Learn with Rosen by reading his blog www.pressthink.org and following him on Twitter @jayrosen_nyu.

Hashtags to Explore

- #advertising
- #converged
- #leadgen
- #mashup
- #nativead
- #nativeadvertising
- #outboundmarketing
- #sponsoredcontent

Maximize Marketing Impact with Converged Media

Chapter 10

Drive Sales with Marketing Automation

"We see our customers as invited guests to a party, and we are the hosts. It's our job every day to make every important aspect of the customer experience a little bit better."

—Jeff Bezos, CEO of Amazon

One morning not too long ago, Lisa woke up to a house without hot water and heat. Fortunately it was a mild day in Boston and her family members, among them three teenage daughters, handled the inconvenience well. When she called the large home services company with whom she had as service contract for 15 years, a customer service representative told her that it would be a week before they could investigate what was wrong. When Lisa expressed concern that this was not soon enough, the representative, who had clearly been through customer service training, explained quite nicely that she understood how Lisa felt, but that there was nothing she could do. Every time Lisa made a suggestion, the representative delivered the same response.

After hanging up the phone, Lisa called a local heating company that arrived at her home within the hour. Several hours later, the boiler was fixed, and the heat and hot water were back. Before they left, Lisa transferred her service contract to the local company and cancelled her existing contract.

This is a familiar story and one for which our customers and prospects have very little patience. In a day and age where customer experience makes or breaks a brand, multinational, national, regional, and local brands must all be able to deliver on the essentials that matter to their customers. Plenty of brands are eager to step up to the plate, offering our customers the type of customer experience they have come to enjoy and expect, if we cannot.

How are companies able to deliver remarkable customer relationships at scale? Successful companies are not just sending their employees through customer service training programs to teach them how to handle disappointed customers. They are taking initiative to change the way they operate and communicate in order to create a better customer experience from day one.

As we have seen, one of the ways companies are improving their customer experience is through personalized engagement. Communicating one-on-one with the right message, at the right time, through the right channels is a daunting task, however. It involves capturing and analyzing our prospects' and customers' digital body language and responding to them, individually, with appropriate content that is integrated across multiple channels, based upon their behavior. This can amount to thousands of interactions and decisions daily. For companies with more than a handful of prospects and customers, this cannot be accomplished manually. It requires an intelligent and integrated customer-engagement platform.

Wanted: An Intelligent and Integrated Customer-Engagement Platform

Most marketers recognize the need for a marketing platform that allows us to personalize conversations with our prospects and customers across channels. However, the majority of us currently interact via multiple, disparate software systems. E-mail communications are delivered by one system; social media by another. While we may be getting the message out, technology silos prevent us from creating the type of synchronized and predictive interactions that our prospects and customers are increasingly coming to expect and that lead to increased revenue.

Technology fragmentation also prohibits us from being able to accurately understand the impact of our marketing efforts. Lacking integrated analytics, organizations often employ a first-click or last-click attribution model, which allocates full credit for revenue generated to the first or last interaction leading to a sale. While easy to apply, this model ignores the combination of content and channels that contribute to securing a new lead or customer. Tremendous insight is lost due to this measurement inadequacy. Meanwhile companies like Leapfrog Online are forging ahead, understanding the exact impact of each of their marketing decisions and using this knowledge to disrupt the compensation model of its industry.

Recognizing the need for an integrated customer-engagement platform, myriad companies are building enterprise marketing management solutions. This is a dynamic market in which much consolidation is taking place as companies look to expand their functionality. Players include but are not limited to Act-On, TreeHouse, HubSpot, and Loop-Fuse, as well as SalesForce (ExactTarget/Pardot), Silverpop, Neolane, Marketo, Eloqua (Oracle), Aprimo (Teradata), and IBM Unica.

Debate continues about what comprises the ideal customer-engagement solution. Some companies are committed to building an all-in-one enterprise marketing management solution that, in addition to automating communication with our prospects and customers, manages multiple internal marketing processes including marketing planning and budgets, calendars, workflows and permissions, and content creation. Others are adopting a multi-vendor approach, looking to integrate core-marketing systems into a best-of-breed engagement platform. With few exceptions, there does not seem to be a need for custom-built applications.

It will take some time to sort through this debate; however, according to a recent Forrester survey of digital experience professionals, the tide seems to be turning in favor of best-of-breed platform solutions. Sixty-one percent of respondents agreed that they are looking for best-of-breed applications instead of suite or custom-built approaches.[1] We believe that there are many reasons for this emerging preference. First, the ideal suite does not yet exist. Second, a best-of-breed approach allows companies to maximize the functionality of each component part. Third, most companies have invested too much time and money in existing technology to start from scratch. Given the wide range of solutions available, in this chapter we limit our discussion to the marketing automation platforms.

What Is Marketing Automation?

Marketing automation means different things to people. This marketplace confusion is not surprising. Although marketing automation has been around for a decade, it has changed substantially during that time. There is also a fair amount of residual distrust from earlier marketing process automation attempts that resulted in customer annoyance—e-mail blasts that our customers did not want, but were inexpensive to send, and automated call centers that frustrated our customers rather than resolving their issues.

Today's marketing automation technology is different. It focuses on creating and nurturing demand and ongoing engagement with our prospects and existing customers through personalized engagement. It reaches far beyond yesterday's e-mail blasts to optimize the type of content, the timing of our messages, and the channels in which they are delivered, based on individual customer behavior and preferences. Using business rules, algorithms, and real-time data inflows, marketing automation tools continually evaluate prospects' and customers' behavior to determine the next best action. In so doing, the technology allows companies to streamline and automate marketing processes and to accurately assess the impact of marketing activities.

Can You Benefit from Marketing Automation?

Sanjay Dholakia, CMO of Marketo, one of the leaders in the industry, explains who can benefit from marketing automation, "If you are in the business of selling something to someone, you really need this because buying has fundamentally changed." As we have seen, targeted content, distributed in the right channels with the appropriate cadence, is key to building customer relationships. As a result, all types of organizations, regardless of size, segment, or category, are purchasing marketing automation technology. Big companies like Chrysler, McKesson, and Samsung and non profits like Harvard Business School have installed systems. Small and medium businesses are currently the fastest-growing market segment. In addition to managing leads, B2B marketers are expanding their use of marketing automation across the customer journey to include managing webinars and renewals. For example, for customers with contracts that will

269

soon be up for renewal, we may distribute content out 90, 60, and 30 days before the contract is due, that outline personalized recommendations for how they can enhance the usefulness of our product or service. We may invite those customers who are up for renewal, and have not taken advantage of the knowledge contained within our customer community or our personalized consulting, to give them a try. Many business-to consumer companies (B2C) are also adopting marketing automation to facilitate cross-channel data collection and communication. These platforms scan trigger a follow-up communication from a coffee chain like Dunkin' Donuts, to customers after they have downloaded its app, offering them a free coffee the first time they use the app to make a purchase. eCommerce companies are using marketing automation to manage shopping cart abandonment. Experion has found that bringing "left in the cart" items to the attention of shoppers causes a 20 percent lift in transaction rates over promotional mailings.[2] B2C companies are also applying the lead scoring feature of marketing automation, which we will discuss in more depth in the coming pages, to track and rank their most important influencers. A young brewery tracks its customers' tweets, blog posts, engagement on its website, and Klout score, to determine to whom it will send personal notes.[3] When you have limited time and resources, this ability to prioritize makes a difference.

Business-to-business companies in the high-tech sector were early adopters of marketing automation; the usefulness of the technology to facilitate high involvement purchases, where there was a long sales cycle that involved a fair amount of research, was clear. As in the past, today's marketing automation platforms allow companies to accompany their prospects through the sales cycle, nurturing leads with relevant and increasingly personalized content. Multiple experience paths can be designed to address the varying educational needs of each of our personas—HR might have a different take on the challenge at hand than Marketing or IT—each of which is integrated across channels. Each interaction adds value as it built upon the prospect's existing knowledge of the product or service and reflects actions they have taken—what they may have downloaded or decided not to view—with the goal of moving the relationship forward (see Figure 10.1).

Dear Lisa,

The **Content Marketing** virtual conference is underway and there's still time to join us. You can participate in the sessions, get advice and tips from our sponsors in the exhibit hall, and network with your peers.

Two great sessions are coming up:

- **KEYNOTE: Less Content. Bigger Results**—In this must-attend session, Andrew Davis will show you real-life examples of successful companies (big and small) who have created less content but delivered stunning results. Before our time's up, you'll be armed with three simple secrets that will drive a steady stream of sales right to your door.
- **The Future of Search and Content Marketing**—In what direction are the search engines headed in 2014? Join us for this information-packed session to learn how to leverage your content marketing efforts using the search insights shared.

Enter the virtual conference *fashionably* late.

Figure 10.1 Marketing Automation Acknowledges and Reflects Customers' Behavior

What's Inside the Black Box?

Marketing automation systems differ by vendor. At their core, marketing automation systems include a central marketing database, an engagement engine, and analytic capabilities. Careful evaluation of vendors before making a purchase is key to finding the right match.

Create a Centralized Marketing Database

Personalized marketing is rooted in a deep understanding of our customers. This rich perspective allows us to identify our key prospects and customers, segment them accordingly, and create relevant messaging based upon their behaviors across a variety of channels.

As we might expect, creating a trustworthy 360-degree view of each prospect and customer is not as simple as pressing a button. It requires that we identify, prioritize, standardize, collect, clean, integrate, govern, and secure relevant data from multiple sources. It is worth the effort, because this single view and dynamic system of record becomes a vital enabler for all of our customer experience efforts.

Marketing automation creates a system of record of what has taken place in the early phase of the relationship in much the same way as CRM does for the later stage of the process. Each interaction, whether it takes place online or offline, generates time series data on individual customers—when they visited our store, when they opened an e-mail, when they tweeted something about us, what they chose to view and not view—which creates a robust behavior-based picture of each of our prospects and customers.

When marketing automation systems are integrated with CRM, both marketing and sales can be continually aware of how much is in the pipeline and which specific leads are flowing through. Similarly, when supported by details of our customers' past interactions with us, our call center reps can provide more knowledgable service. For instance, after installing IBM's Unica marketing automation solution, one European financial institution estimated its enhanced revenue and reduced call center expenses in the first year to be 4 million Euros.[4]

Develop an Engagement Engine

Marketing automation platforms provide an engagement engine though which marketers can create and manage our customer interactions across channels. Typical features include e-mail marketing, social media marketing, landing page and form creation, lead nurturing, and prediction and lead scoring. Some marketing automation platforms also include event marketing capabilities–personalized invites, reminders, and follow-up for webinars or live events–as well as PPC and SEO tools, content management, and lead generation.

With these tools, marketers can run polls, virtual events, and referral programs and create new landing pages. Some systems come with predesigned and verified templates to help marketers become productive sooner. By making it easier for marketers to undertake these tasks, marketing automation systems often reduce the need for outside web designers and IT involvement, realizing substantial cost savings. For example, using Marketo's solution, a health care system was able to save significant costs on advertising dollars, equating to a 3,000 percent return-on-investment. What made the difference? A combination of replacing direct mail and print advertising with a targeted e-mail campaign; reducing the need for web designers since landing pages and e-mails could be created without coding skills; and testing of marketing content to maximize impact.[5]

Optimize with Analytic Capabilities

The predictive lead scoring aspect of marketing automation helps us prioritize our prospects and customers and helps us determine how prospects should be stewarded through the pipeline and the next action we should take with our existing customers. A dynamic rank, this lead score is continually updated, reflecting every action that a prospect or customer chooses to take—or not—in addition to demographic data and the source of the lead (some sources may have higher close rates than others). Lead scoring can also be employed to rank our existing customers depending upon their likeliness to purchase, cross-sell, or renew, and their potential influence.

In addition to making ongoing personalized and predictive communications possible, the analytics component of marketing automation also allows us to test, measure, and optimize our efforts and determine their impact on key financial measures. Utilizing A/B testing we can adjust aspects of our content, search terms, other marketing initiatives midstream to enhance our effectiveness. Further, by creating a closed-loop system, a topic we will explore shortly, we can track leads and sales back to their origins, making it possible for us to identify our most frequent interactions and which channels or combination of channels generates the largest return.

Marketo and Google have collaborated to build models that determine the impact of specific search terms on revenue. In the past, search has been evaluated by click-through rates and landing page hits. With these models, marketers can now see which search terms actually convert into revenue. With this knowledge in hand, we can scale back on the search terms used, optimizing our investment in those that deliver.

Maximize Revenue Performance

Marketing automation is increasingly being referred to as *revenue-performance management* technology because of how it positively impact companies' revenue. By capturing and nurturing leads and continually engaging customers in meaningful ways, marketing automation maximizes our revenue as potential prospects or customers no longer fall through the cracks. By providing hard evidence of what works and what doesn't, it enables continuous optimization of our marketing programs.

Marketing automation also enhances the productivity of our marketing and sales staff by aligning both groups around the customer journey. According to Nuclear Research, companies can expect to achieve an increase in marketing staff productivity of between 1.5 and 6.9 percent and an increase in sales productivity by an average of 4 percent.[6] Similarly, Eloqua has found that businesses that are using marketing automation and aligning their sales and marketing activities see a "451 percent increase in qualified leads, a 54 percent increase in sales quota achievements, and a 70 percent increase in sales cycle speed."[7]

Lead nurturing and scoring provide a prime example of how this alignment can be achieved. As we have seen, marketing automation tools operates on the customer experience journey model. To employ the model, marketing and sales must clearly define their roles and expectations for the front end of the customer experience journey. Working together, marketing and sales must create well-defined descriptions of what comprises marketing-qualified leads and sales-qualified leads. They must determine the methodology upon which prospects' interests and sales readiness will be determined and define thresholds for when specific reports should be taken. These definitions bring transparency to the sales process and reduce the finger pointing that murkiness has promoted.

Some companies are choosing to institute Service Level Agreements (SLA) between sales and marketing that incorporate these definitions and include clear targets for marketing regarding lead quantity and quality, and for sales regarding how qualified leads will be pursued. Marketing automation systems help manage the process, by notifying both parties of actions that should prompt pre-agreed-upon behaviors. For example, the system may send a message to sales saying, "We are sending you this lead, which we believe to now be sales qualified. You have five days to respond. If you believe the lead is not sales ready, please recycle." In Dholakia's experience, this process shortens the sales cycle and creates many more win-ready leads.

Prove the Value of Marketing

If we know how our content impacts lead generation, lead nurturing, and sales readiness, we can quantify marketing's impact on revenue. This is a godsend, because the mandate for increased financial accountability on marketing is not going away. A recent study by the Fournaise Marketing Group, which sells products to measure marketing performance, found that 73 percent of CEOs are concerned that marketers "focus too much on the latest marketing trends, but can rarely demonstrate how those trends will help them generate more business for the company."[8] Going forward it will serve us well if we can clearly articulate the effectiveness of our marketing efforts in economic terms that matter to our C-suite such as impact on revenue or profitability.

Marketing automation's closed-loop analytics make it possible for us to quantify marketing's impact on these key financial measurements. How is this possible? Closed-loop analytic reporting helps us to tie every lead, sale, or up-sell to the marketing initiatives that launched them by tracking customers across the customer journey. By assigning a specialized tracking token for each of our marketing initiatives, whether it takes place online or offline, we can determine which touchpoints initially captured our prospects' attention. While this information is key in helping us understand and optimize our early stage marketing efforts, it does not tell us what happened next. The real power comes when we can link the behavior of these anonymous visitors to specific customer profiles. When we have accomplished this, we have closed the loop. We are able to track our customers' behavior across their entire customer experience journey, observing which of our activities produce results. With this knowledge, we can quantify marketing's impact on revenue and profitability.

275

How do we close the loop? By designing our early-stage touch-points with an effective trigger that prompts visitors to click-through to a simple lead-capture form, we create the opportunity to collect their personal information. If we provide enough value so that he or she is willing to take the time to fill in the form, we can make the link, transforming an anonymous visitor into a person with a name.

Knowing how essential this step is, we want to do all we can to simplify the form completion process. Practicing *progressive profiling*, in which we only ask for a minimum amount of information upfront, and continue to add to the profile over time, is an effective strategy. Explaining why the information we are asking is necessary, if it is not readily evident, what the information will and will not be used for, and reassuring people that they can remove themselves from our database at any time, can reduce concerns about spam and privacy.

How do we go from providing a lead-capture form to proving how our marketing efforts are impacting our organization's financial results? Once we have closed the loop, we can readily capture the ongoing behaviors of our leads and customers. We can then measure our impact on revenue by noting how many targets and leads we generated and the number of qualified leads we were able to pass along to sales. Taking it one step further, we can also track the sales that marketing sourced or influenced, quantifying how marketing directly contributed to new business. (By quantifying the number of leads that sales recycles back to us, and garnering an understanding of the supporting reasoning, we can make refinements to the process and improve our future productivity.)

Closed-loop analytics also allow us to evaluate marketing's impact on profitability. Time in the sales pipeline reveals how quickly we are able to convert leads into sales. Our goal, of course, is to accelerate this process, however, we have to take great care not to rush our prospects.

Other profitability metrics to consider applying include our customer acquisition costs (CAC), which reflects the efficiency of the combined efforts of marketing and sales over time. (It is calculated by combining the total sales and marketing cost for a period of time, divided by the number of new customers obtained during the same period. To find marketing's percentage, take marketing's total cost and divide it by the total sales and marketing costs that we used to determine the CAC.) Observing how our CAC changes over time can be a useful starting place to analyze the impact of our efforts. No hard and fast guidelines for interpretation here, just an important trend to note and explore.

Go for Broke

The ability to identify who within our sales and marketing organization has contributed to a new lead or customer relationship creates new incentives and compensation opportunities. For example, with this knowledge marketers can be incentivized on the basis of pipeline development, rather than campaign effectiveness, aligning marketing compensation with revenue generation. Marketo, for example, is able to have both its sales and marketing people work on quotas, sharing in the associated risks and rewards, because it can track the efforts of its marketing and sales personnel with precision.[9] As a result, management believes that it can better manage every aspect of the revenue cycle to maximize profitability.

We recognize that this new way of being evaluated and compensated would be a major shift for marketers; however, it is worthy of consideration because it reflects marketing's increased importance to the sales cycle. By tying the success of our marketing efforts to our impact on revenue, we have the opportunity to position ourselves as key drivers of revenue, rather than primarily creators of expenses. With sales and marketing in alignment around the revenue cycle, we may eventually choose to merge the two departments into one.

Marketing Automation Supports—but Does Not Replace—Marketers

We cannot just buy a marketing automation system and press "go." To yield benefits, marketing automation requires a comprehensive strategy, new processes, and content, and that requires people.

In Dholakia's experience, to successfully adopt marketing automation, companies should:

- View marketing as creating a customer experience journey, rather than executing marketing campaigns, aligning their efforts with today's buyer behavior.

- Be comfortable with data-based decision-making and analytics, and the underlying enabling technology.

- Have a content strategy and skillset around it to generate and nurture leads and drive ongoing engagement. Content remains the fuel that drives marketing automation.

- Develop an effective end-to-end customer process that clearly delineates responsibilities across functions and drives alignment. This includes everything from data capture and quality, to lead management and measurement.

- Determine who will have ongoing responsibility for the system. In Dholakia's experience, this usually falls in marketing operations for large companies and demand generation teams for smaller ones.

While there is an upfront learning curve, marketing automation does not have to be overwhelming. Most vendors have dedicated implementation teams that can get systems up and running, and online resources to provide ongoing support to sales and marketing. Dholakia reminds us that we do not have to reach an über level of sophistication initially. In his experience, companies can crawl, walk, or run, according to their individual needs.

For example, looking to get up and running quickly, a company may decide to create two customer journey tracks at first, one for prospects and one for existing customers. In support of these tracks, they may create three pieces of content for each persona, each piece building upon the prior. (Remember the matrix, which captures content by persona and stage in the journey in Chapter 7?) This amounts to six pieces of initial content that need to be created, if they do not already exist.

Similarly, in terms of linking activity across channels, companies can think big, but start small. Most companies begin with linking e-mails to customers' web activity—specifically, sending content related to the web pages a prospect visited via e-mail. From there companies often add social channels to take advantage of sharing opportunities. Over time mobile and local are being added to the mix, creating contextualized customer experiences. New content and capabilities are continually added, making the platform, and the customer experiences that it enables, that much more useful.

In the following chapter, we will explore ways that companies are engaging their customers throughout the customer experience journey via loyalty and digital couponing programs.

QUESTIONS

- What interests you about marketing automation?
- How does your company currently nurture leads? How is the handoff between marketing and sales accomplished?
- What specific pain points may marketing automation help alleviate?
- What challenges and opportunities do you anticipate in using marketing automation?
- What metrics do you use to evaluate the effectiveness of your marketing efforts? Can you link marketing efforts to key financial goals?
- What is your next step?

RESOURCES

Influencers We Recommend

- *Ardath Albee*. A B2B marketing strategist with more than 25 years of experience, Albee is CEO of Marketing Interactions, Inc. and author of *eMarketing Strategies for the Complex*

(continued)

(continued)

Sale. In addition to strategizing about complex sales, Albee enjoys cooking from scratch and playing with her Australian Shepherd and is an avid blogger. Stay current on her thinking at www.marketinginteractions.com and on Twitter @ardath421.

- *Rob Brosan*. As principal analyst at Forrester in Customer Insights, Brosan spends his days thinking about how to use marketing technology to build customer relationships that differentiate companies from the competition. Subscribe to his insightful blog at http://blogs.forrester.com/rob_brosnan and follow him on Twitter @brosan.

- *Sanjay Dholakia*. As CMO of Marketo, Dholakia knows marketing automation and revenue performance technology as a customer and a marketer. Draw from his expertise, which was garnered in roles such as CEO of CrowdFactory and as CMO of Lithium Technologies, on Twitter @sdholakia and http://blog.marketo.com.

- *Jay Famico*. As research director at SiriusDecisions, a research and consulting firm specializing in helping B2B companies improve their sales and marketing effectiveness through technology, Famico specializes in demand creation strategies. Stay on the cutting edge by following him on Twitter @JayFamico and reading his blog posts at www.siriusdecisions.com.

- *Paul Greenberg*. Author of *CRM at the Speed of Light: Social CRM Strategies, Tools and Techniques for Engaging Your Customers*, Greenberg also serves as president of The 56 Group, a customer strategy consulting firm. Voted one of the most influential people in CRM by *CRM Magazine*, he has been called "the godfather of CRM" and "the Walt Whitman of CRM" by observers of the industry. Learn with Greenberg from his blog at www.the56group.typepad.com and from following him on Twitter @pgreenbe.

- *Brian Halligan.* CEO and cofounder of HubSpot, a marketing software company designed to help businesses transform the way they market their products, Halligan is a pioneer in the inbound marketing world. He is a senior lecturer at MIT and the coauthor of *Inbound Marketing: Getting Found Using Google, Social Media, and Blogs* and the author of *Marketing Lessons from the Grateful Dead.* Named an Ernst & Young Entrepreneur of the Year, Halligan is also an avid Red Sox fan. Follow him on Twitter @bhalligan.

- *David Lewis.* Founder and CEO of DemandGen, a global team of marketing automation, CRM, and lead generation experts. Lewis is the author of *Manufacturing Demand: The Principles of Lead Management.* Learn with Lewis at www.demandgen.com and on Twitter @demandgendave.

- *Charlene Li.* Coauthor of *Groundswell*, author of *Open Leadership*, and founder of Altimeter Group, a research-based advisory firm that helps companies and industries leverage disruption to their advantage, Li is an expert on social media and technology. She was named one of the 100 most creative people in business by *Fast Company* in 2010 and one of the most influential women in technology in 2009. Explore her thoughts at www.charleneli.com and on Twitter @Charleneli.

- *SavvyB2Bmarketing.* This group of 6 "savvy sisters" creates strategic content-based marketing solutions for B2B clients. They are also self-proclaimed content geeks, and have created a robust resource for all things B2B at www.savvyb2bmarketing.com. Follow the sisters on Twitter @savvy_B2B.

- *Lori Wizdo.* Marketing automation and lead-to-revenue management are a primary focus of Wizdo, who is a principal analyst at Forrester. Often published in *CIO Magazine* and *B2B Marketing*

(*continued*)

(continued)

among others, there is much to be learned from Wizdo at www.blogs.forrester.com/lori_wizdo and on Twitter @Loriwizdo.

Hashtags to Explore

- #B2B
- #L2RM (lead to revenue management)
- #LeadGen
- #marketingautomation
- #measure
- #segment
- #UX

Chapter 11

Craft Worthwhile Loyalty and Digital Couponing Programs

"Most people would not care if 73 percent of brands disappeared tomorrow."

—Havas Media

Walgreens wants to become America's first choice as a partner in health and daily living. As the largest drugstore chain in the United States, it has the size to achieve this goal. Its Balance Rewards® program may be just what it takes to earn Americans' hearts and minds—and improve their bodies.

Balance Rewards® uniquely combines traditionally purchase-based rewards with a wellness challenge. Through the program, Walgreens recognizes its customers for maintaining a healthy lifestyle. Members receive points for setting exercise- and weight management goals and for taking specific steps to achieve them: walking, running, and recording their weight. Participants can easily track their progress by syncing wireless activity trackers (Fitbit and BodyMedia) and scales (Withings) with its website or mobile app or by inputting their data manually. Balance Rewards® points can be redeemed for dollars on future Walgreens purchases. A virtual community offers support to Balance Rewards® participants—one member described how the community helped her get back into her walking routine after surviving a car accident—and provides a fun venue for sharing photos of favorite walks and runs.

"By enhancing our loyalty program to further promote healthy behaviors, we're encouraging customers to take steps to help them achieve overall wellness," explains Graham Atkinson, chief marketing and customer experience officer.[1] Over 85 million members have enrolled in the program to date. Of those, about 886,000 are reporting their health activities and have logged over 25 million miles in the program.[2]

Loyalty Programs Are Ubiquitous

Loyalty programs are abundant. Our customers' wallets are stuffed to the brim with loyalty cards and the weight of loyalty tags on their key chains is damaging their car-ignition switches. In the United States alone, program memberships reached 2.65 billion in 2012, an average of 21.9 memberships per household. While programs differ in design, the underlying goal of most loyalty programs is to motivate customers to make repeat purchases. Are the programs working? Is loyalty on the rise? Does loyalty even matter?

Let's tackle the last question first. Loyal customers are one of our most valuable assets. Fred Reichheld, founder of the loyalty practice at Bain & Company and author of numerous books on loyalty, believes that it is virtually impossible to achieve profitable growth without a loyal base of customers. For starters, there is what Reichheld calls the *customer volume effect*. Businesses must have customers to be viable. At any given point in time, a company's customer base is the sum of its new and repeat customers. Without repeat customers, companies would continually have to acquire new customers to stand still, much less grow. As marketers, we can appreciate the effort and resources that would involve. The very thought provokes images from the Ancient Greek story of Sisyphus, the king of Ephyra, who spent his whole life rolling an immense boulder up a hill, only to watch it roll to the bottom, and then begin again.

Loyal customers fuel advocacy. If our customers respect who we are and what we do, they *want* to tell others about us. Their voices can draw prospects to us, encourage them to purchase from us, and improve their experience with us. These voices can also serve as buffers against negative experiences and publicity. In Reichheld's experience, customers' willingness to promote is the strongest single measurable correlation between customers and corporate performance. So compelling is the evidence, he created the Net

Promoter Score (NPS) framework to help companies optimize their customer experience.

Loyal customers are often more profitable. They understand the value that we provide and this understanding is priceless. Often this appreciation reduces our customer's price sensitivity. How many of us need a financial incentive to frequent our favorite restaurant? Loyal customers also tend to spend more. The probability of selling to an existing customer is significantly higher than to a new one: 60 to 70 percent versus 5 to 20 percent.[3] Regular shoppers often become familiar with features that enhance their shopping experience— 1-click shopping and Prime shipping at Amazon have been shown to increase both the number of sales and the average-sales-dollar value.

In addition to decreased price sensitivity, loyal customers can be less expensive to maintain. Depending upon the business, acquisition costs can make new customers 5 to 10 times more expensive than existing customers. Some businesses with high upfront costs can actually get themselves into a cash-flow bind by taking on too many new customers too quickly, especially if customers defect before the company has recouped these costs. Often our customer-service costs decrease as customers gain familiarity with how we operate as well.

Clearly we want loyal customers. Have loyalty programs made headway, or is this a place where we need to focus our attention?

Is Loyalty on the Decline?

Most brands can no longer feel certain about their customers' commitment. Loyalty erosion and customer defection are pervasive. A recent study by Catalina, which works with consumer products brands and retailers, found that for the average top 100 brands in their network, 45 percent of highly loyal consumers either reduced loyalty or completely left the brand within a year. Had these companies been able to avert defections, they would have grown by another 8.5 percent, which is five times greater than the average brand's actual growth rate during the period.[4] That is significant.

Why are customers losing that loving feeling? Tough economic conditions are often cited as a reason for a loss of loyalty—people

Craft Worthwhile Loyalty and Digital Couponing Programs

often go where the best deal is—but that is only part of the story. Globalization has unleashed new competition and removed traditional barriers to entry. E-commerce has made it rare to be the only game in town or to be able to compete on the basis of convenience. Our customers can comparison shop and purchase almost anything from the convenience of their desktop or mobile device. What is more, today's customers have a proclivity to the new. While this seemingly insatiable appetite creates demand for innovation, it wreaks havoc with efforts at being people's first choice again and again.

But loyalty is far from dead. The real problem is not with our customers, but with us. The best way to create loyalty is to understand what really drives our customers' decisions, the itch or job they are trying to scratch or complete, and if this overlaps with our capabilities and priorities, to deliver on it. Reichheld firmly believes that when businesses give their customers superior value, the loyalty problem is generally solved.

How do loyalty programs create superior value? Or do they?

Do Loyalty Programs Promote Loyalty?

For loyalty programs to work, our customers have to actively use them. Active may be defined differently for each of our companies depending upon whether we sell coffee or washing machines. Only 44 percent of loyalty-program memberships in the United States are considered active and that number is falling.[5] As a result, according to the 2011 Colloquy Loyalty Census, one-third of the $48 billion worth of perceived value in rewards goes unused.[6] This suggests that loyalty programs are good at enrolling members, but not as good at keeping them engaged. It also means that companies are spending time, money, and effort offering experiences from which their customers are not deriving any value.

The ubiquity of loyalty programs is partially responsible. Back in 1981, when American Airlines introduced the first loyalty program, they were the only game in town. Establishing a rewards program was enough to steal market share and keep customers engaged. Today having a loyalty program is no longer a source of differentiation as most competitors within the same category have

286

established programs. What differentiates companies now is their overall customer experience and any superior value that their loyalty programs offer.

The structure of the industry also matters. Don Peppers and Martha Rogers have studied the market conditions in which loyalty programs work best. In their book *Enterprise One on One*, they identify two key market characteristics for successful loyalty programs: a few high-value customers who make the vast majority of purchases and little product differentiation.[7] Applying this criteria, airlines are considered a perfect industry for loyalty programs. About 1 percent of their customers do the most traveling and the product is essentially the same for everyone: transportation from here to there. Loyalty programs that provide access to a more pleasurable experiences—business class, pre-boarding, and streamlined security checks—reward their preferred customers and provide incentives for the rest to keep coming back in hopes of receiving similar benefits.

Polygamous loyalty also impacts brand loyalty. Today's customers are often loyal to several brands in the same category. Larry is loyal to several airlines. He has a preferred airline for travel to Shanghai, another for London, and still another for the West Coast. In order to create brand preference, the underlying travel experience would have to change significantly or the associated loyalty program become extremely compelling. Stay tuned to see what Delta is doing.

Conversely, while customers have multiple loyalties in some categories, they may have zero loyalty in others. Dan Fukushima, who as vice president of Sparks Grove, a marketing strategy and creative firm, works with clients to enhance customer loyalty, has found that people are generally loyal to the things that matter to them. If something is not important to them personally, they tend to be category agnostic. Even if they enroll in a reward program, if the product or service does not hold much meaning for them, they will not become active users. Similarly, people's interest in a category may change over time. While our kids are toddlers, we might be highly interested in joining Pampers' or Huggies' loyalty programs. Once they are through that stage, however, most of us will probably turn our attention elsewhere.

Program design can also impact whether customers remain active. Most loyalty programs are structured to offer a discount on current

Craft Worthwhile Loyalty and Digital Couponing Programs

purchases or to allocate points that can be applied in the future. The challenge with a discount-based approach is that customers who tend to like discounts have the lowest loyalty coefficient. In our effort to recruit and reward loyal customers, we may actually be recruiting less-desirable customers. We are creating an affinity toward a reward program, not necessarily to our brands.

Finally, loyalty comes down to the way in which we demonstrate our loyalty to customers: through ongoing remarkable customer experiences. Companies that consistently offer great experiences does not need a loyalty program to keep people coming back—think of Apple. Conversely, no loyalty program can make up for a poor brand experience.

Benefits Beyond Loyalty

Mandates for loyalty programs are reaching beyond customer acquisition to include generating customer data to support one-on-one marketing communication and engagement throughout the customer experience journey. Loyalty programs' proprietary databases provide unique insights into our customers. With insights derived from this regularly refreshed data we can segment our market, create highly targeted messages and offers, measure the impact of our promotions, and observe valuable trends.

Recognizing the link between customer data and its ability to deliver enhanced customer experience, Papa Gino's, which owns the Papa Gino's pizzeria chain and the D'Angelo sandwich shops, developed an integrated framework around its loyalty program that allows it to track buying patterns, monitor the effectiveness of its messaging and offers, and improve critical touchpoints such as wait time on phone or its time-to-delivery.

Similarly, after analyzing data from its loyalty program, a sports shoe retailer realized that many of its lapsed customers had outstanding rewards certificates. After receiving a personalized e-mail from the retailer reminding them of their rewards status, over 20 percent of these customers redeemed their certificates. What is more, these redemptions lead to incremental revenue, as customers redeeming certificates generally spent more than the average sale.

Access to this customer information can fuel contextualization and the ongoing engagement that many of our customers desire. While customer information can benefit every company, Fukushima has found that it has unique value to business-to-business-to-consumer companies (B2B2C) that typically do not have direct contact with their end users. It presents an unprecedented opportunity to understand and engage directly with end users.

Here is the challenge: Most companies have to improve their analytics ability and technology infrastructure to be able to act on customer data they collect through their loyalty programs. According to a 2013 Forrester survey of marketers, only 37 percent of companies have the technology and analytics in place to deliver customized offers to customers across channels.[8]

Strategies for Designing Loyalty Programs

Have a Clear Goal in Mind

Successful programs clearly define what is being rewarded, what behaviors it will drive, and how those behaviors will add value to the business. A surprising number of companies do not take the time to consider these fundamentals and optimize them for their businesses, however. When designing new loyalty-program offerings, Fukushima recommends testing potential ideas through marketing campaigns that mimic the fundamentals. If the idea is successful, it can then be developed into an ongoing program.

Any number of activities can be rewarded. For example:

- Sprint discourages defections by rewarding its customers with an airline mile for each dollar spent. Recognizing its customers' desire for flexibility, the miles are redeemable at five different airlines.

- American Eagle Outfitters, Old Navy, and Best Buy encourage shoppers to come into their stores by rewarding them for simply walking through their doors.

- Looking to harness the insight of its constituent base, JetBlue rewards its customers with points and money for participating

Craft Worthwhile Loyalty and Digital Couponing Programs

in its e-Rewards opinion panel, which helps the airline and its complementary partner brands shape future products.

- Pepsi rewards followers on Twitter (@pepsi) with free music downloads if they include the hashtag #PepsiMusicNOW in their tweets.

- Amazon rewards purchases made by Amazon Prime members and creates a compelling reason to shop with free two-day shipping, and unlimited instant streaming of 41,000 movies and TV episodes, and complementary access to 350,000 eBooks.

Choose Rewards That Our Customers Value

Rewards can be powerful, as long as people value them. Our customers are heterogeneous. While some are motivated by money, others are motivated by recognition, or access to experiences. For example, some American Express cardholders want nothing more than in-game rewards for the popular game League of Legends, as a "thank you" for using their credit card. Others would prefer early-purchase options for tickets to a Justin Bieber concert. Successful loyalty programs build choice into their rewards. This is especially true in the case where the customer is different from the person making the purchase—perhaps a parent purchasing for a child, or someone buying a gift. In that case, rewards need to make sense for the purchaser.

Rewards that leverage our brands in our customers' eyes serve multiple purposes. Customers are rewarded for their behavior while building a deeper commitment to our brands. Members of Peet's Coffee & Tea subscription program, for example, are rewarded with the freshest coffee around. Coffee is roasted in small batches and is shipped to members within 24 hours of roasting.[9]

Powerful emotional connections are made when companies create opportunities for customers to live out their values. Warby Parker's Buy a Pair, Give a Pair program engages customers in its efforts to provide glasses to the almost 1 billion people in the world that it estimates need glasses, but who do not have access to optometrists. During their first three years of operation, the company and its customers distributed over 500,000 pairs of glasses. Similarly, through its

Common Threads Initiative, Patagonia offers its customers the opportunity to resell their Patagonia clothing online through eBay. The program reinforces the brand's attributes of durability, high quality, and eco-friendliness, while making it easier for its customers to justify a new purchase and make a difference.

Unfortunately, most loyalty programs are not keeping up with their customers' preferences. According to Forrester, less than half of loyalty programs leverage personalized offers and even fewer offer experiences.[10]

Tiered Programs Work

When it comes to loyalty programs, status is important. Customers value the opportunity to strive for a goal and to achieve recognition. Generally speaking, the optimal structure for a loyalty program for higher-commitment brands like airplanes and hotels is three tiers: top elite, bottom elite, and no status. To provide the necessary motivation, membership in the top tiers must remain relatively small so that members feel special and convinced that it is worth the necessary effort. However, companies should adopt the structure that works best for their customers. Starbucks, for example, has four tiers and Amazon Prime, two.

Providing a digital platform that allows customers to track their reward status in real time is key. Through its mobile app, Starbucks provides instantaneous-award allocation and notifications of how close its members are to achieving their next status upgrade. It acts as an effective trigger to keep people motivated.

Keep It Simple, Fresh, Fun

People value simplicity. Programs that are easy to understand work best. If our customers see how they will benefit from the program, they are more likely to enroll and remain active. They should be able to clearly identify the benefits of each tier and know what it takes to move up—and down.

Successful programs make rewards readily obtainable so that members feel that their efforts will be rewarded. The combination of a long-term goal (elite status) with opportunities for immediate gratification works well. Sometimes the design of our reward programs can inadvertently frustrate our customers. Points that cannot be redeemed because of excessive blackout dates are a common complaint. Another source of dissatisfaction is a loss of benefits when our customers' consumption habits change. Feeling demoted often sends once-preferred customers into the welcoming arms of competitors and to Twitter.

Ease of use is also important. As we have seen, mobile phones are making it easier for customers to interact with us and improve their brand experience. Google Wallet and Apple's Passbook apps allow companies to showcase their loyalty programs within these apps. The apps facilitate customer engagement through messaging, loyalty-status and reward balance updates, and simplified redemption.

To stay fresh, rewards programs require ongoing engagement triggers. Starbucks recognizes birthdays, texts offers, and introduces its members to new music and apps every week through its loyalty app. The luxury brand Gucci invites its biggest spenders to fashion shows and the Cannes Film Festival. Through its Priceless Cities Program MasterCard offers its members unique outings in various cities. Examples for Chicago include the chance to play catch in the Cubs' ballpark, Wrigley Field, or enjoying a live concert at Shedd's Aquarium.

Geotargeting capabilities, which allow marketers with retail distribution to reach customers who are in the vicinity with special invitations and experiences, create a timely, localized experience. For example, one evening a bar in Delhi texted special discount offers to patrons who were enjoying drinks at the bar. After 10 PM patrons who remained received a follow-up offer for cab service. The next morning they received a third message that thanked them for their patronage and included tips for reducing hangover symptoms. Their effort was a hit; 85 percent of patrons participated, and the bar's responsible-drinking efforts caused a buzz on social media.[11]

Gamification techniques, such as badges and awards, are a fun way to engage repeat customers. The hotel chain Embassy Suites tested several customer-loyalty methods including direct mail, e-mail, and inviting guests to play a game to determine which customer-loyalty methods were the most effective for its business.

The game performed the best, with nearly half of the 5,000 targeted customers participating.[12]

Gamification can also work with business-to-business (B2B) customers. Companies can add gaming features to their customer feedback process to encourage customers to participate. For instance, B2B marketers can create challenges for their customers by asking them to provide a short case study of how their product has impacted their business, or to generate a list of the five key questions prospects should ask before making a similar purchase. Participants are rewarded with a prize upon completion—perhaps gift cards or complementary consulting hours from the company.

Build Complementary Partnerships

Strategic partnerships with organizations that share the same customers, but address complementary needs, can increase the value of loyalty programs. Delta is blazing the way.

One of the most irritating moments for any traveler, but especially for frequent business travels, are flight delays that make connections between flights challenging. To ease the stress of these moments for its preferred customers—Diamond Medallion Status travelers who have at least 125,000 frequent flyer miles—Delta teamed up with Porsche to meet these elite customers on the tarmac with a Porsche Cayenne to escort them to their next flight. A member of Delta Elite Services explained the impact of this special touch to *NBC News*, "It really turns their frown into a smile."[13] As one customer who benefitted from the ride explains, "It feels like the airline cares."

Extending its customer care beyond the confines of the airport, Delta has teamed up with Starwood Hotels and Resorts to provide VIP customers with immediate, fully reciprocal perks to make their overall travel experience more pleasant. The first of its kind, the Crossover Rewards program lets Delta- and Starwood-preferred customers enjoy each company's most exclusive benefits—including late checkout, free Wi-Fi, priority boarding, and free baggage check—in addition to points accumulation. Customers love the ability to combine two travel accounts into a single program as evidenced by boosts in new memberships and usage.

Get Clear on the Costs

Loyalty programs cost money. Fukushima warns that the costs are not always obvious. In addition to the cost of administering the program, there are the costs associated with the rewards themselves, which can become higher than anticipated with higher-than-expected redemptions. Loyalty programs create liabilities that impact companies' financial reporting.

That having been said, for some companies, there may be costs associated with not having a program. If loyalty programs have become basic attributes, brand features that customers have come to expect, having a program may be the cost of doing business. In the service of gathering customer data, some companies may choose to run their loyalty programs as loss leaders in the short run, until the insight generated contributes to their overall bottom line.

Measuring Loyalty

There are several approaches to measuring loyalty. Some companies focus on customer retention, which measures how long customers stick around. As we noted in Chapter 4, this metric is generated from a backward glance, when there is very little opportunity to turn the situation around. Other companies use repeat sales, up-sells, and cross-sells as a proxy for loyalty. These numbers capture important behavior, but they miss the mark when it comes to understanding underlying attitudes and perceptions that may impact future purchases.

To get at the emotional components of loyalty, some marketers measure customer satisfaction, operating under the assumption that satisfied customers will be loyal and continue to buy in the future. Unfortunately, too many times companies have found that their very satisfied customers defect. Polygamous with their affection, customers may be loyal to other brands as well.

Another popular metric is the Net Promoter Score (NPS), which asks customers: How likely are you to recommend our company/product/service to your friends and colleagues? NPS captures sentiment as well as some expectation for the future and has been found to correlate with revenue growth. Companies like

Apple, American Express, GE, and Intuit use the metric; proponents say it successfully motivates the organization around improving the customer experience. We are all for that.

Customer effort scores address the simplicity factor. This process asks customers, "How much effort did you personally have to put forth to solve a problem with the company?" Companies that use this metric like the fact that it is rooted in an actual experience and measures a key performance indicator that impacts retention.

Engagement metrics assess how involved our customers are with us. The metric recognizes both the emotional and functional components of a purchase decision. Companies that employ this method believe that customers who are more emotionally invested in a brand are also more loyal. PeopleMetrics' *Most Engaged Customer Study* confirms this hypothesis, finding that businesses with higher engagement levels enjoy higher profits, return on investment, and share of market.[14]

Share of wallet is becoming an increasingly valued metric as it tackles the question of how important our brands are relative to other brands in the category. In an environment characterized by promiscuous loyalty, the winning ticket is being the preferred brand. Guided by this strategy, our goal is not to improve overall customer satisfaction, but to improve those factors that will improve our rank relative to the competition. (The Fogg and Kano models from Chapter 4 can be helpful in ascertaining this.) To improve our rank, our research must uncover why our customers use competitive brands: what are they looking for in those alternatives that we do not offer.[15]

What about Digital Couponing?

Frugal behavior is the new black, according to research conducted by the management consulting firm Booz & Co. Americans continue the value-conscious shopping habits they developed during the 2008 economic downturn, a practice that Booz & Co. believes will be an "enduring shift in U.S. consumer spending and behavior."[16] These habits include shopping at discount stores, purchasing online, buying less expensive private-label brands, and clipping coupons. Americans are not alone in this behavior. A Euromonitor survey from 2011 found that three-quarters of British consumers also expressed a strong interest in finding bargains, as did a majority of Brazilians, Germans, and French. This was not the case with Indian, Chinese, and Japanese consumers surveyed, however.[17]

Paper coupons have traditionally been used to bring in new users and garner incremental volume from price-conscious market segments. Digital versions are successfully doing both. A study conducted by Knowledge Networks found that digital coupons are attracting more new buyers than print by a margin of 35 percent.[18] Younger segments of the population that have not traditionally been coupon clippers are among them. Digital coupons also have higher incremental redemptions (77 percent versus 68 percent for print). The most prolific users tend to be traditional couponers—large families and baby boomers on fixed incomes. The one drawback to digital coupons: they yield lower return on investment for companies because of their higher redemption rates and distribution costs.

Digital coupon users say that they "enjoy the hunt" and the sense of gratification that comes from spending their money wisely. They also find digital coupons easy to use. A quick Internet search can yield results on dozens of websites, which can be printed out or saved on mobile devices to redeem in stores. Coupon apps like SnipSnap[19] and PushPins[20] simplify the process even further, organizing coupons, creating grocery lists, tracking spending, alerting shoppers to expiring coupons, and even transforming pictures of coupons and offers into scannable mobile images for use at checkout. Other apps like Coupon Sherpa[21] extend exclusive deals to their users and employ geolocation features to direct shoppers to the closest deals. Some brands choose to distribute their coupons directly on their social media sites to drive traffic to their digital properties and to capture customer data. A study by Syncapse found that 42 percent of Facebook fans surveyed said they became a fan of a brand in order "to get a coupon or discount."[22]

Segmentation is key in an environment where a growing portion of the population describe themselves as value conscious and/or coupon enthusiasts. Being able to differentiate our marketing messages, offers, products, and experiences, makes it possible for us to effectively service those markets that we have chosen to target.

In our next and final chapter we turn our attention to how we can spread customer-centricity throughout our ecosystems so that every component is working toward delivering the customer-experience differential.

QUESTIONS

- How loyal are your customers? How do you know?
- Has your customers' loyalty been increasing or decreasing? If so, can you identify why?
- Does your company have a loyalty program? If so, what behaviors does it reward? Are these behaviors linked to key drivers of your business?
- If your company has a loyalty program, how is it using loyalty data to improve your customer experience? Is it working?
- How price sensitive is your customer base? Are you able to differentiate your marking efforts to reflect value preferences?
- What is your next step?

RESOURCES

Influencers We Recommend

- *COLLOQUY*. The self-proclaimed voice of loyalty marketing, COLLOQUY provides a worldwide audience of 30,000+ marketers with consulting, news, editorial, educational, and research services. Follow COLLOQUY on Twitter @colloquy and explore their resources at www.colloquy.com.

- *Loyalty 360*. "The loyalty marketer's association," Loyalty 360 is a clearinghouse and think tank for all things loyalty. The organization offers a variety of resources including job boards, résumé banks, conferences, and webinars, in addition to aggregating articles and blog posts from leaders in the industry. Follow Loyalty 360 on Twitter @Loyalty 360 and peruse their extensive resources at www.loyalty360.org.

(continued)

Craft Worthwhile Loyalty and Digital Couponing Programs

(continued)

- *Fred Reichheld*. Recognized by *Consulting* magazine as one of the 25 Most Influential Consultants in its 2003 annual survey, Reichheld is a partner on FranklinCovey's Customer Loyalty Consulting Team. The founder of Bain & Company's loyalty practice, Reichheld created the Net Promoter Score (NPS). He is also the author of many books including *The Ultimate Question*. His work has appeared in the *Harvard Business Review*, the *Wall Street Journal*, the *New York Times, Financial Times, Fortune, BusinessWeek, and The Economist*. To learn more about NPS see www.netpromotersystemblog.com or follow him on Twitter @Fred Reichheld.

Hashtags to Explore

- #loyalty
- #customerloyalty
- #customersatisfaction
- #NetPromoterScore
- #NPS
- #shareofwallet

Chapter 12

Ignite Customer-Centricity Everywhere

"The largest enemy of change and leadership isn't a 'no.' It's a 'not yet....'
Change almost never fails because it's too early. It almost always fails because
it's too late."[1]

—Seth Godin

With 30 brands distributed in thousands of stores across several channels, a beverage manufacturer was eager to see how it might better
align the distribution of its products with the demand of each of its
retail partners. Ideally the mix of brands selected and the quantity and
package sizes delivered would be optimized for each individual store.
Further, promotional materials would be customized to reflect the
specific preferences and themes that resonated with each local store's
customer base.[2] Being one step removed from the end-user, the manufacturer lacked essential knowledge about demand for its products,
making it impossible to precisely match supply with demand and
enhance the relevance of its marketing efforts.

Fortunately, that is not the end of the story. By forming a tighter
alignment with its retail and media partners, the beverage manufacturer was able to optimize inventory and maximize revenue and profitability across its broader partner ecosystem. Although each member of this demand chain played a different role, they ultimately
served the same end-user. As a result, each had access to unique
customer insight. Working with the Cambridge Group, a subsidiary
of the Nielsen Company that focuses on understanding demand and
developing a growth strategy to capture it, the group was able to
consolidate each organization's proprietary data, constructing a more

complete understanding of their shared customer. With this information, the network was able to optimize each member's performance and that of the entire ecosystem. This in turn improved the overall customer experience, providing the ecosystem with a distinct competitive advantage over its competitors. We can all drink to that!

Customer-Centricity Is a Systems-Level Opportunity

As important as it is for marketers to retool themselves, individual marketers learning new skills is not enough to deliver remarkable customer experience. As we have seen, a highly synchronized ecosystem-wide effort is necessary to realize the customer-experience differential, which requires a greater level of organizational maturity than we have had in the past. As a result, customer-centricity demands that we develop new organizational competencies. Given their interdependent nature, these new competencies must be developed in chorus, with learning taking place across traditional business silos, not only as individuals or departments.

The type of learning is complex. In most cases we are operating on a frontier, without the benefit of already established material. As a result, we have to learn by doing, which requires us to get comfortable with real-world experimentation. This can be both invigorating and terrifying. We are also learning in diverse groups, characterized by entrenched points of view and differing ways of evaluating success. We have to create the conditions that will encourage people to think anew and across boundaries, in a timely way, with a goal in mind, and to take ownership of the results.

Managing the learning process of ecosystems is beyond the scope of most marketers' job descriptions, not to mention beyond our area of expertise; however, as stewards of our customers and champions of the customer experience, our job is to catalyze the effort if it has not yet caught fire. Fostering a shared vision for customer-centricity across our own organizations is a good place to start.

A Shared Vision for Customer-Centricity

A shared vision can catalyze our organizations to deliver remarkable customer experiences. This vision offers a common identity and sense of purpose. It enables collaboration, experimentation, and creativity, sparking something bigger than the sum of the organization's parts to come to life.

Peter Senge, who directs the Center for Organizational Learning at the MIT Sloan School of Management, describes shared vision as the answer to the question, "What do we want to create?"[3] Rick Kash, the vice chair of the Nielsen Company, describes this vision as a company's "thesis for winning."[4] In Kash's experience, all truly outstanding leaders have a thesis for winning. Without this shared mental model, organizations flounder; they cannot learn. In today's marketing environment, organizations that cannot learn, and learn quickly, don't survive.

What might a thesis for winning focused on customer-centricity look like? It depends upon the individual organization, its customers, and its broader ecosystem. An effective shared vision is not boilerplate; it is homegrown, unique to each company, and will change over time as opportunities for creating shared value shift. An effective thesis for winning focused on customer-centricity answers several questions: Why is customer experience vital in the marketplace? What does customer-centricity look like for us? What type of experiences do we want to deliver? How will we get there? Why will this approach work?[5]

Don't Go It Alone

Marketing cannot create nor activate this vision alone. In order for our thesis for winning to make a difference, broad senior management support is essential. For many companies, a customer-centric thesis for winning represents a fundamental cultural conversion and necessitates changes in organizational structure, operations, infrastructure purchases, governance practices, metrics, hiring criteria, and reward systems. Ultimately, it is the CEO's role to prioritize and champion the effort, articulating the shared vision and engaging the entire organization and broader ecosystem around it. Even if marketing or a CCEO, or CIO, has a mandate for managing the customer experience, in the absence of CEO support, customer-centricity will not happen; there are just too many forces acting against it. In our experience, most CEOs understand the necessity of being demand driven.

Ignite Customer-Centricity Everywhere

The challenge is in envisioning how it will manifest itself and getting there.

CEO support is essential, but not sufficient. For customer-centricity to take a hold of our organization, the vision reaches far beyond the C-suite. Every employee must understand the vision, its relative importance, and how they contribute to its success. They must also be empowered and energized to take ownership of the outcome.

Build the Vision

Story making can help build this shared vision. When we talk about story making, we are not talking about creating passively absorbed content: an edict from on high. Rather, we are envisioning experiences that invite our employees and business partners into the process of writing the next chapter of our collective corporate story that describes where we are headed and how we are going to get there. This type of shared story making harnesses our employees and business partners' ideas and creates an emotional connection to the emerging vision. Although it can generate a lot of noise in the process, in the end it yields a better vision, authorship throughout our ecosystem, knowledge of how people's work contributes to the vision, and enthusiasm for the undertaking.

IDEO's Maker Experiment

We can learn much from the design firm IDEO about how to build a vision and create a pro-learning environment. To rethink its own identity, and explore new ways of imagining corporate identity in general, IDEO is undertaking a maker experiment and has invited all of its employees to contribute to the process.

Michael Hendrix, who co-leads IDEO's Boston studio and is spearheading the effort, explains the impetus for the experiment, "Brands need expressive and flexible identities." IDEO has evolved from a well-defined services organization to a platform model; the brand must reflect this evolution. The company's work at the d.school, ideo.org, and open.ideo are "the beginning moments hinting at a broader diversification of IDEO's expression in the Ignite

Customer-Centricity Everywhere world. Hendrix also explains that "IDEO is a global company with local and personal expression. For example, the Boston studio may express the IDEO brand differently than the Singapore studio." Rather than trying to control the brand and require people to conform, the company awants to acknowledge and celebrate this diversity in expression.

The "Brand New IDEO" experiment is designed to be open, inclusive, and flexible, reflecting the IDEO-brand itself. Another distinguishing feature of the experiment is that the re-envisioning process is being conducted publicly on Twitter (#brandnewideo) and on Tumblr.[6]

Incorporating many of the tenants of design thinking, the experiment has several phases, each of which begins with a challenge to the IDEO community and concludes with a synthesis of the ideas generated, which forms the basis for the next stage's challenge. The initial phase was designed to inspire. A challenge was issued to IDEO employees inviting them to participate in an idea-generating process by responding to six broad themes. Paul Bennett, IDEO's chief creative officer, describes these themes—Talisman, Powers of 10, Writer's Block, Code Junkies, Alternative History, Biological—as "an intuitive stab at where we think we are going as a set of disciplines, but also just looking at our work broadly."[7] IDEO employees from around the globe embraced the challenge by chewing on the themes and posting ideas, examples, and inspirations in a variety of platforms, which can be viewed at www.sixthemes.tumblr.com.

Several weeks later a concept phase began with a make-a-thon in which every employee was asked to put aside his or her agendas and spend the day thinking about IDEO. Working from this well of inspiration, a smaller core team of communication designers was then charged with creating a "high-resolution response that would not necessarily be right, but that would at least be provocative and move the conversation forward."[8] The Brand New IDEO experiment continues. Design concepts and prototypes are currently being created and tested, to further flesh out ideas. Stay tuned.

Fostering a Pro-Learning Environment

What does it take to create a creative, pro-learning environment that can realize our shared vision? Much has been written about fostering

303

organizational learning during the past several decades. After synthesizing the research, management professors David Garvin, Amy Edmondson, and Francesca Gino have identified three broad building blocks that are essential for organizational learning and adaptability:

1. A supportive learning environment.
2. Concrete learning processes and practices.
3. Leadership behavior that provides reinforcement.[9]

To help organizations identify their learning styles and assess how well they meet the criteria for being a learning organization, the authors created an online diagnostic instrument, the Learning Organizational Survey, which is available at www.los.hbs.edu. The tool scores companies on the basis of each building block and provides corresponding benchmarks, providing a helpful basis for discussion.[10] How can we use this framework to improve our companies' customer experience?

Create a Supportive Learning Environment

A pro-learning environment thrives on inquiry and dialogue. It respects differences and values trial and error. Employees of pro-learning organizations *know* that their companies want to tap their insight and hear what they have to say, even if it is controversial or unpopular. In fact, they know that asking questions, admitting mistakes, and building upon the ideas of others is *essential* to their success and the success of their organization. Employees must also be ready to reciprocate the hospitality, listening to, respecting, and enhancing the ideas of others.

A pro-learning organization is also committed to experimentation. Its leaders encourage employees to develop hypotheses, design metrics to evaluate them, and create opportunities to test their theories in the real world. Failures and successes are viewed as equally important evidence upon which future iterations will be constructed.

The increased demand for transparency that we are seeing in the marketplace is also resident in pro-learning organizations. Like a window that can be seen though, transparency implies openness, free communication, and accountability. Openness around our efforts makes it possible for the entire organization to learn from the efforts of multiple smaller groups. What can we all learn about the hypothesis that was tested? What alternatives were considered? What can we learn from the process that was undertaken? How might we improve? Transparency is also a litmus test for how committed organizations are to learning. How does an organization really feel about failure? How serious is the organization about disrupting the status quo?

Learning takes time. A pro-learning environment creates a sense of urgency while avoiding a feeling of being rushed. Finding the appropriate cadence for new initiatives is important as people cannot learn when they feel overloaded. This is indeed a challenge in a rapidly changing landscape when people often already feel overwhelmed.

Concrete Learning Processes and Practices

Learning is fueled by information flows. In this age of big data and analytics, there is no shortage of information about our customers and their experience with our brands, which can provide external evaluations of our efforts. The challenge is to employ the technology, processes, and incentives to collect the data, understand it, and share it with relevant people across our ecosystem, in as close to real time as possible, so that it can be acted upon. Integrating our marketing systems internally, and in some instances with those of our business partners, so that we can see the effectiveness of our efforts in near real time, will provide data streams for this process. Empowering our frontline employees with analytical tools that allow them to test additional hypotheses moves decision-making closer to the market, increasing our organizations' opportunity to learn and our ability to act.

To be effective, we also need to facilitate communication across our organization and ecosystem. Enterprise social-networking technologies, which are essentially internal social media, promote reflection, learning, and the sharing of insight. Unfortunately, many employees (71 percent) believe that it is easier to locate knowledge on the web than it is to find it within their internal Web 2.0 systems.[11]

According to a recent *Altimeter Report*, one of the reasons that enterprise social networks have mixed results is because companies approach them as a "technology deployment and fail to understand that the new relationships created by enterprise social networks are the source for value creation."[12] There is much to be gained from improving the effectiveness of these tools and facilitating their adoption across our organizations.

Web 2.0 tools cannot do it alone. As John Maeda, the former president of Rhode Island School of Design, explains, "Until you can serve pizza or drinks over the web, a social media portal to create collaboration will be so-so."[13] We need to also create spaces that facilitate creative collaboration. Understanding this, Google has intentionally designed its corporate headquarters to foster innovation. The Googleplex campus includes swimming pools and sand volleyball courts, a giant projection of real-time Google search inquiries, and cafeteria lines whose length have been optimized to foster serendipitous interaction, collaboration, and fun. These are the qualities that set innovative companies apart from their peers according to John Sullivan, a workplace consultant and management professor at San Francisco State University.[14]

Just up the road at Airbnb headquarters, the conference rooms have been designed to be precise replicas of its four most popular travel rental spaces—a man cave in Berlin, a modern apartment in Hong Kong, a loft in Soho, and a mushroom-shaped cabin in Aptos, California. These prototypes are fun, stylish, and readily accessible guideposts of what currently works for everyone at the company that is involved in designing and delivering customer experiences.[15]

In the absence of such purposefully designed spaces, we can create the conditions that foster innovation and collaboration by simply bringing diverse groups together temporarily in a space, giving them a compelling challenge, and creating ground rules to encourage collaboration in much the same way as IDEO does in its design-thinking process. Amy Edmondson, a professor of management at Harvard Business School whom we met earlier in the chapter, studies organizational learning and refers to this process as teaming. A verb, teaming differs from team, which is a noun. *Teams* are static, stable units. *Teaming*, on the other hand, brings people together temporarily, and in a fluid fashion, to achieve a goal. Why is teaming important for a pro-learning environment? Edmondson has found that "organizations thrive, or fail to thrive, based on how well small groups within organizations work."[16] Twenty-first-century organizations are often charting new paths, learning by doing. Teaming is what makes this learning possible.

While it is exciting to be part of something that is new and vital to the future of the organization, incentives are often necessary to encourage participation and prioritize customer-centric activities above other activities. Defining clear and measurable metrics that reflect the essential drivers of our unique customer experience, around which our organizations can rally, ensures that everyone is working toward the shared vision. Recognition and other cultural rituals that reward and celebrate customer-centricity may be employed.

Model Desired Behavior

Remember the old adage, "Do as I say, not as I do"? It does not apply here. Garvin, Edmondson, and Gino have found that organizational learning is *strongly* influenced by the behavior of leaders. Leadership at all levels needs to live and breathe learning about, designing, and delivering remarkable customer experiences.

What does this look like? This is a question every company has to answer for itself depending on what it wants to encourage. For HubSpot, having its senior people keep their fingers on the pulse of the market through direct social media involvement it important. Brian Halligan, CEO of HubSpot, has created multiple Twitter streams to stay in touch with the people he most cares about. In addition to the HubSpot timeline and his own, his customized streams include people who are mentioning him and HubSpot on Twitter; HubSpot customers and leads when they mention HubSpot; and a stream that displays tweets from anyone in his database that mention HubSpot and a competitor in the same tweet.[17] This participation shows both the company's employees and the market that leadership is serious about customer experience.

Incorporating customer-centricity as a criterion for evaluating new corporate initiatives puts our money where our mouths are. This

307

justification does not have to be a deep analytical undertaking, but rather a simple discussion about the potential impact of a proposal on the customer experience. Actively engaging with employees, encouraging sharing of results, modeling inquiry and acceptance of multiple points of view, providing funding for experimentation, embracing small wins and losses, and having a bias toward smart action facilitates our organization's ability to live into enhanced customer-centricity.

Where Do We Begin?

The guiding principle for our efforts is: Think Big. Start Small. Scale Fast. A good place to begin to rally our organizations around customer-centricity is with a well-defined, finite, and cross-functional project. Identifying and remedying a pressing need, perhaps a negative component of our customer experience of which we are aware, may be a fruitful place to start. Using teaming, we can conduct a touchpoint analysis, drilling down to identify where our system is breaking down, and identifying and implementing remedies for the situation. Or we may choose to proactively explore our most important market segment's customer experience journey, systematically evaluating and improving components of that customer experience. Perhaps we form a team to identify and consolidate the data resident within our organizations, or we build out our content, or to identify and evaluate how marketing automoation may improve our contextualization efforts. As we begin to think in terms of customer experience, the possibilities will emerge in seemingly endless supply. Determining some vehicle for prioritization of our efforts will be key. Wherever we choose to begin, utmost care must be taken to make this a positive experience for everyone involved as this first undertaking will create expectations and perceptions. In addition to tackling this initial project, there are multiple ways that marketers can work with other C-level leaders within the organization to build momentum, a discussion of which follows.

Build a Data-Oriented Partnership with Our CIOs

Today's CMOs and CIOs need to reinvent themselves and their roles. As we have seen, to be successful, our organizations need tech-savvy

CMOs and marketing-savvy CIOs. We cannot meet our customers' heightened expectations for personalization, manage highly complex marketing processes, or evaluate the success of our efforts in the absence of additional technology infrastructure. Although marketing has successfully carried out shadow IT—software purchases made without IT's direct involvement—given the number of systems that need to be integrated in order to deliver remarkable customer experience, today's CMO needs to collaborate directly with the CIO. Our organization's backend has to mesh seamlessly with the front end and across multiple systems and touchpoints to deliver.

Similarly, CIOs need to collaborate with marketing to remain relevant to their companies. Traditionally CIOs have been responsible for organizational priorities such as security, cloud data, governance, compliance, and privacy. This is only a fraction of the tasks that today's CIOs are being called upon to carry out, however. Gartner's 2012 survey of CIOs from 41 countries and 36 industries found that enterprises realize on average only 43 percent of technology's business potential. "Digital technologies provide a platform to achieve results, but only if CIOs adopt new roles and behaviors to find digital value," explains Mark McDonald, group vice president and Gartner Fellow. "CIOs require a new agenda that incorporates hunting for new digital innovations and opportunities, and harvesting value from products, services and operations."[18] The mandate is clear. While important, it is no longer enough for CIOs to focus only on their traditional responsibilities.

To facilitate alignment, CMOs have to be able to clearly articulate their goals for data analytics and technology purchases and come to an agreement with their CIOs on overall areas of focus. These priorities should reinforce the company's overall growth objectives. CIOs must be prepared to help CMOs select and deploy marketing software to allow their companies to compete in an increasingly contextualized marketing environment.

In addition, some companies are relocating marketing and IT to be in close proximity to each other—a few steps rather than an ocean away. Becoming bilingual in each other's domain can help to bridge the divide and establish mutual respect. Understanding the metrics upon which the other is evaluated and creating new metrics that align the efforts of both departments is essential.

Ignite Customer-Centricity Everywhere

Creating a hybrid role, such as a marketing technologist that acts as a liaison between the two areas, is bearing fruit for some organizations. With a background in both technology and marketing, this person has an understanding of how technology can deliver better customer experience. The marketing technologist at the financial services company Nationwide, for example, facilitated role definition early on, identified the talent needed to set up their customer analytics initiatives, and built a proprietary customer information system. Today, in addition to running the analytics group, the marketing technologist also serves as the project manager for any and all marketing-related IT projects. "We have a strict policy that if you want to interface with IT and get funding for something, you have to go through the marketing technologist," CMO Matt Jauchius explained in an interview with *Insurance & Technology*.[19] Other companies are creating shared marketing and technology groups that act as internal digital agencies. Forrester Research has observed that marketing strategists, designers, and technologists often comprise these digital innovation teams.[20]

Increasingly companies are also changing reporting structures for both marketing and IT. USAA has chosen to have both marketing and IT report to its chief customer officer. Emerson Electric has its CMO, CIO, and customer support group report to a chief innovation officer. Reporting structures make a difference. Imagine how a CIO's priorities might shift depending upon whether he or she reports to a CFO, who is rewarded for cost cutting and efficiency, or a chief innovation officer, who is rewarded for exploring and unlocking future demand.

Align Marketing and Sales

Sales and marketing misalignment is an old story. However, as we have seen, if the two functions are organized around the customer experience journey, their goals are better aligned. Further, when marketing automation software is integrated into customer relationship management systems, there is hard data to show the impact both functions are having on leads and sales. Creating a sales and marketing Service Level Agreement (SLA) that details specific pipeline goals for marketing and sales commits both departments to work together.

Compensation strategies that link performance to these goals provide equivalent incentives for both departments. Some companies are even merging the two departments under one revenue-focused umbrella. GE, for example, has consolidated its marketing, sales, and communications teams to create a more holistic experience around its customers.[21]

Bring Our CFOs into the Process

We are in a game-changing moment. To take advantage of it, our companies have to be willing to fund the future, even as we are creating it. As we have seen, technology purchases in support of more data-driven and personalized customer experience are likely to be plentiful in the years ahead. To build necessary support to fund these and other marketing-related purchases, marketers need to keep our CFOs informed of what we are doing. Using language that CFOs understand and value, we need to demonstrate marketing's contribution to the company's overall financial objectives. How are our customer experiences impacting revenue and profitability? How are our efforts building our pipeline and making revenue more predictable? How will new investments (not expenditures) enhance customer-centricity?

As we explore new frontiers, we may have to put aside traditional metrics, in favor of developing new ones. To bring accountability to the process, we can work with our CFOs to build an understanding of the true drivers of remarkable customer experience for our businesses, establish valid metrics that capture them, and develop financial models that link our efforts to our company's overall business results. These metrics can be applied broadly across our organizations to align our efforts and provide a common set of evaluation tools.

Work with HR to Address the Skills and Culture Gap

The customer-centricity opportunity in front of us is not all about technology. It also requires smart, talented people who are adaptable, eager to learn, and have customer-centric values. It favors ambidextrous thinkers—marketers with technical capabilities, data scientists that understand business, creatives that can write code—who are

311

comfortable crossing domains and integrating seemingly conflicting forces. It puts a premium on those individuals that are flexible enough to thrive as part of diverse teamings and who will not chafe from the structure of a metrics-driven environment. Finding and recruiting these people is a challenge. Creating the conditions in which they will flourish within our organizations is a larger challenge still.

The immediate task at hand for most HR departments is finding the right talent to tackle the challenge of big data and analytics. More than 60 percent of respondents in Spencer Stuart's CMO Summit Survey "indicated that their marketing teams did not have the right talent in place to leverage data and analytics."[22] McKinsey estimates that by 2018 the United States could face a shortage of 140,000 to 190,000 people with appropriate analytical skills and 1.5 million managers and analysts with knowledge of how to glean insight from data and reflect it in decision making.[23]

What is our plan? How do we avoid being squeezed? As marketers we need to collaborate with IT and HR to determine what kind of analytic talent we need. Do we have the necessary data scientists to build relevant models and find insight in the data to allow us to deliver the kind of customer experience we want? In addition to recruiting the right analytic talent, how will we get our existing managers up to speed in order to be able to understand and apply data and analytics and to drive our business results?

Coordinate across Our Ecosystem

As we saw in the case of the beverage manufacturer, when we can move beyond our organization to coordinate our customer-experience efforts across our broader ecosystem, there is even more value to be gained. As information is shared in real time and plans are coordinated, manufacturers, retailers, and marketing partners can optimize around the customers that we collectively service. Each member of the network performs better as a result of this collaboration. When we realize this level of sophistication, we will be optimizing our customer experience from top to bottom and left to right. It will be like a soccer team playing in the World Cup, collaborating seamlessly on the field to score goals, or like the human body's 12 systems working together to create a living, breathing human being. This is not just a dream of what may be possible someday. As we have seen, it is already happening.

What might this look like for our business? What would it take for us to be in the position to coordinate our efforts? How might we benefit? How might our customers benefit? How close are our competitors to realizing this strategic advantage?

The Customer Is at the Center

Back in 1991, Regis McKenna, the chairman of the marketing consulting firm by the same name, wrote an article for *Harvard Business Review* titled, "Marketing Is Everything." In it he declared that "the 1990s will belong to the customer."[24] He spoke of companies that were boldly moving away from a strategy of changing customers' minds to fit their products, toward a more flexible approach that focused on changing their products to fit customers' requests, describing this shift as moving from the "any color as long as it's black" school of marketing to the "tell us what color you want" school. McKenna concluded by describing the pivotal role that marketing would play in the future as a result of this new customer orientation, writing, "That is why marketing is everyone's job, why marketing is everything and everything is marketing."[25]

What started in the 1990s is now coming to fruition. This is good news for marketers. Our primary area of focus—our customers—is essential to our organizations' future success. Our ability to ignite and deliver the customer experience differential is today's source of competitive advantage. All we have to do now is decide to take on the challenge and run with it.

QUESTIONS

- What does customer-centricity mean to your organization? Who are its champions?
- What would you describe as the drivers of customer experience that most impact your business results?

(continued)

313

(continued)

- How would your customers describe the customer experience factors that are most critical to them?
- Is your company willing to change the way it operates?
- What are the costs of not changing your strategy?
- What is your next step?

RESOURCES

Influencers We Recommend

- *The Cambridge Group*. A demand-driven consulting agency, The Cambridge Group, which is a subsidiary of Nielsen, has worked with many companies to identify and satisfy current, emerging, and latent demand. Learn from their thought leaders at www.thecambridgegroup.com and from following them on Twitter @TheCambridgeGrp.

- *Amy Edmondson*. A professor of Leadership at Harvard Business School and author of *Teaming: How Organizations Learn, Innovate, and Compete in the Knowledge Economy*, Edmondson is known for her work on teaming and learning processes in organizations. Learn more from Edmondson at www.hbs.edu/admondson and by following her on Twitter @AmyCEdmondon.

- *Regis McKenna*. One of the best-known marketers in the United States, McKenna founded the marketing firm, Regis McKenna, Inc. in Silicon Valley in the 1970s. He was named one of the 100 people who made Silicon Valley what it is today by the *San Jose Mercury News*. McKenna has written five books on technology business strategies including *Total Access: Giving Customers What They Want in an Anytime, Anywhere World*. To keep up to date on his insights, see www.regis.com.

- *Peter Senge.* A senior lecturer at the MIT Sloan School of Management, and the Founding Chair of SoL, the Society for Organizational Learning, whose purpose is "to discover, integrate, and implement theories of practices for the interdependent development of people and their institutions," Senge is the author of *The Fifth Discipline: The Art and Practice of the Learning Organization*, and coauthor of *The Dance of Change* and *Schools That Learn*. Learn with Senge on Twitter @SoLFlash and at www.solonline.org.

Hashtags to Explore

- #businesslearning
- #collaboration
- #demandchain
- #knowledgemanagement
- #mentalmodels
- #organizationallearning

Notes

Chapter 1: The 10 Essential Skills Every Marketer Needs

1. Gerald Puccio, Marie Mance, Laura Barbero Switalski, and Paul Reali, *Creativity Rising* (New York: ICSC Press, 2012), 16.

2. "Committed to Connecting the World: Statistics," *ITU*, accessed November 3, 2013, http://www.itu.int/en/ITU-D/Statistics/Pages/stat/default.aspx.

3. Google, "The Zero Moment of Truth," *Google Think Insights*, April 2011. http://www.google.com/think/research-studies/the-zero-moment-of-truth-macro-study.html.

4. Peter Boatwright and Jonathan Cagan, "'Amazon Is Amazing,' That's What People Find Themselves Saying," *Built To Love* (blog), http://builtto love.wordpress.com/2010/10/20/amazon-is-awesome-thats-whatpeople-find-themselves-saying/.

5. Harley Manning, "When It Comes to Total Returns, Customer Experience Leaders Spank Customer Experience Laggards," *Forrester Research* (blog), September 14, 2012, http://blogs.forrester.com/harley_manning/12-09-14-when_it_comes_to_total_returns_customer_experience_leaders_spank_customer_experience_laggards.

6. Tim Hurson, *Think Better* (New York: McGraw Hill, 2008), p. 105.

7. Ibid.

8. Clayton Christensen, Scott Cook, and Taddy Hall, "Marketing Malpractice: The Cause and the Cure," *Harvard Business Review*, December 2005, http://hbr.org/2005/12/marketing-malpractice-the-cause-and-the-cure/.

9. J. Josko Brakus, Bernd H. Schmitt, Lia Zarantonello, "Brand Experience: What Is It? How Is It Measured? Does It Affect Loyalty?" Journal of Marketing, Vol. 73, 52–68, (May 2009).

10. "Best Experience Brands 2013," Jack Morton Worldwide, www.slideshare.net/jackmortonWW/best-experience-brands.

11. Ibid.

12. Ibid.

13. Peter Dahlstrom and David Edelman, "The Coming Era of On-Demand Marketing," *McKinsey Quarterly*, www.mckinsey.com/insights/marketing_sales/the_coming_era_of_on-demand_marketing.

14. "Best Experience Brands 2013."

15. Megan Burns, Forrester Research, Inc. Report, "The Customer Experience Index, 2013," *Forrester Research, Inc.*, January 15, 2013.

16. Harley Manning and Kerry Bodine, *Outside In* (New York: Houghton Mifflin, 2013), p. 26.

17. American Express, "Social Media Raises Stakes for Customer Service," (Press Release), May 2, 2012, http://about.americanexpress.com/news/pr/2012/gcsb.aspx.

18. "Best Experience Brands 2013."

19. New Realities 2012, *Jack Morton Worldwide*, http://www.slideshare.net/jackmortonWW/jac-knew-realities.

20. Bryan Yurcan, *"USAA Develops Cross-Channel Capabilities to Improve Customer Experience,"* Bank Systems & Technology, http://www.banktech.com/channels/usaa-develops-cross-channel-capabilities/240144401.

21. "Committed to Connecting the World: Statistics," *ITU*, accessed November 3, 2013, http://www.itu.int/en/ITU-D/Statistics/Pages/stat/default.aspx.

22. A study conducted by Jack Morton Worldwide found that understanding is the second most important driver of customer experience; the first is utility. Jack Morton Worldwide, "Best Experience Brands: A Global Study," http://www.slideshare.net/jackmortonWW/best-experience-brands-a-global-study-by-jack-morton-worldwide-10365627.

23. Jay Baer, *Youtility: Why Smart Marketing is about Help not Hype* (New York: Penguin Group, 2013), p.187.

24. To see pictures of the laser soccer fields, see http://www.nikeblog.com/2013/06/27/watch-fc427-mipista-nike-laser-soccer-field.

25. For more information about the "paradox of choice" see Schwartz's TED talk: http://www.ted.com/talks/barry_schwartz_on_the_paradox_of_choice.html.

26. http://stylewhile.com/.

27. Google Shopper Marketing Council, "Mobile In-Store Research," April 2, 2013, http://www.slideshare.net/pricepoints/mobile-instore-research google-shopper-marketing-marc-apr-2013.

28. http://www.sprooki.com/.

29. "Best Experience Brands 2013."

30. http://www.statisticbrain.com/attention-span-statistics/.

31. Brian Steinberg, "Study: Young Consumers Switch Media 27 times an Hour, Adage.com, http://adage.com/article/news/study-young-consumers -switch-media-27-times-hour/234008/.

32. Everlane, "Introducing Radical Transparency," Everlane.com, accessed December 9, 2013, https://www.everlane.com/about.

33. John Maeda, "If Design's No Longer the Killer Differentiator, What Is?" *Wired*, http://www.wired.com/opinion/2012/09/so-if-designs-no-longer -the-killer-differentiator-what-is/.

34. "Dove Real Beauty Sketches," *Dove*, accessed November 3, 2013, http:// realbeautysketches.dove.us/.

35. Havas Media, "Meaningful Brands," HavasMedia.com, accessed December 17, 2013, http://www.havasmedia.com/meaningful-brands.

36. Seth Godin, "How to be Remarkable," Seth's Blog (blog), January 2007, http://sethgodin.typepad.com/seths_blog/2007/01/how_to_be_remar .html.

37. "The Greatest Customer Service Story Ever Told, Starring Morton's Steakhouse," Peter Shankman (blog), August 17, 2011, http://shankman .com/the-best-customer-service-story-ever-told-starring-mortons -steakhouse/.

38. Research conducted by the Center for Creative Leadership found that learning agility is not only vital for long-term leadership potential, but it is also a much better predictor of future performance than focusing exclusively on past performance, skills, and abilities. For more informa- tion see: www.ccl.org/leadership/pdf/research/LearningAgility.pdf.

39. Reid Hoffman and Ben Casnocha, *The Start-Up of You* (New York: Crown Business, 2012), 189.

40. MCorp Consulting, "Commercial Debt," (case study), http://mcorpcon sulting.com/resources/case-studies/commercial-debt/, accessed Decem- ber 27, 2013.

41. Jonathan Gordon, Jesko Perrey, and Dennis Spillecke, "Big Data, Analytics, and the Future of Marketing," *Forbes*, July 22, 2013, http://www.forbes.com/sites/mckinsey/2013/07/22/big-data-analytics-and-the-future-of-marketing-sales/.

42. IBM, *The Interactive Marketing eBook*, Somers, NY: July 2011, http://lideratis.com/resources/white_papers/IBM-the-interactive-marketing-eBook.pdf.

43. Elana Varon, "Agility in Action: How Four Brands Are Using Agile Marketing," CMO.com, http://www.cmo.com/articles/2013/5/19/agility_in_action_ho.html.

44. To experience FlavorPrint firsthand go to www.mccormick.com/Flavor Print.

45. Douglas Turpel and Andy Warner, "Cross-Channel Marketing Trends and Strategies for 2014," (Webinar), Experion, January 14, 2014, http://www.experian.com/marketing-services/cross-channel-marketing-trends.

46. L'Oréal, "CC The Transformation," *More* magazine, September 2013, 6–7.

47. Mike Wittenstein, "The One App Feature No Retailer Should Be Without," *Mike Wittenstein: Gets to the Heart* (blog), www.mikewittenstein.com /blog/the-one-app-feature-no-retailer-should-be-without/.

48. "Meijer Expands Digital Coupon Program," *Progressive Grocer*, www .progressivegrocer.com/top-stories/headlines/regional-supermarket -chains/id39719/meijer-expands-digital-coupon-program/?icid=home page.

49. www.sethgodin.com.

50. www.ScottMonty.com.

Chapter 2: How Organizations Are Adapting to the Customer-Centric Era

1. "Sam Walton: Bargain Basement Billionaire," Entrepreneur.com, October 8, 2008, http://www.entrepreneur.com/article/197560.

2. Paul Hagen, "The Rise of the Chief Customer Officer," *Forbes*, http://www.forbes.com/2011/02/10/chief-customer-officer-leadership-cmo-net work-rise.html.

3. Ibid.

4. Bryan Yurcan, "USAA Develops Cross-Channel Capabilities to Improve Customer Experience," *Bank Systems and Technology*, December 18, 2012, http://www.banktech.com/.

5. "Media Lab Conversations Series: IDEO's David and Tom Kelley," MIT Media Lab, www.media.mit.edu/events/2013/07/23/media-lab -conversations-series-ideos-david-and-tom-kelley.

6. Linda Tischler, "Dynamic Duos: PepsiCo's Indra Nooyi and Mauro Porcini on Design-Led Innovation," *Fast Company*, October 2013, http:// www.fastcodesign.com/3016310/pepsico-indra-nooyi-and-mauro-porcini.

7. Saul Kaplan, *The Business Model Innovation Factory*, (New Jersey: John Wiley & Sons, 2012).

8. John Maeda, "How to Design a Better World." CNN Opinion, December 16, 2012, http://www.cnn.com/2012/12/16/opinion/maeda-good-design.

9. "Social Media Raises The Stakes for Customer Services," AmericanExpress .com, http://about.americanexpress.com/news/pr/2012/gcsb.aspx.

10. Jay Arthur, "Turning Dissatisfied Customers into Evangelists," Know Ware.com, http://www.qimacros.com/knowware-articles/dissatisfied -customer-evangelist.

11. Sarah Karmali, "Burberry & Google, Sitting in a Tree," *Vogue News*, www .vogue.co.uk/news/2013/06/12/burberry-kisses—send-a-burberry-kiss -google-technology.

12. Brad Tuttle, "Give Disney Visitors Hi-Tech Wristbands and They Spend More Money," *Time Magazine*, http://business.time.com/2013/07/19 /give-disney-visitors-hi-tech-wristbands-and-they-spend-more-money/.

13. "Connecting Everything: A Conversation with Cisco's Padmasree Warrior," *McKinsey Insights & Publications*, www.mckinsey.com/insights /high_tech_telecoms_internet/connecting_everything_a_conversation _with_ciscos_padmasree_warrior.

14. Steve Olenski, "Is Brand Loyalty Dying A Slow and Painful Death?" *Forbes*, www.forbes.com/sites/marketshare/2013/01/07/is-brand-loyalty -dying-a-slow-and-painful-death/.

15. Chris Harrison, "OmniTouch: Wearable Multitouch Interaction Everywhere," www.chrisharrison.net/index.php/Research/OmniTouch.

16. Om Malik, "Now That's What I Call Window Shopping," *Gigaom* (blog), http://gigaom.com/2012/10/01/now-thats-what-i-call-window-shopping/.

321

Notes

17. To experience what Google Glass is like, watch the YouTube video available at www.google.com/glass/start/how-it-feels/.

18. For a listing of seven TED talks on 3D printing, see http://blog.ted.com /2013/02/07/7-talks-on-the-wonder-of-3d-printing/.

19. For more information see Lisa Harouni's TED talk, *A Primer on 3D Printing* available at www.youtube.com/watch?v=OhYvDS7q_V8. Create and share designs, or just see what's cooking, at www.shapeways.com, www.makerbot.com, and www.thingiverse.com.

20. Ben Paynter, "Making Over McDonald's," *Fast Company*, www.fast company.com/1686594/making-over-mcdonalds.

21. To see photos from the Red Bull diving competition in Boston, go to http://www.boston.com/news/local/massachusetts/gallery/diving_off _ica/.

22. James Manyika, *Big Data: The Next Frontier for Innovation, Competition, and Productivity*, McKinsey Global Institute, May 2011.

23. Ibid.

24. Jeff Bertolucci, "Big Data Skills Scarce Among Marketing Pros," *Information Week*, www.informationweek.com/big-data/news/big data-analytics -big-data-skills-scarce.

25. Ibid.

26. Jeff Bertolucci, "Big Data ROI Still Tough to Measure," *Information Week*, www.informationweek.com/big-data/news/big-data-analytics/big-data -roi-still-tough-to-measure/240155705.

27. Ibid.

28. Jake Wengroff, "CMO & CIO: Art + Science = Success," CMO.com, www .cmo.com/articles/2010/9/8/cmo--cio-art--science--success.html.

29. Gary Vaynerchuk, *The Thank You Economy* (New York: HarperCollins, 2011).

30. Jackson Phillips, "Scott Bedbury's Bestowed Industry Wisdom," www .bloggingaboutads.wordpress.com, www.bloggingaboutads.wordpress .com/2012/02/16/7-bedburys-bestowed-industry-wisdom/.

31. Tina Seelig, *inGenius: A Crash Course on Creativity* (New York: Harper-One: 2012), 19.

32. Tim Hurson, *Think Better* (New York: McGraw Hill, 2008), 73.

Chapter 3: Build a Successful Marketing Career (Hint: Standing Still Is Extraordinarily Risky)

1. Andrew S. Grove, "A High-Tech CEO Updates His Views on Managing and Careers," *CNN Money*, http://money.cnn.com/magazines /fortune/fortune_archive/1995/09/18/206087/index.htm.

2. Ella L. J. Edmondson Bell, *Career GPS: Strategies for Women Navigating the New Corporate Landscape* (New York: HarperCollins Publishers: 2010), 1.

3. Murphy, W. M. & Kram, K. E. (2014). *Strategic Relationships at Work: Creating Your Circle of Mentors, Sponsors, and Peers for Success in Business and Life.* New York: McGraw-Hill.

4. Zachary Reiss-Davis, "In Business Everybody Uses Social Media for Work; The Question Is How," *The Forrester* (blog), http://blogs.forrester .com/zachary_reiss_davis/13-07-17-in_business_everybody_uses_social _media_for_work_the_question_is_how?cmpid=pr:soc:tw:Shout+786615.

5. Ibid.

6. www.marketingprofs.com/bsc/welcome.asp#ixzz2cpVNAefF.

7. The statistics about LinkedIn are taken from http://press.linkedin.com /about.

8. Gary Vaynerchuk, *Crush It!* (New York: HarperCollins, 2009), 32.

9. Grove, "A High-Tech CEO."

10. For more information about various online options see www.nytimes .com/2012/03/28/technology/for-an-edge-on-the-internet-computer-code -gains-a-following.html?pagewanted=all&_r=0.

11. For more information see www.one.laptop.org.

12. To learn more, see www.kliptownyouthprogram.org.za.

13. Tina Seelig, *inGenius* (New York: HarperCollins, 2012), 4.

14. Leslie A. Perlow, "Are You Sleeping with Your Smartphone?" *Harvard Business Review Blog Network* (blog), www.blogs.hbr.org/2012/05/are -you-sleeping-with-your-sma/.

15. "Infographic: State of Modern Creativity," *iStock*, www.istockphoto.com /article_view.php?ID=1587#.UlflpCgRjO8.

Notes

16. Victoria Craig, "Parking Lot to C-Suite: SeaWorld CEO's Splashy Success," *Fox Business*, www.foxbusiness.com/business-leaders/2013/06/04/from -bottom-to-top=seaworld-ceos-splashy-success.

17. Wendy Murphy, "The New Rules of Mentoring," *Babson Insights*, (May 2012), http://www.babson.edu/executive-education/thought-leadership /leadership/Pages/new-rules-of-mentoring.aspx.

18. Carter and Silva; Sylvia Ann Hewlett, Kerrie Peraino, Laura Sherbin, and Karen Sumberg, "The Sponsor Effect: Breaking Through the Last Glass Ceiling," *Harvard Business Review Research Report*, December 2010.

19. Catalyst, *Sponsoring Women to Success*, August 17, 2011, 7–8.

20. Adam Bryant, "Don't Compete with Colleagues. Embrace Them," *New York Times*, www.nytimes.com/2012/02/26/business/susan-credle-of-leo -burnett-usa-on-sharing-ideas-at-work.html?pagewanted=all&_r=0.

21. For more information about Dweck's ideas and her book *Mindset*, see http://mindsetonline.com.

Chapter 4: Design Valuable Customer Experiences

1. For more information see: www.warbyparker.com.

2. To read more about the class trip adventures, see: www.warbyparkerclass trip.com/.

3. Tim Brown, *Change by Design* (New York: HarperCollins, 2009), 42.

4. Ibid., 16

5. Ibid., 43.

6. Sarah Thurber, *What's an Idea?*, Brightnow, www.brightnow.eu/articles /show/whats-an-idea.

7. Brown, 87.

8. Brown, 82.

9. Tom Kelley and David Kelley, *Creative Confidence* (New York: Crown Business, 2013), 253.

10. For more information on reactance, see Dillard, J., & Shen, L. (2005). On the nature of reactance and its role in persuasive health communication. Communication Monographs, 72, 144–168 and Bushman, B.J. (1998). Effects of warning and information labels on consumption of

full-fat, reduced-fat, and no-fat products. *Journal of Applied Psychology*, 83, 97–101.

11. Brad Tuttle, "Amazon Prime: Bigger, More Powerful, More Profitable than Anyone Imagined," *Time*, http://business.time.com/2013/03/18/amazon -prime-bigger-more-powerful-more-profitable-than-anyone-imagined.

12. Ibid.

13. For more information see: www.vogue.com/vogue-daily/article/vogue instafashion-our-first-instagram-photo-shoot/#1.

14. For more information see: www.digitaltrends.com/social-media/where -did-throwbackthusday-come-from/#ixzz2grJwIO5b.

15. Steve Rosenberg, "Monitoring Only Like a Marketer Is Losing You Online Sales," *Marketing Profs*, June 20, 2013, www.marketingprofs.com /articles/2013/11006/monitoring-only-like-a-marketer-is-losing-you-online -sales.

16. Jeremiah Owyang, *Altimeter Research Theme: The Dynamic Customer Journey*, www.web-strategist.com/blog/2012/05/21/altimeter-research -theme-the-dynamic-customer-journey/.

17. Noriaki Kano, Nobuhiko Seraku, Fumio Takahashi, Shin-ichi Tsuji, "Attractive Quality and Must Be Quality," *Journal of the Japanese Society for Quality Control* 14(2), 147–156, 1984–04–15 (http://ci.nii.ac.jp/Detail /detail.do?LOCALID=ART0003570680&lang=en). [in Japanese].

Chapter 5: Find Actionable Insight in Big Data and Marketing Analytics

1. Laura McLellan, "2013: The Year Marketers Are Expected To Be Strategic," Gartner (blog), December 8, 2012, http://my.gartner.com/portal /server.pt?open=512&objID=202&mode=2&PageID=5553&resId=1871 515.

2. MG Siegler, "Eric Schmidt: Every 2 Days We Create as Much Information as We Did Up to 2003," *Tech Crunch* (blog), http://techcrunch.com/2010 /08/04/schmidt-data/.

3. Michael Wu, "Big Data Reduction 1: Discriptive Analytics," *Lithosphere: Science of Social Blog*, http://lithosphere.lithium.com/t5/science-of -social-blog/Big-Data-Reduction-1-Descriptive-Analytics/ba-p/77766.

4. Michael Wu, "Big Data Reduction 2: Understanding Predictive Analytics," *Lithosphere: Science of Social Blog*, https://lithosphere.lithium.com/t5

/science-of-social-blog/Big-Data-Reduction-2-Understanding-Predictive -Analytics/ba-p/79616.

5. Michael Wu, "Big Data Reduction 3: From Descriptive to Prescriptive," *Lithosphere: Science of Social Blog*, https://lithosphere.lithium.com/t5 /science-of-social-blog/Big-Data-Reduction-3-From-Descriptive-to-Presc riptive/ba-p/81556.

6. Personal e-mail from Dr. Wu to the writers, January 2014.

7. Thomas Davenport and D. J. Patel, "Data Scientist: The Sexiest Job of the 21st Century," *Harvard Business Review*, http://hbr.org/2012/10/data -scientist-the-sexiest-job-of-the-21st-century/.

8. Bill C. Pink, "How Big Data Liberates Research," *Millward Brown*, www .millwardbrown.com/Insights/PointsOfView/Big_Data/Page1.aspx.

9. Author interview with Bill Pink, August 2013.

10. SCRIBE, "The State of Customer Data Integration 2013," *Scribe*, www .scribesoft.com/state-of-cdi-2013-report.

11. Rick Kash and David Cahloun, *How Companies Win* (New York: Harper-Collins, 2010)

12. James Taylor, "The Case for Centralized Customer Decisioning," IBM Software Thought Leadership (White Paper) New York: IBM Corp, July 2011.

13. For more information about measuring CLTV and customer equity see Peter Fader, *Customer Centricity* (Philadelphia: Wharton Digital Press, 2012).

14. V. Kumar, J. Andrew Peterson, and Robert Leone, "How Valuable is Word of Mouth?" *Harvard Business Review*, October 2007.

15. GroupHigh, "Chuck E. Cheese's Takes Family Entertainment to a New Level With Blogger Outreach," GroupHigh.com, www.grouphigh.com /customer-case-studies-chuck-e-cheeses-takes-family-entertainment-to-a -new-level-with -blogger-outreach, accessed December 28, 2013.

16. Andrew McInnes, "Taking VoC Programs to the Next Level," *Forrester Research, Inc.* (blog), May 16, 2011, http://blogs.forrester.com/andrew _mcinnes/11-05-16-taking_voc_programs_to_the_next_level.

17. Gartner, *Key Findings From US Digital Marketing Spending Survey 2013*, www.gartner.com/technology/research/digital-marketing/digital -marketing-spend-report.jsp.

18. Thomas Davenport and Jinho Kim, *Keeping Up with the Quants, Your Guide to Understanding + Using Analytics.* (Boston: Harvard Business Review Press, 2013).

19. Jean Paul Isson and Jesse Harriott, *Win With Advanced Business Analytics Analytics* (New Jersey: John Wiley & Sons, Inc., 2013), 47–48.

20. CMO Council, "CMO Council Finds Big Data Critical to Customer-Centricity Cultures," CMO Council Press Release, April 2, 2013, http://www.cmocouncil.org/press-detail.php?id=4335, accessed January 2014.

21. Thomas Davenport, "Analytics 3.0: Measuring Business Impact from Analytics and Big Data," Webinar, Harvard Business School, www.slideshare.net/boscolg/analytics-30measurable-business-impact-from-analytics-big-data.

22. D.C. Denison, "Should You Start a Big Data Project?" Acquia.com (blog), March 11, 2013, http://www.acquia.com/blog/should-you-start-big-data-project.

23. Lyris, "Mind the Digital Marketing Gap: New Findings by Lyris & the Economist Intelligence Unit," (infographic), Lyris Connections Blog, June 12, 2013, http://blog.lyris.com/mind-the-marketing-gap-new-findings-from-eiu-2.

24. Bill Franks, "Helpful or Creepy? Avoid Crossing the Line with Big Data," *International Institute for Analytics*, http://iianalytics.com/2013/05/helpful-or-creepy-avoid-crossing-the-line-with-big-data/.

25. Kashmir Hill, "How Target Figured Out a Teen Girl Was Pregnant Before Her Father Did," *Forbes*, www.forbes.com/sites/kashmirhill/2012/02/16/how-target-figured-out-a-teen-girl-was-pregnant-before-her-father-did/.

26. For more information see: www.amazon.com/gp/help/customer/display.html/?nodeId=13316081.

27. "VRM Vision," *Project VRM*, http://cyber.law.harvard.edu/projectvrm/VRM_vision.

Chapter 6: Employ Entrepreneurial Thinking for Discernment and Agility

1. Leonard Schlesinger, Charles Kiefer, and Paul Brown, *Just Start: Take Action, Embrace Uncertainty, Create the Future* (Boston: Harvard Business Review Press, 2012), 47.

2. Taken from an interview with the author.

3. Fast Company Staff, "Airbnb," *Fast Company*, www.fastcompany.com /node/136.

4. Paras Chopra, "The Ultimate Guide to A/B Testing," *Smashing Magazine*, www.smashingmagazine.com/2010/06/24/the-ultimate-guide-to-a-b -testing/.

5. HubSpot, 2013 State of Inbound Marketing Report, http://cdn2.hubspot .net/hub/53/file-30889984-pdf/2013_StateofInboundMarketing_Full Report.pdft=1366805568000.

6. Austin Carr, "Risky Innovation: Will Starbucks's Leap of Faith Pay Off?" *Fast Company*, www.fastcompany.com/3009040/risky-innovation-will -starbuckss-leap-of-faith-pay-off.

7. Nathan Olivarez-Giles, "Starbucks Is Reportedly Dominating Mobile Payments in North America," *The Verge*, www.theverge.com/2013/6/4 /4396750/starbucks-app-mobile-payments.

8. Darrell Etherington, "Mobile Payment at U.S. Starbucks Locations Crosses 10% as More Stores Get Wireless Charging," *TechCrunch* (blog), http:// techcrunch.com/2013/07/26/mobile-payment-at-u-s-starbucks-locations -crosses-10-as-more-stores-get-wireless-charging/.

9. Nicholas Drew, Saras Sarasvathy, Stuart Read, and Robert Wiltbank, "Affordable Loss: Behavioral Economic Aspects of the Plunge Decision," *Strategic Entrepreneurship Journal* 3, no. 2: 105–126 (2009).

10. Kathleen M. Eisenhardt, "Making Fast Strategic Decisions in High-Velocity Environments," *Academy of Management Journal* 32: 543–576, (1989).

11. Benjamin Franklin, *The Private Life of the Late Benjamin Franklin* (London: J. Parsons, 1793).

12. "Junto (club)," *Wikipedia*, http://en.wikipedia.org/wiki/Junto_(club).

13. "Collaborative Innovation Network," *Wikipedia*, http://en.wikipedia.org /wiki/Collaborative_innovation_network.

14. Jeff Bullas, "20 Stunning Social Media Stats Plus Infographic," Jeff Bullas.com (blog), September 2, 2011, http://www.jeffbullas.com/2011/09 /02/20-stunning-social-media-statistics/.

15. To learn more about this cause and effect relationship, see Frederick Reichheld, *The Loyalty Effect* (Boston: Harvard Business School Press, 1996).

16. "'Like' Me: The Dynamics of Public vs. Private Social Media," *Communi-space*, www.communispace.com/dynamics-of-private-vs-public-social -media/.

17. "Android Will Account for 58% of Smartphone App Downloads in 2013 with iOS Commanding a Market Share of 75% in Tablet Apps," *ABI Research*, www.abiresearch.com/press/android-will-account-for-58-of -smartphone-app-down.

18. Dominique Pahud, "Collaboration and Networks: Huffington Post" (blog), July 16, 2012, http://www.huffingtonpost.com/dominique-pahud /collaboration-andnetwork_b_1677782.html.

19. Vijay Govindarajan and Chris Trimble, *Reverse Innovation* (Boston: Harvard Business Review Press, 2012).

20. Ibid, 6.

21. For more information see, www.healthcitycaymanislands.com/.

22. "Despite Recovering Economies, Customers Still Frugal," Fox Business, September 12, 2013, http://www.foxbusiness.com/economy/2013/09 /12/despite-recovering-economies-consumers-still-frugal/.

23. Max Nisen, "Sheryl Sandberg's Essential Business Reading," *Business Insider*, March 18, 2013, http://www.businessinsider.com/sheryl-sandbergs -essential-business-reading-2013–3.

24. To learn more about scrums see www.scrumalliance.org/why-scrum /scrum-for-the-agile-organization.

25. Mike Cohen, "Sprint Retrospective," Topics in Scrum, Mountain Goat Software, www.mountaingoatsoftware.com/agile/scrum/sprint-retrospec tive.

26. Kirsten Knipp, "Get Agile: Running a Market Team Like a Startup," *Hub-Spot*, http://blog.hubspot.com/blog/tabid/6307/bid/13703/Get-Agile -Running-a-Marketing-Team-Like-a-Startup.aspx.

27. For more information see: www.businessinnovationfactory.com/projects /elab.

28. Issie Lapowsky, "Arianna Huffington's Rule for Success: Dare to Fail," *Inc*, www.inc.com/magazine/201302/rules-for-success/arianna-huffington -dare-to-fail.html.

29. Jeff Siebel, "For President, I Want the Guy Who Failed," *Harvard Business Review* (blog), http://blogs.hbr.org/2012/08/for-president-i-want-the -guy-w/.

329

Notes

Chapter 7: Create a Content Experience Strategy That Delivers

1. Jay Baer, "Is Youtility the Future of Marketing?" *Convince and Connect* (blog), http://www.convinceandconvert.com/integrated-marketing-and -media/is-youtility-the-future-of-marketing/

2. To view this classic Coca-Cola ad, see www.youtube.com/watch?v= xffOCZYX6F8.

3. "What Is Content Marketing?" Content Marketing Institute, http://content marketinginstitute.com/what-is-content-marketing/.

4. To see her City Guides, go to http://www.toryburch.com/city-guide -landing-page/cityguide_landingpage.html.

5. "Definitive Guide to Lead Nurturing," Marketo, 2009, www.marketo.com /_assets/uploads/definitive-guide-to-lead-nurturing.pdf.

6. Love Flo? To view your favorite Flo commercials go to http://www .progressive.com/commercials/.

7. Joe Pulizzi, "2013 B2C Content Marketing Research: Benchmarks, Bud- gets, and Trends," Content Marketing Institute, http://contentmarketing institute.com/2012/11/2013-b2c-consumer-content-marketing/.

8. Arianna Huffington, "Burnout: The Disease of Our Civilization," Huff- ington Post (blog), August 21, 2013, www.huffingtonpost.com/arianna -huffington/burnout-third-metric_b_3792354.html

9. "Current Realities 2013," *Jack Morton Worldwide*, www.slideshare.net /jackmortonWW/new-realities-2013.

10. Larry Freed and Eric Feinberg, "The Forsee Experience Index (FXI): 2013 U.S. Retailer Edition, *Forsee*, http://www.foresee.com/research -white-papers/_downloads/foresee-experience-index-2013-us-retail -edition.pdf.

11. For more information see http://www.llbean.com/parkfinder.

12. Jeff Bullas, "21 Awesome Social Media Facts, Figures, and Statistics for 2013," *Jeff Bullas Blog*, www.jeffbullas.com/2013/05/06/21-awesome -social-media-facts-figures-and-statistics-for-2013/.

13. Google and Nielsen, "Mobile Search Moments," Google Insights, www .google.com/think/research-studies/creating-moments-that-matter.html.

14. Google, "What Users Want Most from Mobile Sites Today," Think Insights. September 2012, http://www.google.com/think/research-studies/what-users-want-most-from-mobile-sites-today.html.

15. Ibid.

16. Yesmail Interactive, "Study: Almost Half of Brand Emails Opened on Mobile Devices," August 19, 2013, http://www.yesmail.com/company/news/study-almost-half-brand-emails-opened-mobile-devices.

17. "Gartner Says Mobile App Stores Will See Annual Downloads Reach 102 Billion in 2013," Gartner, www.gartner.com/newsroom/id/2592315.

18. Meat Pack, "Hijack," YouTube, www.youtube.com/watch?v=CekUwaPKUUM.

19. Check out *The GE Show* firsthand: www.ge.com/thegeshow/most_popular.html.

20. Coca-Cola Journey, www.coca-colacompany.com.

21. Mass Relevance, "Mass Relevance Releases New Research: Social Integration Drives Consumer Engagement, Trust," www.massrelevance.com/press-release/mass-relevance-releases-new-research-social-integration-drives-consumer-engagement.

22. "The New Rules of Digital Engagement," Gleanster, www.gleanster.com/reports/the-new-rules-of-digital-engagement.

23. John D. Sutter, "NRA tweeter was 'unaware' of Colorado shooting, spokesman says." CNN.com, http://www.cnn.com/2012/07/20/tech/social-media/nra-tweet-shooting/.

24. "Howard Schultz's Memo to Starbucks Employees," *Seattle Times*, http://seattletimes.com/html/businesstechnology/2004194019_webhowardmemo21.html.

25. Gleanster, "The New Rules of Digital Engagement," www.gleanster.com/reports/the-new-rules-of-digital-engagement.

26. Joe Pulizzi, "2013 B2C Content Marketing Research: Benchmarks, Budgets, and Trends," http://contentmarketinginstitute.com/2012/11/2013-b2c-consumer-content-marketing/.

27. Zabisco, "Infographic of Infographics," August 11, 2011, http://www.zabisco.com/blog/?p=2766.

28. Ibid.

Notes

29. Casey Henry, "What Makes a Link Worthy Post—Part 1," *The Moz Blog*, http://moz.com/blog/what-makes-a-link-worthy-post-part-1.

30. Dan Zarrella, "[Infographic] How to Get More Likes, Comments and Shares on Facebook," *Dan Zarella: The Social Media Scientist*, http://danzarrella.com/infographic-how-to-get-more-likes-comments -and-shares-on-facebook.html.

31. Oli Gardner, "An Infographic is Worth a Thousand Stats," (infographic), unbounce.com, http://unbounce.com/content-marketing/an-infograph icis-worth-a-thousand-stats-infographic/.

32. Warby Parker, "On this Day in Warby Parker History, 2013 Annual Report," Warby Parker, www.warbyparker.com/annual-report-2012.

33. Eloqua, "Want to Learn More about Marketing Automation? Start the Conversation," www.eloqua.com,/contnet/eloqua/en/home/featured -content/intro-marketing-automation.html.

34. "Marketing Infographics," Pinterest, www.pinterest.com/aschottmuller /marketing-infographics/.

35. Ann-Christine Diaz and Shareen Pathak, "10 Brands That Made Music Part of their Marketing DNA," Advertising Age, September 30, 2013, http://adage.com/article/special-report-music-and-marketing/licensing -10-brands-innovating-music/244336/.

36. Nora Aufreuter, Julien Boudet, and Vivian Weng, "Why Marketers Should Keep Sending You Emails," *McKinsey Insights & Publications*, January 2014, http://www.mckinsey.com/insights/marketing_sales/why_market ers_should_keep_sending_you_emails.

37. To see how Postwire works see www.postwire.com/.

38. David Taintor, "Top Digital Publishers Praise Yahoo!'s Tumblr," *AdWeek*, www.adweek.com/news/press/top-digital-publishers-praise-yahoos -tumblr-deal-149793.

39. Ian A. Michiels, "Top 3 Ways to Increase Your Organizations Social Intel-ligence," Gleanster (blog), October 10, 2011, http://blog.gleanster.com /2011/10/10/top-3-ways-to-increase-your-organizations-social -intelligence.

40. David Taintor, "Top Digital Publishers Praise Yahoo's Tumblr Deal."

41. Chad Hallert, "Chad Hallert: SEO Tips for Your Small Business," RGJ.com, www.rgj.com/article/20131103/BIZ15/311030005/Chad-Hallert-SEO-tips -your-small-business.

42. Larry Kim, "Think Nobody Clicks on Google Ads?" *Wordstream Blog*, www.wordstream.com/blog/ws/2012/07/17/google-advertising.

43. Aimee Picchi, "Durex Condoms' Social Media Strategy Goes Wrong," Money.MSN.com, June 4, 2013, http://money.msn.com/now/post.aspx?post=6d7eac81-29b0-4b9f-8f13-123fc39d31b1.

44. Peter N. Golder, "Five Things to Consider When Taking Your Brand Global," *Tuck*, July 30, 2013, http://www.tuck.dartmouth.edu/newsroom/articles/five-things-to-consider-when-taking-your-brand-global.

45. "When Multiculture Is the Culture," *Nielsen*, www.nielsen.com/us/en/newswire/2011/when-multicultural-is-the-culture.html.

46. Ibid.

47. Danny Sullivan, "Google Still World's Mose Popular Search Engine by Far, But Share of Unique Searchers Dips Slightly," Search Engine Land, February 11. 2013, http://searchengineland.com/google-worlds-most-popular-search-engine-148089.

48. China Internet Watch, "China Search Engine Share in November 2013," http://www.chinainternetwatch.com/category/search-engine.

49. Sullivan, "Google Still World's Mose Popular Search Engine by Far, But Share of Unique Searchers Dips Slightly."

50. Joe Pulizzi, "2014 B2B Content Marketing Research: Strategy IS Key to Effectiveness, October 1, 2013, http://www.google.com/search?client=safari&rls=en&q=content+marketing+institute+B2b+research+2013&ie=UTF-8&oe=UTF-8.

51. Joe Pulizzi, "2014 B2C Content Marketing Research: Strategy Influences Success, October 15, 2013, http://contentmarketinginstitute.com/2013/10/2014-b2c-consumer-content-marketing.

52. Joe Pulizzi, "2014 B2B Content Marketing Research: Strategy Is Key to Effectiveness."

53. Joe Pulizzi, "2014 B2C Strategy Influences Success."

54. Chad Brooks, "7 Social Media Tips for CEOs," *BusinessNewsDaily*, http://mashable.com/2013/05/31/ceo-social-media-tips/.

55. Ibid.

56. Skyward, "Transform Your Content Marketing: Advice and Tips from Brand Experts" Webinar, http://www.skyword.com/webinar-transform-content-marketing-advice/.

57. Deloitte, "Making the Maximum Impact," Deloitte, 2013, http://mycareer.deloitte.com/us/en/students/programsinternships/undergraduate/alternativespringbreak.

Chapter 8: Engage Customers via Social Communities

1. To read about KP's multiple awards, see http://share.kaiserpermanente .org/category/awards/.

2. To learn more about how Kaiser Permanente's Innovation Consultancy has used design thinking to develop KP MedRite, Nurse Knowledge Exchange, and Painscape, please go to http://xnet.kp.org/innovation consultancy/.

3. "Center for Total Health," Kaiser Permanente, http://centerfortotalhealth .org.

4. Mary Meeker and Liang Wu, "Internet Trends D11 Conference," *Kleiner Perkins*, May 29, 2013. http://www.slideshare.net/kleinerperkins/kpcb -internet-trends-2013

5. Vala Afshar, "50 Powerful Mega Trend Statistics For CIOs and CMOs," *Huff Post Tech* (blog), www.huffingtonpost.com/vala-afshar/50 -powerful-mega-trend-st_b_3975786.html.

6. Cooper Smith, "10 Social Media Statistics That Should Shape Your Social Strategy," *Business Insider*, www.businessinsider.com/strategic-social -media-statistics-2013–7.

7. Burson-Marsteller, *Global Social Media Check-Up 2012*, http://sites .burson-marsteller.com/social/default.aspx.

8. Ibid.

9. Ibid.

10. Burson-Marsteller, *Global Social Media Check-Up 2012*.

11. "Social Media Report 2012; Social Media Comes of Age," Nielsen, www .nielsen.com/us/en/newswire/2012/social-media-report-2012-social -media-comes-of-age.html.

12. "Facebook Statistics," *Statistic Brain*, www.statisticbrain.com/facebook -statistics/.

13. Ibid.

14. Brett, "Stream Social Q1–2013," *Global Web Index*, www.globalwebindex .net/Stream-Social.

15. Ibid.

16. Jeff Bullas, "20 Stunning Social Media Statistics Plus Infographic," *Jeff-Bullas.com* (blog), www.jeffbullas.com/2011/09/02/20-stunning-social -media-statistics/.

17. "Asian Insight," *Race Point Group* (blog), http://asianinsight.racepoint group.com/.

18. WeChat, www.wechat.com/en/.

19. Mxit, http://site.mxit.com/.

20. "YouTube: Statistics," YouTube, www.youtube.com/yt/press/statistics .html.

21. Shea Bennett, "How Brands Are Using Twitter's Vine: Statistics, Facts & Tips, Mediabistro, September 3, 2013, http://www.mediabistro.com /alltwitter/vine-facts-tips_b48833.

22. Cooper Smith, "Here's Where All Those Teens Fleeing Facebook are Going," *Business Insider*, January 17, 2014, http://www.businessinsider .com/heres-where-the-fleeing-facebook-teens-are-going-2014-1.

23. Kurt Wagner, "Why We Heart It Could Be the Next Big Social Network," *Mashable*, January 13, 2014, http://mashable.com/2014/01/13/we-heart -it/#:eyJzIjoidCIsImkiOiJfdXh2cm9xY3E1bHNkdG1wdjNwMHBfIn0.

24. "Key ICT Indicators for Developed and Developing Countries and the World (Totals and Penetration Rates)", International Telecommunications Union, Geneva, February 27, 2013. www.itu.int.

25. To learn more about Internet black holes go to Reporters Without Borders (www.rsf.org) and examine their World Press Freedom Index.

26. Kathryn Zickuhr, "Who's Not Online and Why," *Pew Internet*, www .pewinternet.org/Reports/2013/Non-internet-users.aspx.

27. "Press Release: Leading Corporations Believe in Corporate Purpose, According to the Burson-Marsteller/IMD Power of Purpose Study," *Burson Marsteller*, www.burson-marsteller.com/Newsroom/Lists/Press Releases/dispform.aspx?ID=933.

28. Cotton Delo, "This Brand Hired a 16-Year Old to Build Its Following on 28." Snapchat, AdAge.com, January 16, 2014, http://adage.com/ article/digital/build-a-brand-snapchat-hire-a-16-year/291124/25. Hub-spot, 2013.

29. HubSpot, 2013 State of Inbound Marketing Annual Report, http://www .stateofinboundmarketing.com/30.

30. Laurie Sullivan, "Pinterest Leads Consumers from Pin to Purchase," MediaPost, www.mediapost.com/publications/article/171459/pinterest -leads-consumers-from-pin-to-purchase.html?edition=45223#axzz2hk2 FruAf.

31. Mashable, "9 Breaking News Tweets That Changed Twitter Forever," October 31, 2013, airingnews.com, http://www.airingnews.com/articles /138089/9-Breaking-News-Tweets-That-Changed-Twitter-Forever.

32. Brian Anthony Hernandez, "MTV's 'Teen Wolf' Facebook Game Is Feast for Fans in First 5 Weeks," *Mashable* (blog), http://mashable.com/2012 /07/29/teen-wolf-the-hunt-facebook-game/.

33. Apple Support Communities, https://discussions.apple.com/index.jspa.

34. To see how it works, go to https://quickbooks.lc.intuit.com/.

35. Roxane Divol, David Edelman, and Hugo Sarrazin, "Demystifying Social Media," *McKinsey Insights & Publications*, www.mckinsey.com/insights /marketing_sales/demystifying_social_media.

36. Simply Measured, "Customer Service: What's Working on Twitter," http:// simplymeasured.com/blog/2013/06/18/customer-service-whatsworking -on-twitter-study.

37. Echo, "2012 Global Customer service Barometer," http://about.american express.com/news/docs/2012x/axp_2012gcsb_us.pdf.

38. Simply Measured, "Customer Service: What's Working on Twitter."

39. Lithium, "Consumers Will Punish Brands That Fail to Respond Quickly," (Press Release), October 29, 2013, http://www.lithium.com/news-room /press-releases/2013/consumers-will-punish-brands-that-fail-to-respond -on-twitter-quickly.

40. Marion aan 't Goor, "What Top 5 Social Brands on Twitter Are Doing Right," *Viral Blog*, www.viralblog.com/social-media/what-top-5-social -brands-on-twitter-are-doing-right/.

41. Bruce Horovitz, "Doritos Going Global with Super Bowl," *USA Today*, www.usatoday.com/story/money/business/2013/09/11/doritos-frito-lay -super-bowl-marketing-crash-the-super-bowl/2798693/.

42. Kim Vallee, "Fans Influence the Outcome of Continuum's Season Finale," *Sidekick Labs*, http://sidekicklabs.com/fans-will-determine-continuums -season-finale/.

43. Dan Hyman, "Pearl Jam Superfan Creates Band's Setlist," *Rolling Stone*, www.rollingstone.com/music/news/pearl-jam-superfan-creates-bands -setlist-20120706.

44. Kevin Ehlinger, "Inbound Marketing—How Universal Launched Harry Potter World by Only Telling 7 People," *Th!nk Creative Digital Marketing*, April 27, 2012, www.thinkcreativedigital.com/blog/bid/136596/Inbound

-Marketing-How-Universal-Launched-Harry-Potter-World-by-Only
-Telling-7-People.

45. Extole, www.extole.com.

46. Everlane Unedited, Tumblr, January 2013, http://tumblr.everlane.com
/post/39579159486/oh-my-goodness-this-everlane-t-shirt-feels-like,
accessed December 14, 2013.

47. "Gartner Says the Vast Majority of Social Collaboration Initiatives Fail Due
to Lack of Purpose," Gartner, http://www.gartner.com/newsroom/id
/2402115.

48. Ibid.

49. "10 Best Practices for Managing Online Communities," Communispace,
www.communispace.com/best-practices-managing-online-communi
ties/.

50. "Gartner Says Organizations That Integrate Communities Into Customer
Support Can Realize Cost Reductions of Up to 50 Percent," Gartner,
www.gartner.com/newsroom/id/1929014.

51. "The Rules of Community Engagement," Communispace, www.communi
space.com/research/featuredresearch.aspx.

52. Details of Godiva story taken from conversation with Diane Hessan and
http://www.communispace.com/godiva.

53. Communispace, Godiva (Case Study), http://www.communispace.com
/godiva.

54. "Community Health Index for Online Communities," Lithium, www
.lithium.com/pdfs/whitepapers/Lithium-Community-Health-Index_v1AY
2ULb.pdf.

55. For more information see www.communityroundtable.com/research
/community-maturity-model/.

Chapter 9: Maximize Marketing Impact with Converged Media

1. Tim Brown and Barry Katz, *Change by Design* (New York: Harper Business, 2009). p. 241.

2. Peggy Wang, "31 Home Decor Hacks That Are Borderline Genius," Buzz-
Feed, www.buzzfeed.com/peggy/cheap-and-easy-decorating-hacks-that
-are-borderline-geniu.

3. Rebecca, Lieb, "The Converged Media Imparative," Altimeter Group (blog), July 19, 2012, http://www.altimetergroup.com/2012/07/the-con verged-media.

4. Brian Anthony Hernandez, "Pepsi Unwraps 'Pulse' Digital Dashboard for Pop Culture," *Mashable*, http://mashable.com/2012/04/30/pepsi-pulse -live-for-now/.

5. "Sponsor Your Page Posts," Facebook, www.facebook.com/notes /facebook-marketing/sponsor-your-page-posts/10150675727637217.

6. Jay Rosen, Twitter post, December 21, 2013, 8:46 p.m., https://twitter.com /jayrosen_nyu/status/414572505194459136.

7. Dianne Molina, "Real-Time Marketing Spotlight: General Electric #IWantToInvent," *Twitter Blog*, https://blog.twitter.com/2013/real-time -marketing-spotlight-general-electrics-iwanttoinvent.

8. Esther Zuckerman, "Sesame Street Successfully Wins the Internet with Monstrous Reveal on Twitter," *The Atlantic Wire*, www.theatlanticwire .com/entertainment/2013/01/sesame-street-grover-twitter/61599/.

9. "Grover's 'There's A Monster At the End of This Twitter Conversation," Huff Post Comedy, January 30, 2013.

10. To learn more about the event see http://www.youtube.com/2daysbeat.

11. Dmitriy Molchanov, "Study: The Value of Promoted Trends," *Twitter Advertising Blog*, September 11, 2013, https://blog.twitter.com/2013 /study-the-value-of-promoted-trends.

12. Tom, "INFOGRAPHIC: Native Advertising Effectiveness Study by IPG Media Lab and Sharethrough," *Sharethrough Says Blog*, www .sharethrough.com/2013/05/infographic-native-advertising-effectiveness -study-by-ipg-media-labs/.

13. "How Native Ad Campaigns Are Shaping Up," *eMarketer*, www .emarketer.com/Article/How-Native-Ad-Campaigns-Shaping-Up/1010 064.

14. Tom, "INFOGRAPHIC: Native Advertising Effectiveness Study."

15. "Leading Marketers Recognize 'Native Advertising' as a Powerful Dis- tribution Vehicle for Brand Content," Sharethrough, www.sharethrough .com/native-advertising-research/.

16. Responsys, "Responsys Research: Mobile Marketing Can Help Retail- ers Cut Through The Clutter," (Press Release), December 3, 2013, investors.responsys.com/releasedetail.cfm?ReleaseID=811110.

17. Lauren Johnson, "Adidas Philippines Campaign Sees 1.27pc CTR With Mobile Game, Rich Media," *Mobile Commerce Daily*, www.mobile commercedaily.com/adidas-philippines-campaign-sees-1–27-ctr-with -mobile-game-rich-media.

18. Michael Fleischman, "TV Ad Targeting Now Generally Available; Lifts Brand Metrics and Engagement," *Twitter Blog*, https://blog.twitter.com /2013/tv-ad-targeting-now-generally-available-lifts-brand-metrics-and -engagement.

19. John Branch, "Snow Fall," *New York Times*, www.nytimes.com/projects /2012/snow-fall/#/?part=tunnel-creek.

20. Epsilon, "Consumer Survey Results Reveal Direct Mail Preferred Channel for Receipt of Brand Communications," (Press Release) December 1, 2011. http://www.epsilon.com/news-and-events/press-releases/2011 /consumer-survey-results-reveal-direct-mail-most-preferred-channel-re.

21. Jack Morton Worldwide, *New Realities 2013*, slide 10, www.slideshare .net/jackmortonWW/new-realities-2013.

22. Nielsen Press Release, "Fourth Screen Network Audience Report," www .nielsen.com/content/dam/corporate/us/en/reports-downloads/2010 -Reports/On-Location-Fourth-Screen-Report.pdf.

23. Jennifer Bergen, "Korea's Tesco Reinvents Grocery Shopping with QR Codes," *Geek blog*, www.geek.com/mobile/koreas-tesco-reinvents -grocery-shopping-with-qr-code-stores-1396025/.

24. To see a video of how Tesco's virtual shopping market works go to www.youtube.com/watch?v=3Mqcb7RoN4Y.

25. David Griner, "Shadow-Activated QR Code Actually Useful and Cool," *Adweek*, www.adweek.com/adfreak/shadow-activated-qr-code-actually -useful-and-cool-139975.

26. To see a video about the Sunny Sale campaign see: www.youtube.com /watch?v=EvIJfUySmY0.

27. National Centre for Domestic Violence, "Drag Him Away," (Video), http://www.youtube.com/watch?v=EEKC-Yu-LeQ28.

28. E2MA and CMO Council, "E2MA & CMO Council Release Global Study on Exhibit & Event Marketing," April 22, 2013, http://www.e2ma.org /news/123017.

29. Moiz Syed and Saad Pall, "Coke's Small World Machines: From Pakistan with Love," *Unbottled* (blog), June 19, 2013, http://www.coca-colacompany.com/coca-cola-unbottled/cokes-small-world-machines-from-pakistan-with-love.

30. Coca-Cola, "Coca-Cola Small World Machines."

31. Syed and Pall, "Coke's Small World Machines."

Chapter 10: Driving Sales with Marketing Automation

1. Anjali Yakkundi, Forrester Research, Inc. Report, *The State Of Digital Customer Experience Technology, 2013*, Forrester Research, Inc., May 9, 2013.

2. Douglas Turpel and Andy Werner, "Cross-Channel Marketing Trends and Strategies for 2014," (Webinar), January 2014, http://www.experian.com/marketing-services/cross-channel-marketing-trends-for-2014.html.

3. Mathew Sweezey, "B2B Marketing Automation Teaches B2C Marketers a New Trick," ClickZ, January 9, 2014, http://www.clickz.com/clickz/column/2321526/b2b-marketing-automation-teaches-b2c-marketers-a-new-trick.

4. Unica, "Unica Customer Successes," ftp://ftp.software.ibm.com/software/in/websphere/smartercommerce/Unica_Customer_Successes.pdf.

5. Marketo, "Christiana Care System" (Case Study), http://www.marketo.com/customers/christiana-care.

6. Marketing Automation Success Center, *Marketo.com*, accessed December 15, 2013, http://www.marketo.com/marketing-automation.

7. Oracle/Eloqua, *Why Marketing Automation? An IT Professional's Guide*, www.eloqua.com/content/dam/eloqua/Downloads/tenet-sheets/O-Eloqua-Marketing-Automation-F.pdf. 2013.

8. The Fournaise Marketing Group, "73% of CEOs Think Marketers Lack Business Credibility: They Can't Prove They Generate Business Growth," (Press Release), June 15, 2011, https://www.fournaisegroup.com/Marketers-LackCredibility.asp.

9. For more information see: www.mpdailyfix.com/wayback-marketing-series-jon-miller-on-being-aggressively-open-and-creating-tons-of-content-waybackmarketing/?adref=nlt081913.

Chapter 11: Craft Worthwhile Loyalty and Digital Couponing Programs

1. "Walgreens Balance Rewards Program Expands Opportunities to Earn Points for Health Behaviors," Walgreens, http://news.walgreens.com /article_display.cfm?article_id=5727.

2. Kate Kaye, "Late to the Loyalty Game, Walgreens Pushes the Envelope," *Crain's Chicago Business*, December 22, 2013, http://www.chicago business.com/article/20131029/NEWS06/131029766/late-to-the-loyalty -game-walgreens-pushes-the-envelope#.

3. Colin Shaw, "15 Statistics That Should Change the Business World—But Haven't," *LinkedIn Today*, www.linkedin.com/today/post/article/2013 0604134550-284615-15-statistics-that-should-change-the-business -world-but-haven-t.

4. *Catalina Losing Loyalty: The Consumer Defection Study*, http://info .catalinamarketing.com/consumer-defection-dilemma-report/.

5. Jeff Berry, "2013 Colloquy Loyalty Census," *Colloquy Talk*, www .colloquy.com/files/2013-COLLOQUY-Census-Talk-White-Paper.pdf.

6. Ibid.

7. Don Peppers and Martha Rogers, *Enterprise One on One* (New York: Currency, 1997).

8. Emily Collins, Forrester Research, Inc., Report, *The State of Loyalty Programs 2013*, Forrester Research, Inc., October 3, 2013.

9. Peet's Subscriptions, Peet's Coffee & Tea, www.peets.com/subscriptions .html.

10. Emily Collins, *The State of Loyalty Programs 2013*.

11. Mark Friedman and Kelly Hlavinka, "Fully Charged: Delivering the Mobile Advantage Throughout the Customer Lifecycle," www.soundbite .com/node/1280.

12. The Embassy Suites Game: Rachael King, "The Games Companies Play," *Bloomberg Business Week*, April 5, 2011, http://www.businessweek.com /stories/2011-04-05/the-games-companies-playbusinessweek-business -news-stock-market-and-financial-advice.

13. Philip LeBeau, "Delta Escorts Elite Fliers to Plane—via Porsche," *NBC News Travel*, October 9, 2013, www.nbcnews.com/travel/delta-escorts -elite-fliers-plane-porsche-8C11363469.

14. People Metrics, *Most Engaged Customers 2010*, www.peoplemetrics.com /wp-content/uploads/2012/06/PeopleMetrics_2010-Most-Engaged -Customers-Study_B2C-Overall-Report.pdf.

15. Timothy L. Keiningham, Lerzan Aksoy, Alexander Buoye, and Bruce Cooli, "Customer Loyalty Isn't Enough. Grow Your Share of Wallet," *Harvard Business Review*, http://hbr.org/2011/10/customer-loyalty-isnt -enough-grow-your-share-of-wallet.

16. Booz & Co, "The New Consumer Frugality: Adapting to the Enduring Shift in U.S. Consumer Behavior," 2010, http://www.booz.com/media /file/The_New_Consumer_Frugality.pdf.

17. "Despite Recovering Economies, Consumers Still Frugal," Fox Business, September 12, 2013, http://www.foxbusiness.com/economy/2013/09 /12/despite-recovering-economies-consumers-still-frugal/.

18. Knowledge Networks, "Digital vs. Traditional Coupons," www.knowlege works.com, 2011, http://www.knowledgenetworks.com/fact-sheets/KN -Trend-Report.pdf

19. For more information on SnipSnap and to read about its money-saving opportunities, see www.snipsnap.it.

20. For more details about Pushpins see www.pushpinsapp.com.

21. To learn more about Coupon Sherpa see www.couponsherpa.com.

22. Max Kalehoff, "The Reasons Consumers Become Facebook Brand Fans," *Syncapse* (blog), June 26, 2013, www.syncapse.com/why-consumers -become-facebook-brand-fans/#.UsDkwCgRj08.

Chapter 12: Ignite Customer-Centricity Everywhere

1. Gareth Goh, "15 Motivational Marketing Quotes by Seth Godin," Insight-Squared.com, September 15, 2013, http://www.insightsquared.com /2013/09/15-motivational-marketing-quotes-from-seth-godin/.

2. Rick Kash and David Calhoun, *How Companies Win* (New York: Harper Collins, 2012), p. 201.

3. Infed.com, Peter Senge and the Learning Organization, http://infed.org /mobi/peter-senge-and-the-learning-organization/, accessed January 30, 2014.

4. Kash and Calhoun, *How Companies Win*.

5. Ibid.

6. Follow the progression at http://sixthemes.tumblr.com/.

7. "Brand New IDEO: Michael Hendrix and Paul Bennett on the Global Design Consultancy's Upcoming 24-Hour Make-a-Thon," *Athenna* (blog), March 21, 2013, http://www.athenna.com/brand-new-ideo -michael-hendrix-and-paul-bennett-on-the-global-design-consultancys -upcoming-24-hour-make-a-thon/athenna/web_design/teoria-de-design/.

8. www.sixthemes.tumblr.com/tagged/followourstory.

9. David Garvin, Amy Edmondson, and Francesca Gino, "Is Yours a Learning Organization," *Harvard Business Review*, http://hbr.org/2008/03 /is-yours-a-learning-organization/ar/1.

10. To access the Learning Organization Survey, go to https://hbs.qualtrics .com/SE/?SID=SV_b7rYZGRxuMEyHRz.

11. Atle Skjekkeland, *AIIM Survey: Collaboration and Enterprise 2.0*, www .slideshare.net/norwiz/aiim-enterprise-20-industry-watch-presentation.

12. Charlene Li, Alan Webber, and Jon Cifuentes, *Making the Business Case for Social Networks*, Altimeter, www.slideshare.net/Altimeter/altimeter -report-making-the-business-case-for-enterprise-social-networks.

13. John Maeda.

14. Steve Henn, "Serendipitous Interaction 'Key To Tech Firms' Workplace Design," NPR.org, March 13, 2014, http://www.npr.org/blogs/alltech considered/2013/03/13/174195695/serendipitous-interaction-key-to -tech-firms-workplace-design.

15. For a tour of Airbnb's headquarters, see http://www.businessinsider.com /airbnb-office-tour?op=1.

16. Amy Edmondson, "The Importance of Teaming," *Harvard Business School*, http://hbswk.hbs.edu/item/6997.html.

17. Brain Halligan, "The CEO's Guide to Listening on Twitter," *HubSpot*, http://blog.hubspot.com/marketing/ceo-guide-to-twitter-listening.

18. Gartner, 2013, www.gartner.com/newsroom/id/2304615.

19. Nathan Golia, "Nationwide CMO: I Have Double-Digit Million Dollar Projects, Insurance & Technology," March 14, 2013, http://www .insurancetech.com/management-strategies/nationwide.

20. Anjali Yakkundi, Forrester Research, Inc. Blog, "The Who, What, Where, and Why of Marketing Technology Groups," Forrester Research, Inc., May 30, 2013, http://blogs.forrester.com/anjali_yakkundi/13-05-30-the _who_what_where_and_why_of_marketing_technology_groups.

343

Notes

21. E. J. Schultz, Jack Neff, "Don't Call Me CMO: Top Marketers Say Job Has Evolved Beyond Title," Adage.com, November 12, 2013, http://adage.com/article/cmo-strategy/call-cmo-marketers-job-evolved-title/245189/.

22. Spencer Stuart, "Bog Data and the CMO: What's Changing for Marketing Leadership?", CMO Summit Survey Results, April 2013, www.spencerstuart.com/research-and-insight/big-data-and-the-co-whats-changing-for-markting-leadership-cmo-summit-survey-results.

23. James Manyika, Michael Chui, Brad Brown, Jacques Bughin, Richard Dobbs, Charles Roxburgh, and Angela Hung Byers, "Big Data: The Next Frontier for Innovation, Competition, and Productivity, *McKinsey Global Institute*, www.mckinsey.com/insights/business_technology/big_data_the_next_frontier_for_innovation.

24. Regis McKenna, "Marketing Is Everything," *Harvard Business Review*, http://hbr.org/1991/01/marketing-is-everything/ar/11.

25. Ibid.

Index

349

Index

352

Index